Measuring the Days

Daily Reflections with
Walter Wangerin, Jr.

Edited by Gail McGrew Eifrig

HarperSanFrancisco
Zondervan Publishing House
Divisions of HarperCollins*Publishers*

POEMS

Acknowledgment is made for permission to reprint material from the following sources: Excerpts from *My First Book About Jesus,* copyright © 1983 by Walter Wangerin, Jr., and from *The Bible for Children,* copyright © 1981 by Walter Wangerin, Jr., reprinted by permission of Checkerboard Press, Inc.; from *As for Me and My House: Crafting a Marriage to Last,* copyright © 1987 by Walter Wangerin, Jr., reprinted by permission of Thomas Nelson, Pubs.; from *In the Beginning There Was No Sky,* copyright © 1986 by Walter Wangerin, Jr., reprinted by permission; from *Reality and the Vision,* copyright © 1990 by The Chrysostom Society, reprinted by permission of Word, Inc., Dallas, TX; from *Una Sancta: A Mass in Thanksgiving for the Unity of the Body of Christ,* copyright © 1986 by Walter Wangerin, Jr.,reprinted by permission; from *Potter,* copyright © 1985 by Walter Wangerin, Jr., reprinted by permission; from *Thistle,* copyright © 1983 by Walter Wangerin, Jr., reprinted by permission; from articles that first appeared in *The Lutheran,* copyright © 1988–1992 by Walter Wangerin, Jr., reprinted by permission.

FIRST EDITION

Library of Congress Cataloging-in-Publication Data
Wangerin, Walter.
   Measuring the days: daily reflections with Walter Wangerin, Jr. / edited by Gail McGrew Eifrig.—1st ed.
      p.   cm.
   "Books by Walter Wangerin, Jr.": p.
   Includes bibliographical references and index.
   ISBN 0-06-069248-0 (alk. paper)
   1. Devotional calendars.   2. Christian life.
   I. Eifrig, Gail McGrew.   II. Title.
   BV4811.W36 1993   92–54691
                                                                CIP

93 94 95 96 97 ❖ MAL 10 9 8 7 6 5 4 3 2 1

Contents

Introduction

It has ever been my notion that the writer by writing is asking for companionship, and the reader by reading is answering, "Yes."

Then each book written becomes at its reading a covenant for a while; but writer and reader remain divided, bound essentially by the business of that single book—a novel, perhaps, or a work of pastoral encouragement, maybe short stories or poetry, or more discursive theology. I've written all these. Each has been bound within its own covers. And then people have in their own time chosen one book or the other, one topic, one genre or another, and met me when I did not know we were meeting. By then I was about some other topic and genre and book.

But now comes something utterly different in my experience, the book that you hold, *Measuring the Days*.

What I particularly appreciate about it is that here the companionship between writer and reader has become the very form and purpose of the book. Day by day you and I can walk together through a host of observations. It isn't just one topic but many. Neither is it just one genre, but a gathering of many sorts of writing—a wider view, then, of my landscape, of myself, of the ways I write and talk and think and believe.

That makes the companionship between us more personal. This is more fully the *person* I am than I might be in a single, circumscribed production of my writing mind. I like that. And if you read these various pieces day by day, then you, too, approach from a variety of moods and situations and needs and attitudes; then you too are more fully the person you are than when you focus but the sharp part of your attention, but a piece of your mind, upon a single work a while. We are more fully *we* in such a collection as this.

And for a moment, recently, I *was* you. We were standing side by side, you and I.

I mean: When I first took in hand the manuscript that Gail Eifrig has woven from so much of my material, and when through her eyes I came newly to my own words, then *I* was the reader saying to the writer, "Yes, I will walk with you a while." And I liked that perspective very much. Gail Eifrig has by a most skillful juxtaposition created something new here, something capable of surprising me. A plowed ground produces new crops—and I am grateful to her for this harvest, a year's worth of food for thought.

So you and I may be readers together, closer in companionship, perhaps, than ever before.

Walk with me.

Words are the touch between us.

And the Word Himself is the life and the light and the grace of any such friendship, ever.

About This Book

If you use this book, you will spend a good deal of time with Walter Wangerin, and perhaps you would like to know whether or not that would be a good idea. (Of course, it is likely that you know his work already, and have picked up this book because you have liked some previous work. If so, then all you need to know is that you will reencounter here that distinctively intense voice in a new way—guiding and contributing to your everyday thoughts.)

If you have not met Walt or his work before, you should take a deep breath and be ready for a big experience, an experience I would describe like this: When, after a day spent lounging about indoors, you step outside for a brisk walk in a blustery fall day, the air strikes you as a challenge. It fills your lungs and makes you breathe deeply. You feel challenged, but refreshed, your head free of cobwebs—you sense that your thoughts are clearer, your emotions cleaner and more understandable. Reading Wangerin is like that.

Walt Wangerin knows you and me. His years as a pastor have given him access to so many people's inner lives. More than that, his writer's heart gives him the skill to point exactly to the place that needs his words. When he writes about our lives—what makes us sad, what makes us feel loved, what gives us joy, what causes our grief—we know we are hearing the truth. And it is a truth grounded in "the knowledge and the fear of the Lord," and a profound love of Jesus Christ.

The life of faith has a thousand different forms, because it has been lived a thousand different ways. And in any one person, the life of faith is always changing. For that reason a book of days can be both engaging and frustrating. I have chosen the selections here because of a rhythm of faith experience that makes a kind of sense. There is variety here— some days are affirmations and a hearty "Amen!" but some express uncertainty and sorrow, some mourn failure, and some celebrate victory. But this rhythm will not always fit yours. For that reason, the user of this book should not always feel bound to the order here, but move around and make its selections his or her own. You will find some passages that become favorites, and will want to write them out, perhaps to keep at work in your desk drawer, or over your workstation, maybe in the car—wherever you spend a lot of time and find yourself in need of refreshment, that sense of opening out into the fresh fullness of the outdoors.

However you use the book, you will find that time spent in Walt Wangerin's company gives you great return. Sometimes he is preaching, sometimes he is counseling, sometimes he is confessing. You will sometimes find yourself disagreeing with a voice that is always emphatic and intense. But you will never find him tedious. You will never hear him saying things that will leave you yawning politely and saying to yourself, "Well, yes, that is what preachers always say, don't they?"

More often than not, you will say, "How did he know I felt that way?" or, even more valuable, "Oh, that describes exactly how I feel—now I understand!"

A word about my editing: For the most part the selections in this book are exactly as they appear in the originals. But in some passages I have cut a phrase or a sentence or more to smooth the reading for this book. To avoid distractions I usually do not indicate the cuts with ellipsis points.

Gail McGrew Eifrig

Publisher's note: A suggested daily Bible reading follows the reading selection for each day.

January

January 1

Meditation on a New Year's Day

Mighty God!

Creator unbegun, unending!

Your works, when I think that they are yours, dazzle me to silence and to awe and aweful prayer.

For I am thrice removed from the knowledge of them, and each remove diminishes me until I am near nothing by your greatness. Yet you love me.

For I may know some little something of the sun, may take its temperature, may track its travels relative to other stars, may date its age, predict its death, observe the windy rage of its digestion in the time between. But what do such solar figures do to the size of me? And what are my own travels and my age and my death beside this brutal fire in the universe? Tiny, tiny, insignificant. My God, the little that I know of your sun, and this but one among a sea of suns, belittles me. How is it that you love me?

For you who made time are not bound by time—except you choose to be.

You embrace me, my dribble of moments. Right now you are standing at my birth, receiving me an infant into this created world. Yet right now you are present for this prayer of mine, prayed between the years. But right now you are establishing the answers of our prayers in our futures, in your present. And right now, right now, dear God, you are waiting at my death, your hands extended, ready to receive me to your kingdom—not only the same God as hears me now, but in the same eternal moment as now I pray!

For you are wonderful beyond describing it. And yet you love me. And still you choose to notice me. And nonetheless, you bend your boundless being, your infinity, into space and time, into things and into history, to find me, to preserve my life.

Abba, Abba, Father!

How is it that you care for me? *Psalm 19:1–14*

January 2

Not Melancholy, but Realistic

Many who read my writings today are inclined to call me "melancholy." They are wrong. Andersen's fantasies schooled me, rather, in realism. I know no resurrection except that first there's been a death. And as a writer, I cannot speak genuinely or deeply of resurrection except I speak the same of death and the sin that engendered death. That I can speak accurately of death without despairing is hardly melancholic. It is liberty— and victory ("O Death, where is thy sting?"). It is the evidence of the fundamental influence which Hans Christian Andersen had upon a child who did not analyze but lived such stories as Little Claus and Big Claus. *Ecclesiastes 7:1–7*

January 3

The Windows of a Fairy Tale

A forehead white with anger, a mouth made stiff—I recognized that woman too. I had met her often in the mornings, in the kitchen; and now I understood (as a child understands these things) her changes and her rages.

This is the explanation which imagination could accept: that I had not one but two mothers, an original and a stepmother, a Mother of the Evening who disappeared not once but ever and again, and a Mother of the Morning who possessed a different nature indeed. What a relief this insight was for me! No longer was my mother's transformation my fault. It was a simple, sad fact of existence—but a reversible fact, since the good and godly mother could spring new every evening, just as I could reread Snow White whenever I wished.

Moreover, even when the loving mother was absent, she still continued to exist—in me! My being was the issue of her prayer, her yearning, her bright red blood, and all her purity. I was the abiding beauty of that mother, which was precisely why the stepmother couldn't stand me. Should I think evil of myself? No. As the graceful offspring of my better mother, my very existence reminded my stepmother of worth and the virtue that she lacked. Not some shame in me, but rather my very innocence enraged the stepmother. I could endure her without guilt, for her anger now became understandable to me. I, the Snow White of the story, had destroyed her self-absorption.

Thus did I peer at the "real world" through the windows of a fairy tale, and thus did I find a certain fantastic sense in all of it, and the sense preserved me. Truly, this explanation of the double mothers is more subtle than I thought it through in childhood. I merely lived it. And I knew on some functional level that Snow White was "just" a fairy tale, that I was engaged in serious pretense. But the comfort it afforded me was actual: I loved better, walked freer, was a better, healthier child on account of it.   *Ecclesiastes 7:8–14*

January 4

Words Make Connection

Words work, as we've said, *within* experience. They are a means of personal participation, of submitting and committing to the encounter. They are dialogue, the dynamic process of both separating and also joining those that encounter one another; for when one talks while one listens, there are two roles, two beings; but when one speaks and the other receives *the same thing,* then two act as one. They are prayer or prophecy or "sweetly questioning" one of the other. They may be the impulses of the experience itself.

This first function of language is, perhaps, no great wonder, being so common—until we realize that this is the function Jesus himself performs. He *is* the means of encounter between God and us. He *is* the speaking of God into our ears. He *is* the Word.   *John 3:1–10*

January 5

Created, Named

This second function of language is divine for the further reason that God uses it, too, and we have received it from him. God not only created the world and the things of it; he also named what he created. Light he named "Day." Darkness he named "Night." He called the firmament "Heaven," the dry land "Earth," and the gathered waters, "Seas." In this way he said, "These things are not me, but they are mine." Too, by the name of the thing he expressed the essence of that thing and declared that this is the way that the thing would be forever. Finally, in the name he designated its correspondence to other things and its purpose for being. What God had made, he also fixed, firmed, affirmed, in the midst of all creation, under his clear ownership.   *Genesis 2:18–20*

January 6

God Must Act First

Words create.

Only God performs this function purely—God, who spoke the cosmos into being. For, before he spoke, there was nothing. And when he spoke, the speaking *was* the thing! His word was not a means, no incantation, no magic to body forth a something influenced by, but separate from, the word that called it. No: his imperative "Let there be light" was itself the light. This is why John later says that the Word is Life and Light; now the person of Jesus, the Word, takes on a mystery too wonderful for words; now we see that when God uses language according to its first function, the means of encounter, he can at the same time create, causing to be what had not been before, speaking into existence the Relationship, the faithing, that the human could not know nor initiate, causing love within that human for himself; now we know why God must act first. *John 3:17–21*

January 7

Sign and Meaning

It is an error to think that the process of faithing transcends the stuff of the world, and therefore to seek God only in the heavenly places. What is hidden is the meaning, not the sign itself. In Jesus' day, many people saw the signs, but misinterpreted. And those who picked St. Paul from the road, in order to lead him to Damascus, knew that something happened, though they couldn't explain it. And when the Father spoke to Jesus, the dull-eared *did* hear; they said, "It thundered."

John 3:11–15

January 8

The Human Whole

Or, to say all this another way: God leads the faither unto himself not in a manner divorced from daily and worldly experiences—in the secret regions of his soul only—but *by means of* the stuff and tumble of physical human existence. It is not a secret piercing of the heart that kills the faithing one, invisible to the eyes of other people. No, it is by the actions of those people themselves; it is in the very intercourse of community and words and feelings, bruisings, touchings, the casual greetings and the catastrophic attackings; it is in the downsitting and the uprising that God shapes the drama which kills the sinner. The spiritual drama of faith is enacted on the stage of this world, bodily and under sunlight. Faithing occurs in the experience of the whole human—the human whole; and though we may outline a general pattern to the drama, naming for it six passages, it is always performed in particularity, with loving attention to each individual actor.

John 2:1–12

January 9

Lord Rooster Meets Lowly Dog

The following selections, through January 31, tell the story of The Book of the Dun Cow, *in which animal characters play out the drama of good and evil in the world.*

In the morning Chauntecleer the Rooster stepped out of his Coop to crow at the sun and to rouse up all of his Chickens. When he was done, on this particular morning, he coughed hoarsely; and then he noticed that he was standing on something warm. He looked down and saw a Dog smiling up at him. The Dog was shaking his head. There were tears in his eyes.

"Such a voice in such a fine small beak," he said.

"Such a headache," said the Rooster, "from such a rug."

Humbly the Dog lowered his head. "Thank you, Doctor," he said.

The Rooster hopped down and strutted away. His tail feathers were flags behind him. "The name is Chauntecleer," he said, "you doormat."

"It's a little thing; a nothing, really," called the Dog behind him, "but there is a name for me, too. Of course there is no beauty in it. If the Doctor wants to call me Doormat instead of Mundo Cani Dog, this Dog will be happy."

From that day forward, Mundo Cani Dog would feel sad if Chauntecleer crowed to the rising sun from anywhere else but from his own sad and lumpy back.   *Job 1:1–5*

January 10

Chauntecleer Explains the World

Crows for laughter and crows for grief; a whooping crow for joy, which made joy come alive and dance right there in the Coop; a soft, insinuating crow for shame, at which the Hens would hide their heads under their wings. He could crow a certain spilling crow when he admired something very much. He could warn the stars themselves with a crow like a bloody alarum, and then the stars themselves would stand on guard. And at the death of someone beloved, Chauntecleer the Rooster mourned the passing by strutting to the roof of his Coop and

there sounding a throaty crow which rolled across the country-
side like the tolling of a heavy iron bell; and then God's creatures would surely pause, bend their heads, and weep.

Crows of pride and crows of glory; crows on the occasion
of a victory or a defeat. And crows, too, for the plain sake of
crowing.   *Job 1:6–12*

January 11

His Crows Bless the Moment

These canonical crows told all the world—at least that section of the world over which he was Lord—what time it was,
and they blessed the moment in the ears of the hearer. By
what blessing? By making the day, and that moment of the
day, familiar; by giving it direction and meaning and a proper
soul. For the creatures expected his canonical crows, and
were put at peace when they heard them. "Yes, yes," they
would say, "the day is our day, because Chauntecleer has
made it ours." That they would say in the morning, grateful
that by his crow the day should hold no strangeness nor fear
for them. And at noon: "The day's halfways over; the best part
is still coming." It was a comfort to be able to measure the day
and the work in it.   *Job 1:13–19*

January 12

The World Crowed into Order

Seven times a day, dutifully, with a deep sense of their importance, and by the immemorial command of the Divine,
Chauntecleer crowed his canonical crows.

At dawn, from Mundo Cani's lumpy back, he crowed a
fresh, green crow which sounded like chilly water and which

awakened the Hens on the spot. When it was time to go to work, he crowed another crow: "A-choo-choo-choo!"—something like a steam engine starting up; and then one couldn't help it; one's wings began to beat and claws would start to scratch the ground, digging for seeds and grubs, and beaks would begin to peck.

At nine o'clock, at noon, and then again at three o'clock the Rooster crowed crows to announce what kind of day was going by. Up went his head, with its comb as red as coral, its beak as black as jet. He listened to the wind; he saw the color of the sky; he watched the scratchers scratching; he considered all the news of all the things which were happening in that day up until that moment—and then he crowed some busy crows about this and that and such and such. Every creature knew the day when Chauntecleer was done with these crows: at nine o'clock, at noon, and then again at three. And kindly did the time pass by.   *Job 1:20–22*

January 13

The Gray Things Explained

The sixth crow came when the sun was going down. A Hen was glad to hear it for several reasons. For one, it sounded something like a compliment; it came across the evening air and patted each one on the back, and it made each forehead cool as if with a breeze: "Good," it said. "Good and better than you did yesterday. Now, stop. Eat supper. And rest easy." And so these were the other reasons a Hen was glad to hear it: Work was done and supper was coming.

But the seventh was the kindest crow of all. This was as quiet as nightfall. This crow was the night at peace upon her nest. This was settle, and rest, and "You are safe," and amen, and "Go, now, to sleep." For "Done," when it is well done, is a very good word.

When Chauntecleer crowed his canonical crows, the day wore the right kind of clothes; his Hens lived and scratched in peace, happy with what was, and unafraid of what was to be; even wrong things were made right, and the gray things were explained. *Job 2:1–6*

January 14

The Threat to Gentle Order

A third word concerning Chauntecleer's crows must now be spoken, though he himself was unaware of it. A third category of crows would, within a year of Mundo Cani's coming to the Coop, burst from Chauntecleer's throat with a terrible power. For an enemy was gathering himself against this Rooster and his land. Within the year Chauntecleer would find his land under a treacherous attack; and then, in that war, this third kind of crowing would become his necessary weapon. Cruel crows; sharp, explosive crows, murderous and thwarting, they would be called "Crows Potens." But Chauntecleer knew nothing of this now: of neither the enemy, nor the war which was to be, nor the killing crows which he had it in him to crow, the "Potens." *Job 2:7–13*

January 15

Earth and Creatures

In those days, when the animals could both speak and understand speech, the world was round, as it is today. It encountered the four seasons, endured night, rejoiced in the day, offered waking and sleeping, hurt, anger, love, and peace to all of the creatures who dwelt upon it—as it does today. Birth happened, lives were lived out upon the face of it, and then death followed. These things were no different from the way they are today. But yet some things were very different.

For in those days the earth was still fixed in the absolute center of the universe. It had not yet been cracked loose from that holy place, to be sent whirling—wild, helpless, and ignorant—among the blind stars. And the sun still traveled around the moored earth, so that days and nights belonged to the earth and to the creatures thereon, not to a ball of silent fire. The clouds were still considered to flow at a very great height, halfway between the moon and the waters below; and God still chose to walk among the clouds, striding, like a man who strides through his garden in the sweet evening.

Job 3:1–10

January 16

The Keepers

Many tens of thousands of creatures lived on this still, unmoving earth. These were the animals, Chauntecleer among them, whom God noticed in his passage above. And the glory of it was that they were there for a purpose. To be sure, very few of them recognized the full importance of their being, and of their being *there*; and that ignorance endangered terribly the good fulfillment of their purpose. But so God let it be; he did not choose to force knowledge upon the animals.

What purpose? Simply, the animals were the Keepers. The watchers, the guards. They were the last protection against an almighty evil which, should it pass them, would burst bloody into the universe and smash into chaos and sorrow everything that had been made both orderly and good. *Job 3:11–23*

January 17

Wyrm!

The earth had a face, then: smiling blue and green and gold and gentle, or frowning in furious gouts of black thunder. But it was a *face,* and that's where the animals lived, on the surface of it. But under that surface, in its guts, the earth was a prison. Only one creature lived inside of the earth, then, because God had damned him there. He was the evil the animals kept. His name was Wyrm.

Deep, deep under the oceans and the continents, under the mountains and under the river which ran from them to Chauntecleer's land, Wyrm crawled. He was in the shape of a serpent, so damnably huge that he could pass once around the earth and then bite his own tail ahead of him. He lived in caverns underneath the earth's crust; he lived in darkness, in dampness, in the cold. He was lonely. He was powerful, because evil is powerful. He was angry. And he hated, with an intense and abiding hatred, the God who had locked him within the earth. And what put the edge upon his hatred, what made it an everlasting acid inside of him, was the knowledge that God had given the key to his prison in this bottomless pit to a pack of chittering *animals!*   Job 3:24–26

January 18

Winter Rain; Damp Souls

At twelve noon on the following day, Chauntecleer the Rooster was to be found plotched upon a mud heap in the middle of a wet and runny field in the middle of a gray, rainy day. His color was spoiled yellow in the rain, and everywhere his feathers stuck to his body.

It is a lesson, how one may pass quickly from the immortal feeling of triumph to the mortal mood of grumpiness. From midnight to noon Chauntecleer had made the transition: He was in a filthy mood.

There was, first of all, the rain. The night had passed; the Rat had disappeared; but the rain had not. *Tap, tap, tap*—through the night and through the morning after it the chilly drizzle had persisted, and the boding clouds hung very near the earth. There was no sun, that sickly day, no cleanliness to crow to. Nothing whatever was solid in such a rain: The earth was slippery, water driveled everywhere, the sky merely dripped, and every standing thing lay down to weep. *Plot, plottery, plot, plot:* The rain fell into the puddles all around him, spinning out foolish circles. Nonsense! Ha and nonsense! Chauntecleer hated the drear rain, and he would have attacked a puddle if it would have done any good. But it wouldn't have—and so he was grumpy. His soul itself was damp.   *Job 9:1–13*

January 19

Suffering Asks, "Why?"

The Widow Mouse is one of the first victims of Wyrm's campaign against the animals. Chauntecleer, as Lord of the animals, tries to rescue her and her babies, the Tags.

The Mouse moved her mouth. Immediately Chauntecleer put his ear close to her mouth, but there wasn't a sound. And when he drew back to see her again, she was looking at him with clear, earnest, pleading eyes. Her eyes said, "Answer me."

"Dear Widow," he said, "I want to love your children. I want to see them living that I may love them. Can someone step from the shore to these branches, or does someone have to swim?"

Again her mouth moved without a sound. Her voice had finally gone away, but her lips were still making the words. Chauntecleer could see what they said. They were not answering his question. They said: "Why should the river move so fast?"   *Job 9:14–24*

January 20

Chauntecleer Saves the Tags: A Small Victory

"Listen to me, children," Chauntecleer said. "Your mother is beautiful. She has a coat as warm as sleep. She has a dry place in which to sing to you. But do please listen to me: She isn't here. And the dry place isn't here."

Perhaps not his words themselves, perhaps his tone and the steady look in his eye, spoke to them. For they looked back at the Rooster, somewhat sadder but less afraid.

"So she sent me to you with this message. Come. Come closer to hear it."

One did wriggle closer. Chauntecleer's heart beat violently.

"She said, 'A Rooster will give his wing to you.' This wing. And I'm the Rooster. Forgive me: I have a bad voice, nothing like your mother's. But that is truly her message. And she said, 'You, my children, must hurry to climb onto his wing.' Do, please, children, climb onto my wing."   *Job 9:25–35*

January 21

He Saw Her Lovely

Chauntecleer rescues another victim, the beautiful Hen, Pertelote.

She was lying unconscious on her back, her small claws balled on top of her. At her throat her feathers were crimson and beautiful. But her tail feathers were lapped in water, and she was wet to the roots. Her beak was open. But she was not dead. And she was so beautiful.

Now Chauntecleer the Ready did a most unready thing: He sat down and stared.

Perhaps if he had first seen her while she walked among a flock of Hens, clucking and pouting, this might not have happened to him. But he saw her in her weakness. He saw her lying open, where anyone in the world could have come by and hurt her. He saw her loose, sleeping, and without protection whatsoever. He saw her truthful, when she was not pretending to be anything else than a purely white Hen with fire at her throat. He saw her when she didn't see him back. He saw her lovely.

Job 10:1–5

January 22

The Coop Recoups

But if mud and a bleak season lay all around, then Chauntecleer's Coop was a warm, blessed island in the middle of it all. This little company of creatures was proof against dreariness, and together they were very happy.

On account of the strange weather, they lived in an unending twilight; yet the Rooster must have had a rising and setting sun on the inside of him, for lauds and prime he always crowed on time; terce, sext, and none he observed ever on the button; vespers and compline he kept as they should be kept—and his small society was kept very well that way.

Chattering and motion and light and warmth filled the Coop, as if it were a little furnace in a dark land. Food went into stomachs; gossip attended every ear; and the good cheer of the morning made waking a pleasant thing, while friendship—which filled the evenings—made sleep a good conclusion. The creatures were happy, because they were busy with good and important matters.   *Job 10:6–14*

January 23

The Mercy of the Snow

But perhaps God looked down from his heaven and had pity upon the Coop, for a merciful change occurred in the rain. It became snow. And where water as rain was mere misery, the same water as snow was a soft delight: A hard freeze made the ground bony and firm; snow followed to whiten and to reveal the gentle contour of that ground; the cold air snapped life into the creatures who ventured forth to walk on it; the forest greeted them, tinkling and clinking as if its great trees had tiny voices—and more than any of that, the Coop became muffled in its warmth, because snow drifted up the outside of its walls.

Now the place was no longer strange to the Beautiful Pertelote, and she sang some clear, haunting melodies. Her singing was like the moon in a wintry night—sharp edges, hard silver, slow in its motion, and full of grace; so it took the place of so much that was missing in those days, for there was no moon.   *Job 10:15–22*

January 24

What Wyrm Hates

The wasted land, the shattered society, the bodies dead and festering, were all great Wyrm's triumph. In one small part of the earth his Keepers had been first weakened and then killed. Their lives, which locked his life beneath them in the earth; their banded peace, which chained him there; their goodly love, which was his torment; their righteousness, which was iron against his will—that fabric had in one place on the earth been torn.

So one part of the earth's crust was softened, and Wyrm rejoiced. Could he but spread that soft, vulnerable area across a continent and to the sea, then he could himself blast through the crust, break free, and gallop through the spheres of the universe. Oh, he would swallow the moon in a gulp. He would bloody the sun. And he would roar almighty challenges to the Lord God Himself. He would spew chaos among the stars; and he would whirl his tail with such power that when it hit the earth, that planet would be cracked from its fixed position at the center of things to spin like nonsense going nowhere. While Cockatrice flew westward above, Wyrm dreamed dreams below: He himself would make of his earth prison a puny mockery. *He* would make it little among the planets and nothing among the suns. *He* would snatch purpose from its being, giving it a loose, erratic, meaningless course to travel. *He* would surround it with cold, empty space. And *he* would cancel heaven from above it.

Oh, how Wyrm hated this round ball, the earth! How he yearned to be out of it forever, to see it a piece of dust, whimpering from the edge of a galaxy for its God! *Job 21:7–16*

January 25

Beryl's Words

Beryl is the nursemaid for Chauntecleer and Pertelote's chicks, the three Pins.

Beryl dearly loved the Pins. She had been proud at their birth. She had been proud at the size of them and the speed with which they learned. And she had burst with pride to be chosen their nurse. No one knew how often she stole to their nests of a night, merely to hear their breathing and to assure herself that they were at peace. No one knew how deeply her heart yearned for them each time they went out of her sight—and for that reason she had never permitted them to leave the yard around the Coop. Did they want something from the forest? Well, then, *she* troubled herself to go and get it, whatever it happened to be. Great was her heart for the children, and great her care for them.

Beryl also had an abiding respect for words. As far as she was concerned, the word for a thing somehow *was* that thing. Therefore she never spoke frivolously what she did not mean to say; and she surely never put into words anything which she did not wish to happen. For the words themselves could trigger it, and then it would happen. To say something was to send the thing itself out into the world and out of her control. It was to curse. She never analyzed this faith of hers; she merely believed it and, with a dreadful care, acted accordingly.

Under her breath she prayed blessings upon the heads of the Pins continually. Continually? Why, she had never *ceased* to pray for them since their birth. With words she was constructing a defense around them, against danger, against disease, against ill will, against misfortune. All alone, in the secret of her soul, she was building their peace and their good growth—and that with *words*. *Job 21:17–26*

January 26

The Dun Cow Comes to the Stricken One

The Pins and Beryl have been killed by Wyrm's agent, Cockatrice.

"O my sons!" Chauntecleer suddenly wailed at the top of his lungs, a light flaring before it goes out: "*How much I want you with me!*"

The dark land everywhere held still, as if on purpose before such a ringing, echoing cry. The dark sky said nothing. The Rooster, with not an effort to save himself, sagged, rolled down the roof, slipped over the edge of the Coop, and fell heavily to the ground. Wind and sobs together were knocked out of him; he lay dazed.

And then it was that the Dun Cow came to him.

She put her soft nose against him, to nudge him into a more peaceful position. Gently she arranged his head so that he might clearly see her. Her sweet breath went into his nostrils, and he assumed that he woke up; but he didn't move. The Dun Cow took a single step back from the Rooster, then, and looked at him.

Horns strangely dangerous on one so soft stood wide away and sharp from either side of her head.

Her eyes were liquid with compassion—deep, deep, as the earth is deep. Her brow knew his suffering and knew, besides that, worlds more. But the goodness was that, though this wide brow knew so much, yet it bent over his pain alone and creased with it.

Chauntecleer watched his own desolation appear in the brown eyes of the Cow, then sink so deeply into them that she shuddered. Her eyes pooled as she looked at him. The tears rose and spilled over. And then she was weeping even as he had wept a few minutes ago—except without the anger. Strangely, Chauntecleer felt an urge to comfort *her;* but at this moment he was no Lord, and the initiative was not in him. A simple creature only, he watched—felt—the miracle take place. Nothing changed: The clouds would not be removed, nor his sons returned, nor his knowledge plenished. But there was this. His grief had become her grief, his sorrow her own. And though he grieved not one bit less for that, yet his heart made room for her, for her will and wisdom, and he bore the sorrow better.

The Dun Cow lay down next to the Rooster and spent the rest of the night with him. She never spoke a word, and Chauntecleer did not sleep. But for a little while they were together.

At dawn Chauntecleer crowed lauds; and then he went alone into his Coop.   *Job 23:1–7*

January 27

Pertelote's Song

The song was beautiful, a new thing in this place and unexpected. The voice was like a single shaft of cool light through so much gloom. It sang "Ah." It was sure of itself. It wound like a purely silken thread around all the thousand animals in the yard. It rose high and yet higher, singing no more than "Ah." "Ah" to the hearts of the thousand. "Ah" unto their Lord. "Ah" as clear and beautiful as the limber sky.

For one wild moment Chauntecleer thought that this was the voice of the Dun Cow, though he had absolutely no reason to think so. He stared out over the assembly to find her. And he did, at the very back, underneath the trees. No, it wasn't her voice. But once again he saw her eyes with a strange clarity, and he perceived where she was looking. The Dun Cow was gazing directly at the singer. Chauntecleer followed her gaze and saw that it was the Beautiful Pertelote who had begun to sing. The lady had found her voice.

When she had risen to a region of crystal beauty, Pertelote turned her song into "Turalay," and it became a ballad. What a shining and peaceful ballad! It settled the entire multitude and, listening, they closed their mouths.

Yet, in the lovely clothing of this ballad, Pertelote told them what she knew of the danger which was approaching. She told them of the serpents which crawled and killed. But because such knowledge came to them in a song, the animals felt equal to this evil, and they did not panic. She told them of the poisonous bite, the dreadful speed with which they flung themselves. Her ballad did not make the serpents lovely. Her ballad hid nothing of their dread. But the music itself spoke of faith and certainty; the melody announced the presence of God. So the evil which the words contained did not panic the animals, and they listened, understanding. She named Cockatrice in her ballad, and she rhymed him with "hiss." And the animals discovered that she had chosen against this abomination and yet had lived; and the animals did not panic.

Chauntecleer looked down upon her of the flaming throat, and he loved her. Mother—no mother anymore; yet she sang. Silent once, but silent no longer; and she sang. O God! Where was there a faith in all the land to match the faith of Pertelote?

And while she sang her lovely melody, for just a moment until it was done, the clouds broke; and then the visible sun touched the tops of the trees, for it shone from the edge of the earth. It turned the white Coop golden; and all the heads of those who listened burned a little bit. And all the ears were filled with light and understanding.

Pertelote finished her song and was still.

Spontaneously in the sun's red glow, in the afterglow of Pertelote's song, the multitude whispered together one massive word: "Amen," as if it were an exhalation from the earth to the spheres. The moment was peaceful and good. In the days to come, Chauntecleer would remember it often and draw strength from it.   *Job 23:8–17*

January 28

Your Cockatrice Is Dead, and I Have Done It!

In the battle, Chauntecleer, armed with Gaff and Slasher, kills Cockatrice.

Chauntecleer lay underneath—Cockatrice, his winding tail, on top of him. Gaff had pierced Cockatrice at the throat. The Slasher was buried deep in his chest. Cockatrice was not dead; but he was dying. Yet his hatred for the Rooster was so intense that he did not back away nor pull the weapons out of his body. Instead he lunged forward, reaching with his beak for the Rooster's neck.

He thrust Gaff entirely through his own throat. The point slid bloody out of the back of his neck. Jerk by jerk he pressed the Slasher ever deeper into his chest. He inched closer to Chauntecleer's face.

The demon's face was just in front of his own—a mirror.

Then hot blood burst out of Cockatrice's mouth, spurting and steaming, and the demon died.

In a rasping, tormented voice, Chauntecleer began to crow the crow of victory. So the animals were set free. They climbed the wall to see what he had done; and when they saw, they were astonished by the thickness and the strength of the demon's tail. But still no one said a word. Chauntecleer was not done.

Slowly he returned to the body, gargling a vehement, crazy crow. Savagely he began to hack at its neck. Into his own beak he took the bare neck bone of the enemy; this he shook with such violence that it broke and the head came away from the body. Chauntecleer raised this head high, and walked.

Across the battlefield he walked. Around the corpses he walked. Wearily, but with the head of Cockatrice above him like a standard which trailed torn flesh, Chauntecleer walked to the river.

At the shore he stretched his neck and cried out: "Wyrm! Oh, Wyrm! Oh, wretched Wyrm! Swallow this thing and gag! Your Cockatrice is dead, and I have done it!"   *Job 38:1–11*

January 29

Losing the Battle

But it is entirely possible to win against the enemy, it is possible even to kill the enemy, and still to be defeated by the battle.

Chauntecleer had not lost his life to Cockatrice, but he'd lost something infinitely more dear. He had lost hope. And with it went the Rooster's faith. And without faith he no longer had a sense of the truth.

When the battle with Cockatrice—sore, exhausting battle—turned out *not* to be the final battle after all, then it was Wyrm and not the Rooster who rejoiced in victory. With seven words Wyrm had more than weakened him, for he was already weak. With seven words Wyrm had made the war an endless thing and every victory a joke. With seven words Wyrm had murdered hope and sent the Rooster mumbling through the windless halls of despair. And with seven confident words Wyrm had struck down the leader of the land, so that the land was no longer proof against his escape. Leaderless, loose, the Keepers would lose their strength. The bond was breaking, the patch frayed at the center of it, the prison gate unlocking. And Wyrm saw freedom in front of him!

For Chauntecleer one thing and one thing only held any meaning now: his own feelings. All of the rest was mere shadow—smiling, mocking shadow.   *Job 38:31–38*

January 30

Mundo Cani Dog Saves the Coop from Wyrm

For one second Mundo Cani crouched, taut upon the cliff, the long horn between his teeth. Then, with a cry, he leaped.

Over the edge, past the mud, missing the rock like a shadow, down and down Mundo Cani fell, the white horn livid in the dark.

The eye had almost begun to turn. But Mundo Cani had aimed himself well, had made an arrow of his fall. He hit the eye hard, with all four feet. He scrambled, grabbed a footing with his sharp claws, raised the horn, and drove it to the butt through the white flesh.

How Wyrm raged then!

Back and forth the body slammed against the sides of the canyon, the earth crack. Howlings ascended, as if the caverns of the earth were all Wyrm's throat, all filled with his hideous dismay. No longer was his vast motion controlled. It was mad, enraged—and blind.

In heaven the clouds ripped asunder like a veil. And the light of the sun plunged down and filled the earth. And Chauntecleer could see. And Chauntecleer, in a world suddenly silent, suddenly bright, grieved.

Behind him neither Coop nor camp nor wall. A desolation.

In front of him, at a good distance from him, a sparkling and peaceful sea. And, finally, between him and the sea, an endless scar east to west in the face of the earth—an angry seam closed.

It was this scar that the little Rooster was watching. But he wasn't seeing the scar at all. Over and over again in his mind—as if it were still happening—he was watching a memory: He remembered that as Wyrm swung himself about so grimly a moment ago, and as the wall was caving in on him, there was a Dog in his eye, stabbing and stabbing that eye with a long horn until the eye was no more than a blind and shredded socket.

Wyrm, and more than Wyrm—that scar had knit Mundo Cani into the earth.

Job 40:1–9

January 31

It Is Not Over

Pertelote explains his guilt to Chauntecleer.

"For what! He went down and it should have been me. So! I've said so. For what else?"

"Oh, Chauntecleer. He *knew* he had to go down. Don't you understand that? There was never any question about who would make the sacrifice. Leader or not, it just wasn't your place to go. Cockatrice was yours; but Wyrm's eye was his. So it was from the beginning. So it had to be. And so he told me when you were raving in the Coop strange things about a Cow. With neither fear nor hesitation he told me this thing, the last thing left to do. He accepted it as destiny. This is not your sin, Proud Chauntecleer; and if you keep saying that it is, you protect yourself against the greater. You are blinding yourself. Penance for what else?"

Chauntecleer shivered all over as the thing pushed its way into his throat. He could say it, perhaps, into a hole in the ground. He could give it word, perhaps, when no one else was around. But to say it to Pertelote—his wife, the one who spoke with Mundo Cani when no one else was speaking to him, and when Chauntecleer himself—

"I despised him," Chauntecleer said.

"So," said Pertelote. "This was your wickedness."

"He was making ready to die for us, and I didn't understand that. I judged him a traitor. I made his last moments lonely, and I despised him."

"Did you think that this was a secret, that you should hide it so long?"

"No."

"But this, Chauntecleer—this is your sin?"

"Yes."

"But now you have said it," Pertelote said, "and that is good. That is the beginning of your life now, because it is the ending of something. Chauntecleer, maybe one day you will say the same to Mundo Cani, and then he will be able to speak his forgiveness in your hearing, and that will complete the matter. Then you will be free of it. Chauntecleer," she said full quietly on the maple limb. She waited until his attention had been turned from his sin unto her. "I love you."

"Thank you," he said foolishly.   *Job 42:1–6*

February

February 1

God Giving Birth

Pastor Cheri baptizes her baby, Hannah, in the congregation of Grace Lutheran Church.

Of course this mother would weep at the baptism of her child, her heart. She was weeping in gladness for her beloved, whom she loved not merely in sentiment, but in most holy doing, with her bones and her blood and her muscle, her womb and her suffering. She was weeping in knowledge—for this was a birth that no one could snatch away from Hannah, a life forever; and this time no one suffered pain but the Savior, no one bled but the Christ; but Cheri knew what sort of pain that was.

Pastor Cheri: *Hannah, I baptize you in the name of the—*

But again, again—I saw Cheri as if there was nothing between us, neither time nor space nor flesh nor worlds, and I recognized in that same moment a most celestial thing:

That *I* was the baby Hannah.

That Cheri was the figure of my God, and God was weeping.

And this is what my heart sang: Holy God, how you have mothered me!

For the crying voice of Reverend Cheri Johnson was precious, was the voice of the Holy One, *bath qôl,* daughter of the voice—of God! Divine the words that she uttered at this second birthing: she was the authority of the love of God, effectual and effectually there. Oh, this was no metaphor nor some image of my mind. This was sacred fact, present and immediate—and I saw how the weeping God had birthed me.

I saw the restless God, pacing and pacing the empyrean, suffering the contractions of my bulking incompletion, my unborn presence, suffering in the deeps and the very elements of uncreated being. I saw God searching for and finally finding the holiest, most merciful posture for bringing me to birth—

I saw the mighty God kneel down.

God knelt in utter humility for a tender parturition, tender to me, hurtful to the tender parts of God. God sank into this world, humble to all of the laws, bowed down to all of its pain. The Word became a flesh that could bleed a human blood.

And having knelt, God groaned and bore me my second time. In pain. I was born in a rain of godly blood: blood that I had caused, for I burst my God, the brow and the palms and the heart of God, in order to be born; but blood my God did not begrudge me, for this was the very life of God upon me. Wash me! Wash me clean.

And even now the maternal God remembers my delivery. I am not lost in the multitude. What mother does not remember the single deliverance of every single child she bore? What mother doesn't whisper the baby's name, remembering? So God loves me and calls me by my name.

1 Samuel 2:1–11

February 2

Mary's Child and Mary's Promise

On the fortieth day after his birth, his parents gathered him up and walked the distance from Bethlehem to Jerusalem. There they purchased two turtledoves in order to perform the appointed sacrifice; and then, for the first time in his life, Jesus was taken to the Temple of the Lord, the house of God.

At once a man stepped forward and stretched out his hands.

"Woman," he whispered. His voice trembled.

"May I," whispered the man, "woman, may I hold him awhile?"

Mary said, "Yes," and the man took Jesus to his own breast as though he were a starving man and the child were bread for him.

"Forgive me," he said, for he wept.

This was Simeon. And this particular moment in his life, this holding of the baby Jesus, was all that he ever lived for. Long ago the Holy Spirit had promised him that he would not die until he had seen the Christ of God. And for all his years Simeon had led a devout and righteous life, waiting, waiting for the consolation of Israel.

Now here it was. And here he was. And he wept with a joy fulfilled.

Suddenly he began to chant a song over the child.

"Now you may let me die, my Lord, in peace according to your word, for my own eyes have seen the bright salvation which you sent for all the people. Light enlightening the nations! Glory for your people, Israel!"

Simeon turned his wet eyes to Mary and Joseph, who marveled at the song he sang. He blessed them both. But for Mary alone he chanted another verse.

"Ah, Mother, by your child shall many stumble and fall. And many in Israel shall rise by him. Bitter will be the arguments surrounding him, for he will reveal the secret thought of many hearts. And a sword," sang Simeon. "Yes, and a sword shall pierce through a mother's soul—yours, dear Mother of the Child. Yours."

One single child did Mary and Joseph bear in their arms as they returned that evening to Bethlehem. But in their hearts they bore a thousand thoughts about him. And they walked in silence by the way. *Luke 2:22–32*

February 3

What is Hell?

Hear, then, of the death those who trust in Jesus shall not die. Hear and tremble and give thanks to God.

It is the Dying Absolute. It is the sundering of every relationship for good, forever, and for all. It is more than the cutting of earthly relationships, for it is the experience of eternal, irrevocable solitude. It is perpetual exile from God. From love. It is, perhaps (though I do not understand this) the death that knows it is dead. Now, finally, one knows what love is, though one is severed forever from loving and being loved. Now one knows God both in goodness and in glory, and fears him, and honors him, and would even believe in him, but cannot, for God has departed from that one eternally. This is the death of every holy alternative: what is, must be the same forever.

It is a divine and solemn irony, for God hath finally granted the sinner, now in his fourth death, what he took from God in the first: complete independence, a perfect autonomy, a singularity like unto nothing in all possibilities—except the singularity of God before he began to create. But he who has died the fourth death is not God; he never could create, and now he can accomplish nothing. He is the god of a little realm that admits one god only, his impotent self. He can only know and despair. He is lost, and "lost" is all he may say of himself forever, no attribute, no other characteristic, no past nor future, that single thing. "I perish." *Apollumai.*

The utter state of solitude is the Dying Absolute. Outer darkness, where there is weeping and gnashing of teeth.

Throughout the generations, its common name has been Hell.   *Matthew 5:21–30*

February 4

The World Imprisoned

It is precisely because of the faith of my father than I can consider the death of my father with clarity and completeness, as well as deaths in all their differences and all their extremities. The legacy of his faith, as it is also my faith, has a thousand returns. It offers a freedom the poor world, imprisoned in ignorance, desperately needs.

The death of our bodies is only the most visible and evident episode in the long drama of dying that began when first we severed ourselves from the Lord of Life. The third death is a gathering of all Secondary Dyings in one final convulsion; therefore it is the climax of the drama—but not the conclusion!   *1 Corinthians 15:54–57*

February 5

Work

And here is the highest and the tightest element of mutuality between ourselves and nature: that our "work" on earth—our actual service to and within creation—approves for each of us our individual value. It is in the Natural Relationship that our lives are proven important. While we are workers at any good labor, we are not meaningless ciphers!

Whatever the present attitude may be, "work" itself was never a curse. Our various jobs, our "work" declares our purpose on earth; it is our conscious, personal participation in the webbing of the universe; it is my relevance. More than that, within the Communal Relationship it becomes our repute and thereby—in the best sense of the term—our glory.

Dear laborers, in the obedient discharge of our labors we are servants of God to God's creation, exercising the Image of God in us.

And this is the sweet return: "That the Lord your God may bless you in all the work of your hands that you do." That particular blessing does not promise some sort of financial prosperity; rather, it promises joy. That you will *like* to work, and that the work itself will be your own supreme self-satisfaction. That by it you shall be assured: you are accounted worthy in the universe. Lo, ye are of more value than many sparrows!   *Genesis 1:28–31, 3:17–19*

February 6

Naming the Loss

When a dear friend discovers some radical difference in himself, some characteristic hitherto hidden; when, for example, he feels convinced that he is homosexual; or when he comes a cropper, poorer than anyone thought and in desperate need—what do we feel then? In the midst of every other emotion, *both* the friend and we ourselves will suffer the radical revision of an old relationship. So what will we feel? Grief. Name that rightly, or anger may turn into accusation, rendering new relationship impossible.

Grief, in such circumstances, is right and righteous. Tears and sadness have their place. But a flat, angry rejection of the other is the doubling of death. He who already has died unto his old self is now cut off by his friend as well. Count: two for him, one single death for you—but your death caused his second death, and that latter was not necessary, if only you had perceived your grief *as* grief.

Thus the "passages" of friends and relatives break the familiar patterns of our lives. "Everything flows," saith the philosopher truly. For good or ill, people change, breaking the relationships we had enjoyed with them, causing us daily to die. Do you begin now to know why thy soul is cast down and sad?   *Ecclesiastes 3:18–22*

February 7
The Question

The question, my children, is not *whether* you will suffer but *how* you will suffer. For either you will take the world's terms as your own and give as good as you get—an eye for an eye, spit for spite, pain in equal measure—

Either, I say, you will rage like the world to save yourself, feeling justified in any counterattack and changing nothing whatever beneath the sun—

Or you will find in unearned suffering an opportunity of the spirit. This is a hard saying, I know. But it is not impossible. The presence of Christ in you can translate suffering into a ladder—a Jacob's ladder with four rungs up toward redemption and four rungs down that holiness might enter the world again. *Ecclesiastes 6:1–6*

February 8

Love, or Self-Pity?

Sham love never perceives the image intrinsic within the other. Rather, it makes up its own image of what she ought to be, then imposes this fiction upon her. When she doesn't conform, sham love might remain resolutely blind to what she is and pretend she *has* conformed, imprisoning her within its restrictive fiction. Or else it will blame her for the failure: "I'm so disappointed in you!" Thus justified, sham love will try harder to force conformity, or will reject her altogether.

One of the plainest signs of the sham in love is self-pity. Another is fear of freedom. Since the goal of sham love is itself, it must control the beloved. In fact, it measures her love by the amount of obedience she gives its will. Therefore, though genuine love takes a genuine joy in the free flight of the beloved, sham love is angered by her slightest act of independence; angered first, then threatened; then frightened by an independence that bodes separation; and finally, if she has flown indeed, sham love falls into the despair of the unfulfilled, the futile.

Listen to the songs of the world and the language they use for love. How often the point of the song is the singer! Listen to the wisdom of the world: "Feeling good about myself, yeah! Self-fulfillment's a birthright, and my worth you must acknowledge and accommodate, just because I AM." Such a demand—though it makes a worldly sense—is exactly the opposite of sacred love, for it makes a god of the self.

Ecclesiastes 4:8–12

February 9

Words for Those Who Comfort the Grieving

Comforting shall require much of the comforter.

No gesture of grief is isolated. *She* may not know why she does what she does. She may fear that her broken emotions and wild compulsions are evidence of a sort of insanity, sudden, inexplicable, estranged, and isolated. Coming from nowhere. In fact, every gesture and every mood is experienced in the stream of all her grieving, which soon reveals a continuum, a necessary form. The comforter can recognize the form according to general human patterns of behavior. Even if the griever "spirals" through the pattern, repeating certain acts again and again with greater or lesser intensity, yet because the comforter can name the behavior he is himself neither frightened nor useless, but remains a stable element in the midst of chaos.

Comforter, know where she's at in her journey *according to the script*. Though you need teach her nothing right now, you are her knowledge: you yourself have become the "knowing" that assures her of sanity and hope and healing, though she *recognizes* none of these things.

On the other hand, do not impose the script upon her, nor presume to know which act she's in without first reading her behavior. Always take your cues from her. By instinct *she* is leading; in patience you are serving.　　　　*John 6:17–27*

February 10

Failure

If self-image is what we think we are, self-esteem is the value we place upon it. We like to like ourselves.

If the self scores well according to standards one admires, then one can admire himself. The relationship is good; he is content. But if the self should fail some significant test, the relationship breaks. He falls out of favor with himself. Can there be a more ruinous break than this, that one should despise his *self?* It is worse than if the eye said to the hand, "I have no need of you." Worse, I say, because this rejection can be total and passionate: the eye saying to the *eye,* the man to the man, "I have no need of you." This is death.

"Standards." One wishes that we would accept the absolute standards of God for a righteous self-evaluation, even the law that is written upon our hearts. Instead, the world sets standards we feign would follow: our peers announce what's fashionable; the media persuade us of style; the expectations of a culture or a community or a corporation become the Law for us.

Standards come from those whom we have allowed to be authorities over us, whose approval we yearn, whether society or business or families or even our own whims and desires.

These, when we feel driven to obey them, become gods in place of the true God, whose standards were established in perfect wisdom and holy love for us. False gods may or may not love us—that doesn't matter. False gods cannot save us—that's what matters, because even from false gods we seek salvation, we seek esteem for ourselves, *we seek to prove ourselves worthy,* by striving to keep the laws they set.

And since the law of any god, whether true or false, requires a perfect obedience, we will fail these laws.

When we fail the laws of the True God, we may receive forgiveness, by Christ's achievement.

But when we fail the laws of false gods, there is no holy option since there is no holy God around: we simply fail. We are severed from standards we honor, from all who honor the same standards, from reputation, from self-esteem, from worth.

To fail is to die. *Ephesians 4:6–14*

February 11
The Strength of the Mighty Deity

If the Gospel seems irrelevant to our daily lives, that is our fault, not the Gospel's. For if death is not a daily reality, then Christ's triumph over death is neither daily nor real. Worship and proclamation and even faith itself take on a dream-like, unreal air, and Jesus is reduced to something like a long-term insurance policy, filed and forgotten—whereas he can be our necessary ally, an immediate, continuing friend, the Holy Destroyer of Death and the Devil, my own beautiful Savior.

How else could the psalmist confront in such terrible detail his own dying, the sundering of vital relationships, and the grief that follows—except in the strength of the mighty Deity, yea, though that Holy One seem so distant?

> *Why art thou cast down, O my soul?*
> *And why art thou disquieted within me?*
> *Hope thou in God:*

for I shall yet praise him,
who is my help
and my God.

Ephesians 2:11–15

February 12
Why Is Wyrm?

This and the selections through February 26 are from The Book
of Sorrows, *a sequel to* The Book of the Dun Cow. *The animals
of the Coop try to live after the first great battle with Wyrm.*

Wyrm, that subterranean Serpent! No one deserved so ruinous an evil underneath her feet. No one had defied him; no
one had sinned enough to justify his presence in the universe. Absolutely no one. Yet, he was; he was; he existed.
Long and foul and putrefying, a single muscle, a massive,
contracting muscle in the round earth. Why? And he hated
God with a furious hatred; but he focused his spite on the Animals, and they were the ones who suffered his cruelty, but
who were they? Animals. Plain Animals, yet he had murdered
them, and all were horrified, and all of them transfixed—all
but one. One. Mundo Cani Dog took him a stick and taunted
Wyrm, ha! And when the Wyrm's eye turned to see this
speck, why, Mundo Cani leaped over the cliff, ha-ha! down
and down the gorge, the earth-crack, Wyrm's hatch, and
landed fighting on the monster's eyeball: pierced it, pierced it,
slashed it to madness, so that the great, slick muscle doubled
on himself, and the earth-crack couldn't stand the spasm; it
collapsed in earthquake; it thundered shut. So Wyrm was
contained. So, ha! Ha-ha to the monster imprisoned again!

So Wyrm crawled the belly of the world. So. But so *what?* He was still alive, for all of that! And he took with him a friend beloved above all others, that humble Mundo Cani. When one went down, they both went down together. Oh, how shall we live without the gentle Mundo Cani? How can we ever be complete again? Oh, Wyrm! Oh, Wyrm!—Oh, fire and fury! Wyrm!

Mighty God, you talk to us! Tell us: *why does Wyrm exist?*

He killed peace.

He killed their deeper trust and sweet security; Hens had rather more suspicious eyes than ever they did in the past. Chauntecleer's Canonical Crows were more needful than ever before, more necessary than the rising of the sun; nonetheless, ironically, they were less believed than ever before; because of the war which came in spite of them. Because of Wyrm.

Oh, Chauntecleer crowed crows nearly baroque for subtlety, intelligence, and beauty; he went extraordinary lengths to make each Crow a something, a memorable blessing each in itself, all tender to the Chickens; but sometimes he wondered whether those lengths didn't measure a personal doubt. And could it be that the grander, more wonderful the Crow on its outside, the emptier it was at its core?

Mighty God, please talk to us. Explain it, explain—

Why is Wyrm?   *Acts 1:6–11*

February 13

How He Wrestled Darkness

In the evening, in the night, twenty-nine Hens sat like globes of fruit in the branches of the maple tree; and seven Mice had dug themselves a new hole at its roots; and a Weasel lurked not far away.

And Chauntecleer crowed, from the lowest branch, a soft, familiar Compline, to make this place and this particular night less alien. This is how he wrestled darkness. And the Hens tucked their heads beneath their wings. They settled down to little homely clucks, and finally to sleep.

Acts 1:12–14

February 14

Fear: Ferric the Coyote

At the edge of the great northern forest, at the foot of steepling pine, low, low down, crouched at his forelegs, up in the rear, grinning, it seems, with all of his teeth—a Coyote is hiding.

He *thinks* he is hiding.

In fact, he's in full view from three sides, with only his butt to the tree trunk; but this is the way he hides: he freezes. Poor Ferric! He's convinced that perfect stillness effects perfect invisibility. And he is not grinning. He's scared. His cheeks go back to his ears when he's scared, and his eyes narrow into two pitiful darts crossing at his snout, and the snout itself seems to sharpen. Ferric! Fear turns him into one long, taut nerve, an arrow fixed mid-flight, or a bowstring which, if it's only touched, would hum at a high pitch: *eeeeeee!*

Ferric has frozen this way often in his lifetime, since life itself is for him a dangerous proposition. The Coyote is cursed with senses too keen for a fainting heart. His ears are dishes; they hear everything. His paws are raw, and his bones are hollow tubes and his skin tympanic; they feel everything, magnified. His eyes are perpetually frighted; they see every twitch in nature, and any twitch may be malicious, for no twitch that he knows doth love him.   *Acts 2:1–13*

February 15

Tiny Between the Seasons

But then, in the following weeks, the weather changed. And Rachel, too, who had never changed before, changed. And Ferric had a whole new riddle set before him in the person of his wife. For her change seemed to have nothing whatever to do with the weather's, and he was confounded.

Winter commenced. Two days after they had gone about scenting a little territory for their own, the winter began with weird, inexplicable shifts, a sort of colliding of the elements, so that Ferric Coyote grew wary; he paced constantly; he started at little noises; he rolled his eyes restlessly.

And he felt silly, since Rachel did none of these things.

But he couldn't help himself. Look: through several days together the winter sky would oppress them with humidity and a steady drizzle, would so laden the air that a Beast could see his own breath, yet he would sweat in the closeness. And pace.

But then in any given night the cold would hit like a fist: sudden, absolute and numbing; and the moisture froze so fast, 'twould seem as with a click; and the north wind might scream across the land, or else the wind would kill by the cold alone, lazily touching all things to ice. Nobody hung his tail outside the Den on such nights, and by morning the muddy world was transfigured. Ferric climbed the stones to find the plains pure sheets of ice, slippery under his paws, the sun blinding him by slanting from its surface, the air crisping his whiskers and stabbing zero to his lungs. He'd gulp, and suffocate. And the great pine trees he found cased in ice, sparkling, tinkling lightly, and yet splitting the limbs by its weight, causing tremendous crashes in the forest. Little Ferric gazed, then, on a cold *Eisreisenwelt*, so lovely and so sepulchral.

Who wouldn't pace nervously at such a spell?
Who wouldn't feel tiny between the seasons?   *Acts 2:14–21*

February 16

Forgiveness Makes a Sin Gone

*The Seven Mice, the Tags, are wakeful because Freitag has—in
trying to cheer the gloomy rooster—imitated Chauntecleer in front
of the Coop. Chauntecleer was not amused.*

But Chauntecleer was right there, listening. He wasn't far
away. "In God's name, tell me," he said, feeling like a stranger.
"Why don't you sleep?"

Samstag whispered, still as though he were not there, "I
think that I will tell him, Wodenstag, on account of, he
asked." And to Chauntecleer: "We stay awake with Freitag, to
keep him company."

Chauntecleer said, "Freitag—" But the mere speaking of
the Mouse's name unmanned that Mouse. He began to cry:
"Hoo-hoo. Hoo-hoo," such a pitiful snuffling and so polite
that Chauntecleer felt gross and clumsy. He truly didn't understand Freitag's trouble, though all the Brothers seemed to.
How long had this been going on? How much had he missed?
And why should tiny Mice protect their Lord—?

The Rooster, by willing it, restrained his own confusion; he
gathered all his care and all his sensitivity into a gentle voice
and spoke for the Mice alone.

"Do you remember?" he asked slowly, "how I took you
from the river long ago, when you were nips about to
drown?"

"Yes," said Wodenstag and Donnerstag and Sonntag. "Yes.
Yes," all of them full of solemnity.

"Do *you* remember, Freitag?"

Freitag said, "Hoo-hoo, yes, hoo-hoo."

"You were so brave, to climb from the river onto my back. Remember? And you trusted me, and that's why I could save you then. Remember, Freitag?"

"Hoo-hoo."

"Do you trust me now, enough to lay your trouble on me? So that I could help you now? I still help, little Tag. I don't hurt Mice. Do you believe that?"

"Oh truly, truly—hoo-hoo."

"Then tell me, why don't you sleep? Why do you cry?"

Freitag fairly wailed, "Because the Rooster is so good. That is the trouble." Then, deep in a wee gloom: "Because I am so wicked. That is the trouble."

Chauntecleer's face burned hot—a rush of shame at this innocent division of good and evil—and he couldn't speak. Freitag could.

Freitag said, "A wicked Creature doesn't have the right to sleep."

"You are *not* a wicked Creature!" Chauntecleer struggled to keep his voice from sounding angry.

"Oh, yes, I am very wicked," sighed the Mouse. "Because—" And then the words tumbled from him: "I made fun of you, Rooster. I mocked you, yes, yes. I walked like you walk, and I crowed like you crowed, and all my Brothers laughed at it, and you would never hurt me, but I hurt you, dear Rooster, because you didn't smile at what I did, but you were kind, you didn't scold me either. You . . . you just . . . you just walked away from me. Oh, Rooster! Hoo-hoo-hoo."

Chauntecleer snatched his head from the Mouses' hole and raised his face to the dark tree-forms beneath the stars, and he wanted to cry. *You just walked away from me.* The wind shrieked a manic winter in the woods. The moon accused him. The Rooster felt naked. Walking away: that was his sin, not Freitag's! Yet that little Mouse accepted the fault without a second thought, because that little Mouse—and here was the worst pain—that little Freitag loved him.

He put his head into their hole again. With fierce restraint, he counted his words like coins. "You think you sinned against me?" he asked.

"It is the way that I am," said Freitag. A bleak answer, a bleak Mouse.

"If you sinned against me," said Chauntecleer, "then it's my right to punish you, isn't it?"

"Yes."

"But not your right at all. You have to accept my will."

"Yes."

"Freitag?"

"What?"

"My will is not to punish you. So you can't punish yourself any more with not sleeping. Freitag?"

"What?"

"My will is to forgive you. I forgive you. There is no sin any more. It's gone. Do you hear me? Forgiveness makes a sin gone, and you are good again. Good Creatures have every right to sleep. Go to sleep, Freitag. Go to sleep, now. Can you go to sleep?"

Freitag took a long time to answer. Oh, God, why couldn't all the world smell as kind and woolen and comforting as a Mouse's hole on a winter's night?

Finally the honest Mouse answered, "I don't know."

Chauntecleer said, "How if I told you one thing else?"

"What?" said Freitag.

"That I love you with all my heart, little Tag."

"Yes," sighed Freitag, infinitely relieved. "Yes, that makes a difference."

Wodenstag asked, "Then we can all go back to sleep?"

Acts 2:22–36

February 17

Pertinax Knows Best!

Pertinax Cobb the Ground Squirrel hadn't minded when Hens and some Mice and a certain Weasel of immoderate length had collected at the Hemlock tree across the Liverbrook—and Chicks of a noxious peep. He stood erect at the porch of his own tunnels, and watched the bustle, and he didn't mind.

Neither did Pertinax mind frightfully when it became evident that they meant to *stay* in the neighborhood.

Pertinax Cobb hadn't minded the golden Rooster either, nor the metronomic regularity of his crowing, because the Bird was beautiful, of a beautiful song, and Cobb fancied himself something of an artist; besides, he valued schedules and self-discipline. He hadn't minded the jolting crow in the early mornings. He hadn't minded the midnight broodings (which necessitated that the Ground Squirrel pop up in moonlight, erect, to watch). He hadn't even minded (though this cost him much patience, not to mind it) that the Rooster never once took a neighborly glance across the stream, in neighborly fashion to greet the neighbor standing there, waiting—

What Pertinax Cobb *did* mind, however, was that at the cold beginning of the winter—when he had expected some relief, since Animals generally retired into a winter's seclusion, allowing other Animals their peace—the whole community began to act as if it were the spring! Boisterous noise! Furious activity! A royal racing about, and a totally untimely scavenging for food. Craziness! The neighborhood was in an uproar, and Pertinax was displeased.   *Acts 2:37–47*

February 18
Thinkings Makes Gloominesses: The Weasel Reflects

Well, this was the joy of the Weasel, to see that Rooster in his glory once again. When Chauntecleer ruled as he should, why then, the world was *right*. Chauntecleer had taught him manners, once upon a time, and he, John Wesley, had learned. Chauntecleer had been the single Creature tougher, scrappier, louder, more boisterous than him; so he had learned. And he was beholden to the one that had civilized him, because lesser should always take its place below the greater. Loyalty! Weasels don't questions loyalty.

But when greater collapses into miserable little puddles, then the whole world is confused, and lesser begins even to question himself! Lesser gets lost.

There had been a period of turmoil for the Weasel, then, when he suspected the sanity of Chauntecleer, for he himself was spinning loose in the universe. "Gloominesses," he was convinced, "blocks the brains. Thinkings makes gloominesses"—two afflictions John manifestly did not suffer— "and them what thinks is them what doesn't do." He had feared the Rooster's melancholy since Russel's death, and even now mistrusted the midnight morbidities of the Cock. Ah, but he forgave them both when the day dawned and his bold Rooster loosed a brazen crow across the land, scuttling a hundred sleeps and scattering Critters abroad in lively obedience. Golden, lordly, unequivocal was Chauntecleer, and loud again, and ruling as he should do. *Acts 3:1–10*

February 19

At Home in the World: Pertelote the Hen Tries to Comfort Her Husband

She gazed at his form, a shivering, haunted husband—but of such remarkable parts. Pertelote breathed a prayer for his peace of mind.

And then she argued for it: "The Tags," she whispered, "laughed today. Is it nothing that you've given someone the security to laugh? And Animals were singing while they worked. Chauntecleer, they enjoyed the day. They were not afraid. Is that nothing?"

"The world is still infected."

"The world—is always troubled, Chauntecleer. That's why good order and friendship are such sweet blessings after all. They make a refuge, don't they? And the worser the world, the better the refuge? The more needful a place and faith against confusion, no?"

"The apple has a grub in it, the earth a tapeworm."

"But we are *here* on the earth. And you are here. And *here* you've made a refuge in spite of the troubles, and that is something extraordinary, Chauntecleer, something quite enough—because what do you call this thing? Why, you call it a home. A home. We are home. Can't you be content with that—and can't you sleep then?" *Acts 3:11–26*

February 20

Times Ordained in Goodness:
The Rooster Crows God's Hours

Chauntecleer crowed the crows.

Animals who had never known of Vespers or Compline before lay down in gratitude and wondered that they felt so comforted. Eating was one thing. It satisfied the yearning of their bellies. But these regular signals of the times ordained in goodness, these cries in a kindred voice, were something else. They enclosed the Animals against the void. They argued that here, at least, existence was not a chancey thing but protected by a destiny—and the destiny loved them, for it came in the song of a Rooster: one alive! They mercied them and satisfied the longing of their souls. If winter hadn't silenced this Priest, then what could winter do to them?

Chauntecleer crowed.

And the Animals slept. *Acts 4:1–12*

February 21

Joy

So then it was that Pertelote lowered her head, and like a child moved very close to him. And it was *he* who swept her into a full and mighty hug, he who buried her head in his breast. Her shoulders began to shake; she was weeping, unashamed. The Animals saw that, and many of them, too, began to weep. But Chauntecleer raised his head above his wife. "Oh!" he said with a grand pride. "Oh, Pertelote!" He closed his eyes below the sky, and then this is what Lord Chauntecleer did: he opened his beak, and he laughed. The Rooster burst into a long peal of rolling, uncontrollable laughter. He breathed, and he laughed again. So then the poor Animals were crying and laughing both at the same time, whose mood had been so dreary till this morning—laughing because the Rooster laughed, crying because their Lady was so glad. And a new sound rose up above the land that day, a deep and throated, holy sound, the whole camp participating, none left out, none louder than the others. And this was the name of the sound: it was Joy.   *Acts 4:13–22*

February 22

Chauntecleer Decides to Battle Again

He crowed constantly. He wanted to lift the spirits of his Animals in spite of the bitter winter; more than that, to convince them of strength and purpose and grandeur and color in their lives, to unify them with the sense of their own significance; but most of all, to proclaim the good news that the Rooster had changed. He'd taken hold again. He was in startling command. The times! The times themselves were changing—and by a single, extraordinary act he, Chauntecleer, would see to the health of the Animals forever. He was taking leave. But he wanted to leave them faithful and whole.

"Mundo Cani shall come out of the depths!" he crowed. "Then who can hurt you, when we have triumphed over Evil, face to face, in his own place? Oh, dear hearts! When Evil is dead, there shall be no Evil any more. And the Dog shall be the sign of it. Watch for the Dog. Remember that I told you to watch for the Dog!"

Bright, incendiary Rooster, scorching the land from the top of a traveling Stag! And the Animals believed in him. They laughed. Their eyes were stars, their voices full of worship, and their hearts burst.

They said, "The spirit of God is upon him." Then who could resist his excitement?

None. Neither two nor two thousand. He asked none of them to go with him tomorrow, because the battle would be his alone. This time *he* would enter the breach. It was his obligation and his oath. But neither did he deny any happy heart the right to attend him, and many talked of going.

Acts 4:23–31

February 23

Pertinax, Homeless

It was snowing, now, in a steady, silent dead-fall, filling all the little burrows of the earth, drifting mildly, blanketing everything with a kind of white amnesia.

Maybe God said, "Let it snow."

Maybe God had meant it mercifully.

But for Pertinax Cobb, who lay in a foreign hole because he couldn't keep pace with the Animals but wouldn't go home without news, for Pertinax beneath the snow, it was oppressive, and he felt so lonely.

The snow kept whiskering the ground above him, like some mammal sniffing the darkness. It sifted across a quiet earth, pretending to be as light as ghosts; but that was a lie because it was heavy after all and made his hole a tiny pocket. He felt the drifts above him. He was a Cobb cut off.

That would have been just fine, if there had been two Cobbs together. Many a winter he and Mrs. Cobb had gnawed nuts in a chamber five feet below the cold, and he had told her stories, and half of them were fictions, but she would say, "You're wonderful, Mr. Cobb," so the fiction had had its truth. But Mrs. Cobb was nowhere near him now. He missed her. And the whispering snow made him miss her the more.

Pertinax was homesick.

Mrs. Cobb was a very important person. He knew that now.

Acts 4:32–37

February 24

Chauntecleer Cannot Win; Evil Is Too Strong

In this way the web was shredding. Keepers who could not keep one another were no Keepers of the Evil any more.

Somewhere Darkness was smiling that night, and Coldness curled in a Cat's repose, content. Because Wyrm had been right: he could not have invaded the Animals frontally, but only by entering at the heart. There had to be complicity of one, then two, and then two thousand. They had to choose for Evil themselves and then, to protect and nourish it within, to justify their choices. Let wrong be right and right wrong. And how? By letting every living Creature believe his choices to be right simply because *he* chose them; then let him, as in a holy crusade, fight for the right against any who threatened it—who were wrong simply because they threatened it. Set Keepers against each other. Then, when the clash began at night, when things began to fall apart because the center could not hold, then Wyrm no longer lurked below the earth in his own sole sphere, oh, no. Then Evil had taken up dwelling among the Keepers themselves. *Spiritus Mundi.* The smell of rot arose from them, and *their* society stank to heaven. And they were Wyrm.

Somewhere Darkness was smiling. The spell was nearly done, the net asunder, and Chaos almost come again.

Acts 5:1–16

February 25

Forgiveness Is Stronger

But Ferric doesn't mean to make it an agony. They are only just two wounded Creatures, lying in the snow together.

"Then how can I blame you? I can't," whispers the Coyote. He crawls closer to the Rooster, using his elbows. "Chanty-clear, I came to forgive you. We should be the same in this, too, don't you think?"

During the next words of the little Coyote, a remarkable change seizes Lord Chauntecleer the Rooster. He lies very still, listening. And then he seems to shrink, curling in on himself, his eyes and his face compressing nearly to nothing. Then, helplessly, he bursts into tears.

"Oh, Chanty-clear, there is a beautiful Cow. When I was hurting the most, this beautiful Cow came to me. And somebody maybe should have punished me, on account of all the troubles that I caused. But she loved me, Chanty-clear. Isn't that a mercy? She touched me, she fed me, she washed me, and that is how she loved me. Then this is how she forgave me: she did the same thing for my daughter Hopsacking. All of the hurts, every one of the hurts, she took away from me with her eyes and with her tongue, and there was no reason for that, but she did it, Chanty-clear. Do you know this beautiful Cow? One horn on her head? She knows you, Chanty-clear. She said that she loves you, Chanty-clear. You especially— Shh, don't cry, Chanty-clear, poor Chanty-clear. You didn't listen to her when she came to you, but that's okay, too, because look: she sent me. This is the main reason why I came. To forgive you. Don't cry. Don't cry. See? I forgive you—"

Chauntecleer the Rooster has delivered himself to grief. He is gulping the air and sobbing like an infant. His tears drill the dirty snow. *Acts 5:17–33*

February 26

The End of This Story. . .

Pertelote lifted up her voice and began to sing to the battlefield. She sang as though she walked the rim of the universe, like the moon, a pale and lovely presence everywhere on earth.

While she sang, the gray Wolf Chinook left the form of Boreas and came to Pertelote and bowed her head and listened, and then there were two women together to make a common memory of the ones they loved. The women bore the same things in their hearts.

While she sang the Animals lifted their heads from sleep and looked at the sky and saw the stars, and these became the blanket for their beds, and they resolved never to forget the song nor the singer.

And far, far away the Brothers Mice pulled their noses from the circle in which they slept. "Listen," they said. "Do you hear that? The dear Lady Pertelote is singing Compline. Oh, she remembered us with a Compline."

And Pertinax Cobb told his wife that the winter was breaking up. She asked him how he could know such a thing, and he answered that he heard the spring. He heard it singing in the air.

And Chalcedony the crippled Hen touched the Fawn to waken her. "Listen, listen, child," she said. "'Tis seldom in a lifetime you shall hear an angel. 'Twould be a pity if you missed the blessing. Listen."

But Pertelote stood in her solitude, singing one thing only, one thing only ringing in her soul:

> *"He woke me from my slumbering;*
> *He taught me how it was to sing*
> > *The songs;*
> *To him my mornings and that part*
> *Of me most holy—oh, my heart!—*
> > *Belongs.*
>
> *"And who was bolder on the ground?*
> *Or who more golden sailed around*
> > *The sky?*
> *Remember thee? Oh Lord, I will*
> *Remember none but thee until*
> > *I die.*
>
> *My dear. My dear.*
> *My Chauntecleer—"* Acts 5:34–42

February 27

And the Beginning of the Next . . .

Last week I took a long walk, some 30 miles through the country beside a two-lane highway, an eight-hour test of my endurance both physical and, as it happened, spiritual.

The day was dreary, cold and gray. From the first light it rained. My breath was a steam, the distance was ever a mist and, except for my hair and my upper body beneath a poncho, I was soaked. But I had set a brisk pace, and I maintained it through these hills of southern Indiana. I had to. If I paused, I froze. There was no dry place in all the world to sit and rest.

Traffic passed me, the tires ripping the liquid road, sounding like silk when it tears. But walkers and drivers exist in separate dimensions. These vehicles were glass and steel, not people. The wind of the big trucks struck me and stung me with spray. I felt solitary after all, and the day grew late.

Then, in dusky light, I glanced to the right, down into a culvert, and was surprised to see a homely sort of familiarity: a face, a brown coat and a creature. I stopped and stepped closer and was suddenly overwhelmed with sorrow. Here was, in fact, a handsome stag cast down into the water. Here Lent began for me.

Clearly the creature was not long dead; its fur had oil enough to keep it from matting in miserable weather. It lay on its back at the shoulders but was twisted down the torso so that its hips were turned aside. The forelegs crossed upon its breast, the delicate hoofs pointing downward. Its face gazed askance, its eyes half open, brown, contemplative. I saw the rim of a gray tongue just beneath its black nose. Neck and throat were long and noble. A noble stag was dead.

Lent. Here was mortality to remind me of my own. *Think, Walt, thou thing of nature like this deer. Observe your ending. Meditate.* And so, in the rain, I did. But this particular reminder betokened more than the natural death. There was a horror here.

Someone had taken a chain saw to the deer's head. Someone had cut it horizontally from the forehead to the temples, and then had cut down from the crown. Someone had taken a wedge-shaped section from the skull of the stag, leaving the brain exposed till birds had eaten it clean away. Some fine hero had taken a trophy of antlers and left the corpus to rot in a culvert.

Oh, my dear! I'm sorry! You don't deserve to die this way—for no other purpose than that some fool should glorify himself, yea, with your horns of glory, with no regard for your life!

But Lent: For me, the void in the skull of the stag was a symbol of sin—the attitude that caused death in the first place and has made of us all a moribund breed in need of salvation. *Forgive me, my dear! I, too, have desired to "be like God"; and I have, for my own benefit, controlled, manipulated, commanded and canceled the minds around me.*

I stood in the rain, considering my complicity in the deaths of deer, of the innocent, the weak and the speechless. The great trucks hissed on the highway behind me. Civilization passed, unaware of the lonely body dropped in this culvert.

Finally, Lent: I saw in the deer's soft, uncomplaining eyes an icon of the rejected Jesus, whose death in perfect isolation was sacrifice for all of us. *Acts 7:51–60*

February 28

To Begin to Remember

"Remember, thou art dust, and to dust thou shalt return."

Ash Wednesday, the day of the personal ashes, the first of the forty days of Lent: Like a deep bell tolling, this word defines the day and starts the season and bids me begin my devotional journey: *Memento!* "Remember!"

Well! But that sounds old in a modern ear, doesn't it? Fusty, irrelevant, and positively medieval! Why should I think about death when all the world cries "Life" and "Live"? The priests of this age urge me toward "positive thinking," "grabbing the gusto," "feeling good about myself." And didn't Jesus himself promise life in abundance? It's annoying to find the easy flow of my full life interrupted by the morbid prophecy that it shall end. Let's keep things in their places, simple and safe: life now, while there is life; death later, when there must be death. . . .

Nevertheless, Memento! tolls the ageless bell. In spite of my resistance, the day and the season together warn: "Remember!"   *Ecclesiastes 12:1–7*

February 29

Spring

Spring: The moist air smelled of loam and the earth. It smelled like flowers even before the flowers had begun to bloom. Chauntecleer had preserved hope in his animals during the storms; so when the storms left, the animals quickly forgot them. And when the new spring air filled up with sweetness and promises, so very quickly the hearts of the Hens were stirred. They clucked, gossiped, joked, giggled, and grinned; they swept the floor with feathered brooms, scrubbed the roosts, poked at cobwebs, dusted with down, and threw every window wide open. Spring! The air puffed through the open Coop and gently tugged at the feathers on their backs. And that was a good feeling. The busy waters outside chuggled and laughed gladly. And that was a good sound. Seven young Mice and three young Chicks tumbled joyfully through the Coop, squealing and falling over each other; and thirty-one Hens didn't mind their games at all.

That was a good time.   *Psalm 138:1–3*

March

March 1

The Temple and the Miniature: Mosquitoes

George Herbert was an English clergyman and poet. He died on
March 1, 1633.

> *They die so easily, these little things;*
> *Flying thread-knots, they've got pine-sliver limbs*
> *And tiny, tiny gardens for eyes. They're*
> *Constructed of bitterness and accident,*
> *You know—every last one of them; so they share*
> *With us the consequence of that moment when God*
> *Would share just nothing with us. You sing your hymns,*
> *Herbert, and I'll sing mine; and the one who sings*
> *Encomiums to a mosquito sings*
> *To that thing where God is not but in spent*
> *Anger. You praise his Presence, George; I'll prod*
> *Around and rummage in his Absence. Between*
> *Us we ought to strike some order on the earth.*
> *You kill, I'll mourn the little creature's little spleen*
> *And look for her to dawdle through a second birth.*
> *George Herbert, we'll get on—and God, then, will have been.*

Proverbs 30:24–28

March 2

Seeing Wholly

In order to comprehend the experience one is living in, he must, by imagination and by intellect, be lifted out of it. He must be given to see it whole; but since he can never wholly gaze upon his own life while he lives it, he gazes upon the life that, in a symbol, comprehends his own. Art presents such lives, such symbols. Myth especially—persisting as a mother of truth through countless generations and for many disparate cultures, coming therefore with the approval not of a single people but of *people*—myth presents, myth *is,* such a symbol, shorn and unadorned, refined and true. And when the one who gazes upon that myth suddenly, in dreadful recognition, cries out, "There I am! That is me!" then the marvelous translation has occurred: he is lifted out of himself to see himself wholly.   *Revelation 1:17–20*

March 3

Mirrors

The reader is encouraged to use these next twenty-two selections as preparation for Easter.

Mirrors that hide nothing hurt me. But this is the hurt of purging and precious renewal—and these are mirrors of dangerous grace.

The passion of Christ, his suffering and his death, is such a mirror. It is my *self* in my extremest truth. My sinful self. The death he died reflects a selfishness so extreme that by it I was divorced from God and life and light completely: I raised my *self* higher than God! But because the Lord God is the only true God, my pride did no more, in the end, than to condemn this false god of my *self* to death. For God will *be* God, and all false gods will fall before him.

So that's what I see reflected in the mirror of Christ's crucifixion: my death. My rightful punishment. My sin and its just consequence. Me. And precisely because it is so accurate, the sight is nearly intolerable.

Nevertheless, I will not avoid this mirror! No, I will carefully rehearse, again this year, the passion of my Jesus—with courage, with clarity and faith; for this is the mirror of dangerous grace, purging more purely than any other.

Romans 6:1–7

March 4

Happiness and Joy

The difference between shallow happiness and a deep, sustaining joy is sorrow. Happiness lives where sorrow is not. When sorrow arrives, happiness dies. It can't stand pain. Joy, on the other hand, rises from sorrow and therefore can withstand all grief. Joy, by the grace of God, is the transfiguration of suffering into endurance, and of endurance into character, and of character into hope—and the hope that has become our joy does not (as happiness must for those who depend upon it) disappoint us.   *Romans 5:1–5*

March 5

Preparing for Joy

In the sorrows of the Christ—as we ourselves experience them—we prepare for Easter, for joy. There can be no resurrection from the dead except first there is a death! But then, because we love him above all things, his rising *is* our joy. And then the certain hope of our own resurrection warrants the joy both now and forever.

For the moment, lay yourselves aside. Become one of the first disciples. And in that skin, consider: what makes the appearance of the resurrected Lord such a transport of joy for you? Consider this in every fiber of your created being. How is it that so durable a joy is born at this encounter?— joy that shall hereafter survive threats and dangers and persecutions, confusions and death, even your own death?

John 20:11–18

March 6

Power Confronts Jesus

Here comes Jesus, closer and closer to me. Ah, the closer he comes, the less I like it. His very existence threatens mine. I've grown used to my way of life. I like the familiarity. I know my place in society, my reputation, my rights and privileges, all of which are comfortable to me. Behold, I am a person of some prominence—small or large, it doesn't matter: I am! This is me. This is my identity.

But here comes Jesus to Jerusalem, the seat of my existence, the place of my authority—and all of this is threatened. I rule here because Rome allows it and because religious tradition sanctifies it. Rome requires an obedient people. Religion authorizes me to hold them in check. But if the people riot, Rome will strip me of power. If religious practice is undermined, I lose identity. If religion here is ruined, why, the whole world tips in confusion and I slide off the edge.

Yet here comes Jesus, at Passover! At the feast of Unleavened Bread! Look how volatile the people are now! Worse than that, he is questioning religious laws developed over the centuries, the very forms by which we order ourselves and know ourselves and name ourselves.

If order is lost, so am I.

If I lose my power and prominence, I lose my identity, my being, my very self. And then I am *not!*

What then? Why, then I must destroy before I am destroyed. Self-preservation is a law of nature. I will arrest this Jesus by stealth and kill him. Because if I do nothing, I will *be* nothing.   *John 18:12–14, 19–24*

To the Woman Who Anointed Jesus

What is your name that I might address my praise to you? I don't know. Were you someone's mother? I don't know. Were you old, bent by years of experience? Were you a prostitute? Or else praiseworthy for purity and virtue? Were you poor, the ointment an impossible expense for you? Or rich, with easy access to a hundred such flasks? I don't know. Mark never says. I know nothing about you save this: that you anointed the head of my Lord.

Ah, but that's enough to know! That deed alone is your identity, your entire being: your self. It memorializes you forever. "What she has *done*," says Jesus, "will be told in memory of her." Woman, now you are that deed, neither more nor less than that deed. I marvel at you. I pray God that I might do—and therefore be—the same.

For what was your gesture? An act of pure love for Jesus particularly. It was an act so completely focused upon the Christ that not a dram of worldly benefit was gained thereby. Nothing could justify this spillage of some three hundred days' wages, except love alone. *Mark 14:3–9*

Who Betrays Jesus?

We sinners are so backward! We invert the true source of our justification. It isn't some preliminary cause, some motive *before* the sin that justifies me, but rather the forgiveness of Christ which meets my repentance *after* the sin. If I did it, I'm responsible, whatever the reasons might be. Motives are incidental to the sin *as a sin* and to its expiation. If by excuses I duck my responsibility, I'll never truly repent, and then the forgiveness of Christ will seem incidental to me. (Oh, what a wretched state that would be!) But if I own my responsibility, own *up* to the sin and so repent, then that forgiveness will justify before God even the most horrendous betrayer of Jesus. Even Judas Iscariot. Even me.   *Mark 14:17–21*

March 9

The Risk of Harboring Jesus

Who will give me room? the Lord Jesus asks today.

If we're experienced, we know the risk. The sophisticated world mocks a meek and sheepish Christian. The evil world hates those in whom Christ shines like a light upon its darksome deeds. Even the worldly church will persecute those who, for Jesus' sake, accuse its compromises, oppose its cold self-righteousness, and so disclose its failure at humble service. It will kill that zeal which threatens its composure.

We know the danger of harboring Christ in a dark world and in a worldly church. They can freeze the one who burns with his bright spirit. They are shamed by a sincerely sacrificial love. They cool their shame by blaming the lover. They cut him from community. They cut him dead.

Yet, *Where is my guest room?* the Teacher asks. And loving him as he loved us, we answer, "Here, Lord. In my heart."

Mark 14:12–16

March 10

Breaking Bread with His Friends, His Betrayers

The Lord Jesus, the same night in which he was betrayed—

When is a mother more inclined to cuddle her children? When they're a nasty, insolent brood, disobedient and disrespectful of her motherhood? Or when they are cuddly?

When will a father likelier give good gifts to his children? When they've just ruined the previous gift, by negligence or by downright wickedness? When they are sullen and self-absorbed? Or when they manifest genuine goodness and self-responsibility?

But the love of Jesus is utterly unaccountable—except that he is God and God is love. It has no cause in us. It reacts to, or repays, or rewards just nothing in us. It is beyond human measure, beyond human comprehension. It takes my breath away.

For when did Jesus choose to give us the supernal, enduring gift of his presence, his cuddling, his dear communing with us? When we were worthy of the gift, good people indeed? Hardly. It was precisely when we were most unworthy. When our wickedness was directed particularly at him.

Listen, children: it was to the insolent and the hateful that he gave his gift of personal love.

In the night of gravest human treachery he gave the gift of himself. And the giving has never ceased. The holy communion continues today.

But in that *same* night he remembered our need. In that *same* night he provided the sacrament which would forever contain his grace and touch his comfort into us.

Oh, this is a love past human expectation. This is beyond all human deserving. This, therefore, is a love so celestial that it shall endure long and longer than we do.

This is grace.   *Mark 14:22–25*

March 11

We Speak with Peter's Words

Hey, look me over, Lord! Check me out! I know I wasn't worth much before—but I've changed, right? I'm your solid citizen now, a solid Christian, loving you and trusting you, forgiving my neighbor as I would be forgiven. Why, I've confessed your name at work, and you know how grim those guys can be. But they know I'm a Christian. They don't curse near me no more. Feel my muscle! Bigger, right? I'm your man! Hey, I'm your disciple!

You will all fall away.

Whoa! You can't mean that! Not *all* of us. Not me! I mean, okay: I know folks who could care less about you, right? Skip church, don't pray but when there's trouble, love their cars more than you. They say they're Christian, but when it comes to the crunch they drop you, Jesus. I pray. I do—daily and long, because I love you! I go to church. I serve on seven boards. I tithe, I fast (though no one knows but you)—I mean, I really *practice* my faith! I visit people in the county jail, right? Look, even though everyone else falls away, I won't!

Truly, this very night before the cock crows twice, you will deny me three times.

No! No, you don't know me! Oh, Jesus, how can you doubt me like that? Me, of all people! Me, who loves you the most! Don't I always speak up for you? Okay, okay—what should I do to prove my love? Tell me! You want me to quit my job? Sell everything? Become a missionary? I mean it! You want me to *die* for you? I will, Lord. I promise, I will. But I'll never, never deny you! *Mark 14:27–31, 66–72*

March 12

The Kiss

There comes an orange snake eastward through the night. A snake of fire, a long snake of torches. Perhaps the disciples glance down from the Mount of Olives and see it and do not understand. Jesus understands. It is a fatal snake. It kills by kissing.

The binding strength of that snake is the armed guard of the Temple and the police of the Sanhedrin. Behold how the servants of God can bite!

But the head of the snake is one of the twelve, a disciple of Jesus.

Suddenly Judas Iscariot appears beside the group of friends who stand outside the Garden of Gethsemane. Smiling. Judas is smiling. Peering into these faces. Looking for . . . no, not for John, not James; no, not for Andrew or for Peter, though he greets them all with familiar nods. He's looking for . . . ah!

The snake coils now into a thick knot of bodies and flame before the disciples. Its scales are weapons, swords and clubs adown its sides. Its silence is tense, dead menace in close proximity—and it stinks of human sweat.

The disciples swallow, nervous and uncertain.

Jesus gazes and waits.

Now, the serpent was more subtle than any beast of the field which the Lord God made. From the beginning its movement was smooth, its manner mild, a murderer even from the beginning, a liar, the father of lies, and the father, so Jesus once declared, of—

The serpent strikes!

Smiling, Judas says, "Rabbi!" and kisses Jesus. A sign of devotion. A sign, for the Temple guard, that this is the one to seize and lead away. A lie.   *Mark 14:43–52*

March 13

What Shall I Prove to Be?

And who, under the same circumstances, am I? Or what shall I prove to be?

It's not as if I haven't been warned. Jesus has spoken at least three times of his suffering and death—and fully as many times he's declared that if I intend to come after him I must deny my *self* and take my cross and follow him. "For those," he said, "who would save their lives will lose them, and those who lose their lives for my sake and the gospel's will save them." Who can forget such words? "Go, sell what you have; and come, follow me." Those words. And these: "The cup that I drink—you will drink."

The cup.

And I, with all his disciples, heard and agreed. "Yes," we said, "we are able to drink that cup." And I meant it! No, I was not lying. I would do anything for Jesus. But that was during the period of words and learning. A sort of prelude, I suppose. Sunday school, confirmation, sermons, study: preparation. A time of pieties and promises.

Well—here comes the cup!

Here's the real world, and the world's at war! And my deeds are my words now, and deeds don't lie.   *Matthew 20:20–23*

March 14

The Definition of Messiah

Oh, what a message comes in the timing here! And what a caution to Christians who want a hero for their Christ!

Only now, finally, does Jesus publicly claim the office of Messiah. *Now!* Why, any fool could choose a better time than this, right? Wrong! Anyone who did would be a fool indeed, for he would pervert the character and the intention of the Christ.

Now is the best time, because this is the Christ: a prisoner and a failure.

From the beginning of his ministry, Jesus charged those who experienced his power to say nothing about it. When he was dazzling crowds, confuting enemies, causing shepherds and lepers and kings to ask, "Who *is* this man?"; when masses were "astonished beyond measure, saying, 'He has done all things well, the deaf to hear, the dumb to speak!'"; even when Simon Peter explicitly confessed, "You are the Christ"—Jesus commanded them "to tell no one about him." Apparently none of this was the real work of the "Christ."

Even when Peter, James, and John saw his celestial glory in the transfiguration—saw Jesus revealed as the fulfillment of the whole Old Testament—he told them to shut up.

The world might have expected a warrior-king, someone triumphant in its own terms. A winner, you know. A hero.

Only when that characterization is rendered absurd and impossible does Jesus finally accept the title "Christ."

Christian, come and look closely: it is when Jesus is humiliated, most seeming weak, bound and despised and alone and defeated that he finally answers the question, "Are you the Christ?"

Now, for the record, yes: *I am.*   Mark 14:55–64

March 15

The Cross Is First

It is only in incontrovertible powerlessness that he finally links himself with power: "And you will see the Son of Man seated at the right hand of power." Because any display of messianic power is far, far in the future—in his and in ours together, on the last day. *The last day of the world, not today!*

This, then, is the Christ that Jesus would have us know and accept and (O Christian!) reflect:

One who came to die.

One who, in the assessment of this age, failed—an embarrassment, a folly, a stumbling block. An offense!

One crucified.

Here in the world, the Christ and his followers hang ever on a cross. The cross is foremost, because a faithless world cannot see past it to the Resurrection.

And even for the faithful the cross must always be first, because the Resurrection is only as real (both in history and in our hearts) as the death is real. *Mark 15:21–32*

March 16

How Does Christendom Triumph?

What then of our big churches, Christian? What of our bigger parking lots, our rich coffers, our present power to change laws in the land, our political clout, our glory for Christ, our triumphant and thundering glory for Christ? It is excluded! All of it. It befits no Christian, for it was rejected by Jesus.

If ever we persuade the world (or ourselves) that we have a hero in our Christ, then we have lied. Or else we are deceived, having accepted the standards of this world.

He came to die *beneath* the world's iniquity. The world, therefore, can only look *down* on him whom it defeated—down in hatred until it repents; but then it is the world no more.

Likewise, the world will look down on us—down in contempt until it elevates the Christ it sees in us; but then it won't be our enemy any more, will it?

Mark 14:65, 1 Corinthians 4:7–13

March 17

Jesus Doesn't Leave Us

Peter is paralyzed between the good that he would and the evil that he is.

I see this. I recognize this. I cannot divorce myself from this—for Peter's moral immobilization is mine as well! I am in the courtyard with him, watching. I, too, am good and evil in terribly equal parts—and helpless.

Two things alone can break the impasse for Peter and me.

1. The dreadful, merciful word of the Lord, which calls a sin a *sin* and mine: my fault, my own most grievous killing of Christ in my life to keep that life my *own*.

When Peter's denial reaches such extremes that he draws down death in "a curse on himself" (the logical end of all our sinning!) Jesus intervenes: "And immediately the cock crowed a second time, and Peter remembered" what Jesus had said. Peter may have left Jesus; but Jesus—by wonderful means of remembering him, rooster's crows like sacraments—has not left Peter.

2. Our sorrow when we see the sin, our personal repentance.

Rather than striking back at the Lord, spitting on him, blindfolding and despising him, we rush out to a private darkness, Peter and I. In the alleys, in the shadows of Friday's dawning, we break down and burst into tears.   *Mark 14:66–72*

March 18

Which Would We Choose?

This, precisely, is the timeless choice of humankind.

If they choose the latter, they choose humanity over divinity. They choose one who will harm them over one who would heal them.

If they choose Barabbas, they choose the popular revolutionary hero, the swashbuckler, the pirate, merry Robin Hood, the blood-lusty rake, the law-flout, violence glorified, appetites satisfied, James Bond, Billy Jack, Rambo, the celebrated predator, the one who "turns them on," over one who asks them to "deny themselves and die." They choose (voluntarily!) entertainment over worship, self-satisfaction over sacrificial love, getting things over giving things, being served over serving, "feeling good about myself" and having it all and gaining the whole world and rubbing elbows with the rich rather than rubbing the wounds of the poor—

The choice is before them. And they think the choice is external, this man or that man. In fact, the choice is terribly internal: this nature or that one, good folks or people essentially selfish and evil, therefore. It's an accurate test of their character. How they choose is who they are.

Behold a people in desperate need of forgiveness.

Mark 15:6–15

March 19
Why Does He Reject the Pain-Killer?

Jesus is on the cross.

He shakes his head. He will not drink from her cup. He will in no wise dull his senses or ease the pain.

And so we know. What are the feelings? What has the spirit of Jesus been doing since Gethsemane? Why, suffering. With a pure and willful consciousness, terribly sensitive to every thorn and cut and scornful slur: suffering. This he has chosen. This he is attending to with every nerve of his being—not for some perverted love of pain. He hates the pain. But for a supernal love of us, that pain might be trans-figured, forever.

Or what has the Lord been doing since Gethsemane? Drinking. Not from the woman's narcotic cup, but from the cup the Father would not remove from him: drinking. Swallow by swallow, tasting the hell therein, not tossing it down in a hurry: "So that by the grace of God he might taste death for every one."

Or what has the Lamb been doing since Gethsemane? Bearing our griefs. Carrying our sorrows. By the stripes he is truly and intensely receiving, healing us all.   *Mark 15:16–23*

March 20

To Be Sin

Maybe none shall see with more terrible clarity the sorrow of our Lord than the apostle Paul: "For our sake," he writes, "God made him to be sin who knew no sin, so that in him we might become the righteousness of God" (2 Corinthians 5:21). He does not write: "To bear our guilt," as though a good man became better by substituting himself for our punishment. Severely, Paul writes, "God made him to *be* sin." Jesus has become a bad man, the worst of all men, the badness, in fact, *of* all men and all women together. Paul does not write, "To bear our sin," as though Jesus and sin are essentially separate things, the one a weight upon the other for a while. No, but "to *be* sin": Jesus is sin! Jesus is the thing itself!

Beneath a blackening sky, Jesus has become the rebellion of humankind against its God.   *Mark 15:33–39*

March 21

What God Thinks of Sin

My God, why hast thou forsaken me?

Who answers him?

The thunder is silent. The city holds its breath. The heavens are shut. The dark is rejection. This silence is worse than death. No one answers him. No, not even God. Not even God, his Father, because he who has become hateful in his own eyes now is hateful likewise to God, his Father.

Jesus. Him. It is against *him* that heaven has been shut.

In this terrible moment of storm, the loss of light for humanity is at once the loss of love and life for its Christ. He has entered the absolute void. Between the Father and the Son now exists a gulf of impassable width and substance. It is the divorce of despising. For, though the Son still loves the Father obediently and completely, the Father despises the Son completely because he sees in him the sum of human disobedience, the sum of it from the beginning of time to the end of time. He hates the Son, even unto damning him.

Revelation 6:12–14; Mark 15:33–39

March 22

What the Centurion Sees

The centurion whirls around and sees Jesus, so suddenly dead upon that battle cry of triumph—and whispers with the solemn weight of a personal confession, whispers in a late day's dawning, "Truly, this man—"

Here is a paradox, both impossible and true. This once we can have it both ways and can delight in the manic breaking of the rules of the universe. This once the creatures can rise up *in* creation to peer *beyond* creation through a magic window at the Uncreated One, the Creator. Here, in the conjunction of impossibilities. Here, on Golgotha.

And here is a door through which God has crossed infinity to enter our finite existence, flooding the dungeons with light. Here is a door through which we by faith may enter Heaven, a doorway made of nails and wood, a crossing, a cross.

Christ's unseeing *is* our sight.

His solitude is the beginning of human communion with God.

For it is on Golgotha that a centurion spins around and stares at the man in the middle, just as that man dies, exactly as Jesus gives up the ghost and slumps forward from the cross.

But all at once that centurion sees as though light burst upon his eyes, as though the veil between bright heaven and dark earth had been torn in two from the top to the bottom. The centurion sees better than he did: he sees God! He sees the very nature of the love of God! The dying of one is the other one's window, and what has been veiled is now revealed, and a pagan whispers with the solemn weight of conviction, confession, faith: "Truly, this man was the Son of God!"

Revelation 1:17,18; Mark 15:33–39

March 23

It Is Finished

Joseph of Arimathea buries Jesus' body.

Somewhere a woman delivers a long, soft, terrible sigh to the world. Who is that?

The door to the tomb is a hole in stone no higher than a human waist. Joseph enters backward, bent down, bearing the shoulders of Jesus. The centurion, on his knees, keeps the legs from dragging dirt.

"Thank you," says Joseph. His voice echoes in the hollow rock. "Thank you. This is enough."

He disposes the body alone, then, and emerges into the darker part of evening. The sun has set. The sky is empty. The air is absolutely still.

There is a descending groove in the stone ledge below the sepulcher's door. Joseph rolls a flat stone down this groove. A single, slow revolution will bring it flush to the hole. No animals will desecrate this body.

There are two sounds in the dusk: the grinding of stone in stone—and once more the soft sigh, a low, compulsive, wordless sigh. Who is that?

Then the door is closed. The deed is done. It is finished.

Mark 15:40–47

March 24

Waiting for Easter

Alleluia!
I see thee, and I do not die!
I see me in thy seeing eye!
As thou art life, in Life am I,
In Love, in Christ and crucified.
　　Alleluia!
　　Alleluia!
　　Alleluia!

　　　　　Amen.

Revelation 1:12–16; Mark 16:9–15

March 25

The Drama of Faith

Ah, little children! Faith is not yet surcease, nor hiding, nor retreat, nor an island in the waters. Ah, children, you cheapen it by your chatter, judging some to be "in faith" and others "out of faith" as though it were a fixed condition and you, the "faithful" had the right to make distinctions, as though faith, once experienced, were ever thereafter the same. Oh, dear children, "faithing" is neither a stone nor doctrine nor any product of your desiring. It is, rather, the frightful thing: a *drama,* wherein God is the protagonist, the first and greater wrestler, while we are the antagonist, Jacob at Peniel, terribly, terribly deep in the night.   *Hebrews 11:1–12*

March 26

God's "Huh!"

Forsythia is a pure yellow light. Even when I look away from them, bushes of the bright forsythia still sting my seeing.

Dogwood among the naked trees is a humble triumph, its pastel explosions, white petals with drops of red which the ancients took for the blood of Christ. Not in groves, but here and there the wood erupts in a muted, dogwood awakening.

The redbud tree is a haze of softer violet, almost as if the air itself were lightly stroked and blushing. The redbud is beautiful. In her there is no violence or pride, although she is royal. The redbud is the clemency of God. So who stroked the air to wake her red? God. Who breathed modesty into a tree? God.

The Lakota Sioux of the northern Plains believed that the buffalo cow, when she calves, exhales a fine red dust. *Huh!*

she bellows, and a red cloud blows from her mouth; and this is the labor and this is the loveliness of birthing. So God says *Huh!* in the spring of the year, and softly the redbud appears like smoke on the forest air.   *Psalm 117*

March 27

Springtime's Arena

Springtime is not the source for our creed of resurrection. But springtime was the arena for Christ's resurrection, which hallowed it and filled an otherwise futile season, a fraudulent promise, with meaning and a holy truth.

In Christ the whole of creation has proof of redemption, both we and nature together. But nature is quicker to praise, more obedient to reflect, profounder, grander, more faithful to demonstrate the certitude of that redemption and the coming fact of resurrection. Creation too, you see, shall obtain the glorious liberty of the children of God. Nature knows it, although unknowingly. Nature shows it—where my eyes can see.

Therefore this Easter I will go out and find the signs of Easter among these muter children of God.

I will apply to my brother forsythia. Bright and yellow, his light is my illumination: Christ has risen! The darkness has not overcome him!   *Psalm 107:31–38*

March 28

Death Serves Life

Spring: The earth, when you walk on it, is soft and takes your footprint willingly. It holds the rain and waits for seed. The rivers are rising, and the streams know how to laugh, and a white-tailed deer is listening, her head held high, her milk vein swollen, her body heavy with young.

Spring: The whole of creation is not groaning. Right now creation does not travail in pain. For a little while creation is eager with life and bursting with hope.

Spring is Easter! Resurrection is reality. Jesus Christ, in fact, rose living from this ground.

And although creation for the rest of the year may suffer thorns and thistles, the curse on the ground for our sake and our sinfulness; although summer and fall may reinforce its subjection to futility, and winter kill the abundance it labored to produce, nevertheless, at Easter creation enjoys a respite. Now it is not in bondage to decay. Instead decay becomes a compost nourishment. Life is not subject to death, but death serves life. The green shoot feeds on autumn's leaves. Humus is the richest scent on a springtime air.   *Psalm 145:13–16*

March 29

Her Tears, His Blood

This and the following two entries comprise the complete story "Ragman."

I saw a strange sight. I stumbled upon a story most strange, like nothing my life, my street sense, my sly tongue had ever prepared me for.

Hush, child. Hush, now, and I will tell it to you.

Even before the dawn one Friday morning I noticed a young man, handsome and strong, walking the alleys of our City. He was pulling an old cart filled with clothes both bright and new, and he was calling in a clear, tenor voice: "Rags!" Ah, the air was foul and the first light filthy to be crossed by such sweet music.

"Rags! New rags for old! I take your tired rags! Rags!"

"Now, this is a wonder," I thought to myself, for the man stood six-feet-four, and his arms were like tree limbs, hard and muscular, and his eyes flashed intelligence. Could he find no better job than this, to be a ragman in the inner city?

I followed him. My curiosity drove me. And I wasn't disappointed.

Soon the Ragman saw a woman sitting on her back porch. She was sobbing into a handkerchief, sighing, and shedding a thousand tears. Her knees and elbows made a sad X. Her shoulders shook. Her heart was breaking.

The Ragman stopped his cart. Quietly, he walked to the woman, stepping round tin cans, dead toys, and Pampers.

"Give me your rag," he said so gently, "and I'll give you another."

He slipped the handkerchief from her eyes. She looked up, and he laid across her palm a linen cloth so clean and new that it shined. She blinked from the gift to the giver.

Then, as he began to pull his cart again, the Ragman did a strange thing: he put her stained handkerchief to his own face; and then *he* began to weep, to sob as grievously as she had done, his shoulders shaking. Yet she was left without a tear.

"This *is* a wonder," I breathed to myself, and I followed the sobbing Ragman like a child who cannot turn away from mystery.

"Rags! Rags! New rags for old!"

In a little while, when the sky showed grey behind the rooftops and I could see the shredded curtains hanging out black windows, the Ragman came upon a girl whose head was wrapped in a bandage, whose eyes were empty. Blood soaked her bandage. A single line of blood ran down her cheek.

Now the tall Ragman looked upon this child with pity, and he drew a lovely yellow bonnet from his cart.

"Give me your rag," he said, tracing his own line on her cheek, "and I'll give you mine."

The child could only gaze at him while he loosened the bandage, removed it, and tied it to his own head. The bonnet he set on hers. And I gasped at what I saw: for with the bandage went the wound! Against his brow it ran a darker, more substantial blood—his own! *John 4:5–10*

March 30

The Ragman's Sorrow

"Rags! Rags! I take old rags!" cried the sobbing, bleeding, strong, intelligent Ragman.

The sun hurt both the sky, now, and my eyes; the Ragman seemed more and more to hurry.

"Are you going to work?" he asked a man who leaned against a telephone pole. The man shook his head.

The Ragman pressed him: "Do you have a job?"

"Are you crazy?" sneered the other. He pulled away from the pole, revealing the right sleeve of his jacket—flat, the cuff stuffed into the pocket. He had no arm.

"So," said the Ragman. "Give me your jacket, and I'll give you mine."

Such quiet authority in his voice!

The one-armed man took off his jacket. So did the Ragman—and I trembled at what I saw: for the Ragman's arm stayed in its sleeve, and when the other put it on he had two good arms, thick as tree limbs; but the Ragman had only one.

"Go to work," he said.

After that he found a drunk, lying unconscious beneath an army blanket, an old man, hunched, wizened, and sick. He took that blanket and wrapped it round himself, but for the drunk he left new clothes.

And now I had to run to keep up with the Ragman. Though he was weeping uncontrollably, and bleeding freely at the forehead, pulling his cart with one arm, stumbling for drunkenness, falling again and again, exhausted, old, old, and sick, yet he went with terrible speed. On spider's legs he skittered through the alleys of the City, this mile and the next, until he came to its limits, and then he rushed beyond.

I wept to see the change in this man. I hurt to see his sorrow. And yet I needed to see where he was going in such haste, perhaps to know what drove him so.

The little old Ragman—he came to a landfill. He came to the garbage pits. And then I wanted to help him in what he did, but I hung back, hiding. He climbed a hill. With tormented labor he cleared a little space on that hill. Then he sighed. He lay down. He pillowed his head on a handkerchief and a jacket. He covered his bones with an army blanket. And he died. *2 Corinthians 5:1–5*

March 31

The Ragman Lives

Oh, how I cried to witness that death! I slumped in a junked car and wailed and mourned as one who has no hope—because I had come to love the Ragman. Every other face had faded in the wonder of this man, and I cherished him; but he died. I sobbed myself to sleep.

I did not know—how could I know?—that I slept through Friday night and Saturday and its night, too.

But then, on Sunday morning, I was wakened by a violence.

Light—pure, hard, demanding light—slammed against my sour face, and I blinked, and I looked, and I saw the last and the first wonder of all. There was the Ragman, folding the blanket most carefully, a scar on his forehead, but alive! And, besides that, healthy! There was no sign of sorrow nor of age, and all the rags that he had gathered shined for cleanliness.

Well, then I lowered my head and, trembling for all that I had seen, I myself walked up to the Ragman. I told him my name with shame, for I was a sorry figure next to him. Then I took off all my clothes in that place, and I said to him with dear yearning in my voice: "Dress me."

He dressed me. My Lord, he put new rags on me, and I am a wonder beside him. The Ragman, the Ragman, the Christ!

Philippians 2:6–11

April

April 1

The Little Dyings

The first death, the cause of all deaths (since God remains the source of all life), is then manifested in the host of little dyings we suffer during our conscious lives on earth. These are the breakings of those relationships that are life for us: sunderings from other people; the hurtful divisions between ourselves and the rest of God's creation; the serious severance of self from self, when one in earnest sorrow whispers, "I hate myself," and another, "I'll never, never be what I want to be. . . ."

This act, while still we walk on earth, is the seeming longest; it runs through countless scenes, as many scenes as we have days to live. But the nearer we come to its ending, the shorter the act begins to feel. Here is "the human condition." Here we suffer grief with loud cries and conscious particularity.

But here, dear prodigals—if all of our lesser dyings finally persuade us of the death to come ("I perish here with hunger"), if we let the grief do what God intends for grief to do (that is, to begin a healing, renewing, a resurrection)—here, I say, we may by faith arise and return to the Father to confess: "I have sinned against heaven and before you. . . ." And God, says Paul, "who is rich in mercy, out of the great love with which he loved us, even when we were dead through our trespasses, [will make] us alive together with Christ." *Luke 15:11–21*

April 2

Three Liturgical Colors, and Time

The first of the first day's dawn was white,
That detonation of Time—white;

That primal verb and the birth of being,
Fiat! from the yawp of God,
Was a shout of light,
Was a perfect howl of progenitive light—white!
And in between,
The whole earth springeth green.

Then this shall be the evening
End of Time's long westering—
When the phenomenal noun dispredicates
And the growl of God has closed debate
And the light descends in separates—
This: universal purple gloom.
But in between,
The whole earth springeth green.

And the Lord's intrusion in Time was white,
The re-murmuring of the First Word, white;
Then that advent requires a swaddling white.
But the King's conclusion's imperial;
For the Judge shall conjugate us all;
Oh, that advent demands a purple pall.
Yet in between—
All in between—
The whole earth springeth green.

Wheat, and the young vine, green;
Shoots, and the small stalk, sweetly green;
And the tree unfolds and flattens high
A gang of hands to weave the sky,
An audience applauding light—
And green! Ten thousand leaves are busy green!
For the grace of the spacious Time between
Is the whole earth, springing green.

All in between,
The good earth springeth green.

> *Genesis 1:3; Joel 2:12–14; Revelation 22:1, 2*

April 3

Something Must Endure

If everything flows, we are lost. We have no control in the world; and worse, the world that controls us is, to us, a mystery. Then we are no more than chips spinning in a flood. We are lost, and we lose everything, too: we can keep nothing that we cannot name, not ourselves or our own identities. We cannot speak truth because we can't speak of anything truly if it changes between our seeing and our speaking it. When our words are meaningless, our hands are powerless; and the horror is that we cannot even know what crushes us.

Oh, we demand our nouns to declare—or else to effect—the fixedness of things.

Look: even I am pretending fixedness in this very act of writing a book for you, supposing my words still to contain some meaning by the time you come to them to bleed them of that meaning. And I trust the pretense, that not all the blood's run out before your arrival. I would grieve to think that I wrote corpses, or that all I wrote Time turned to lies.

Something must endure. With every significant act attempted, we pray: something must endure. *John 1:1–5*

April 4

Why Fiction Is True

Of his character, the Rev. Orpheus:

This man is an example of one moving through the passages of faithing, but he is not exemplary. He is drawn fully human, as anyone experiencing the full length of a relationship with God must be fully human: faulty, sinning some sins consciously and others unconsciously, sometimes very clear about his own condition, sometimes fearfully obtuse, yet able, withal, to love sincerely and to believe in the Lord God on many levels.

Surely, I do not enjoin the reader to be like him. Nor ought anyone to seek in him an ideal. Rather, I say: as this Orpheus does, so do we enact a drama with our God. And even as we are, every one of us, complicated individuals of ingenious slights and devisings, baffling even ourselves, so is he. He is not always to be trusted; but his story is. Trust the story. Orpheus, though unique, is at the same time one among a countless throng which includes you and me, each unique as well.

The fact that this story is a fiction makes it universally true.

Matthew 13:34, 35

April 5

Nouns and Things

We desire our nouns to declare the fixedness of things.

We desire nouns *because* they presume the fixedness of things: general categories, particulars in a general category, variations on those particulars, stages in which the variations might be caught and assessed—but always, always at our meeting them, fixed. Named. It comforts us.

A stone's a stone and ever a stone will be. If we return tomorrow and find that stone cracked in two, well, then there are three stones dwelling in our memory, one twice the size of either of the others. And all three participate in the unchanging (Platonic) ideal *Stone*. We will have them solid nouns because we couldn't live forever in the violent moment of the cracking, whose beginning and whose ending are different one from the other, whose ending we cannot know when we are at the beginning—unless, of course, we comprehend the laws that stone-crackings obey, and then we have nouned a process after all, fixing it. We've nouned a verb, as it were. We do that to comfort ourselves; we identify and codify "natural" laws to comfort ourselves: laws are the nouning of terrible verbs.   *Exodus 3:13–15*

April 6

Freezing the Fluid

This is what a sonnet is: it is a cameo, a little stone, a tiny house of the poet's desire containing a thought, an image, love itself, the thing he hopes has not become mere memory but which survives the same *on account of* his expression of the thing. Stop the world!

"Love is not love," Shakespeare says,

> *Which alters when it alteration finds,*
> *Or bends with the remover to remove:*
> *O, no! it is an ever-fixed mark,*

he says, and then he ends his sonnet with a self-conscious irony which, by its exaggeration, shows the frightfully destructive effect of alteration, verbs, and change: his craft, his fixed place in history thereby, his very being and love itself dissolve:

> *If this be error and upon me proved,*
> *I never writ, nor no man ever loved.*

He wrote, all right, despite his protestation (and his error). He wrote as all of us use words: to catch and to fix the things we would not lose, to preserve the subtlest and the loveliest of things, to freeze the fluid.   *1 Thessalonians 5:21*

April 7

Faith and Words About Faith

Faith is relationship. But relationship dies in doctrines about it; at least it hides the while. Neither faith nor love, despite our desire, abides the fixing. It is Shakespeare's sonnet *about* love which is fixed, not the loving itself. His words I may know; but love I must encounter on my own, when I myself breathe *Thou*. Love must be loving. Likewise, it is only our words *about* faith that remain fixed, not the faith itself. Faith is personal and must be faithing. In time our words about faith shall fall nearer our desiring than they do the truth.

Genesis 22:1–8

April 8

Ceremonies

"Might we not find ourselves in fact on the road to Emmaus with Cleopas?" Christendom has been repeating, "I think so" for some time now. And Christendom has meant more than a doctrine, since its assent has been preserved in an action: "Take, eat," and "Believe, and be baptized."

And yet, as far as individual Christians are concerned, here is an irony: the very ceremonies which would translate us to the day of the death of Jesus, and into that death, the very sacraments which would *un*define defining times, we do ourselves regulate. We dominate them, instead of allowing their dominance over us, and so forestall the threatful, consuming experience of bereavement. We do not want to be on the road to Emmaus! Let us, rather, consider grief without truly grieving.

Ceremonies are controlled experiences. They occur at ecclesiastical choosings, despite the agency of the Divine. They obey a rubric. Their gestures are fiercely ritualized. And we

participants have often been more passionate about our inter-
pretations of the event (distancing ourselves by committing
ourselves to a strictly, safely, human dialogue), have been
more passionate in arguments regarding the practice (sprin-
kling? submersion? wine? juice? close? closed? doctrinal
agreement?) than passionate in and for and by the event itself, than passionate a-practicing it.

No, we fear to lose control. We fear fluidity. And we would
not want to find ourselves on the road to Emmaus desolated
by the death of Jesus.   *Luke 24:13–17, 25–32*

April 9

Verbs Are Fire

When we believe in faith's fixedness, then we have come to
believe in words, in words, in the nouns and the commission
of our nouns—in doctrines, but not in God. We believe (a sad
tautology) in the activities of our own minds; we depend
upon definitions (but who can rope the Infinite?); and might-
ily, by our own passionate commitment, we persuade ourselves that these words are not hollow. To the degree that we
fear fire and the fury, to that degree we need the nouns. And
to the degree that we need them, even to the same extreme
degree do we fight for the familiar doctrine. Fight? Why, we
rage against the destroyers, those with bright and glorious
faces, the verbs.   *Job 42:1–6*

April 10

Faithing: The New Verb

Faith, if ever it is to be a noun, is properly the whole play,
from the first scene to the last, done up and done. But we do

not know that last until we are there, until we have come to it both through and by our tribulation. (God knows; but we don't know as we are known.) Therefore, while we are still involved in it, we cannot truly use the fixing noun. "Faithing" allows—appallingly, it presumes—change.

But having heard that, hear too the blessing it implies:

When the relationship between the Lord and us is troubled; when we cry, as surely we will in the deep sincerity of our souls, "There is no God!" then, if all we had for definition were the noun *faith,* we would have to judge ourselves faithless, fallen from the faith, cast out. And that were the worst of deaths to die. On the other hand, if it is faithing which we are experiencing, and if this desolated cry arises from one scene in a long and fluid play, then even the desolation may have its place in the changing relationship, caused by previous action, causing actions subsequent; then despair may be an episode in the drama. And then we are not fallen from the faith, but rather falling within it—and even this, dear child, may be *of* the faith.   *Psalm 22:1–5*

April 11

God's Silence; God's Speech

Faithing is dying into a living God and not a stone, neither a calf nor an icon, neither a principle nor an ideal, neither a temple nor a tradition nor a statute, neither a memorial nor an objective. The God *autonomous,* the God *a-nomos* altogether, the God eternally the same, this God is, by a paradox, also one who walks the garden in the cool of the evening and then, some years later, announces to the Baptist: "It is fitting for us to fulfill all righteousness." Holy and jealous—yes, he is. But merciful as well. Hidden, yes. Supernal and above all worlds, yes. And silent therefore: so silent that the Psalmist wailed. "Thou hast forsaken me!" So silent and so still that the eerie stillness seemed, to Elijah on Horeb, to make its own sound—a sound of the absence of sounds. Silent, yes. And yet he is a speaker as well, words and sentences and discourse flowing from his mouth, a voice, a speaking voice: the Word!

1 Kings 19:8–14

April 12

Changing

Two things happened on the Holy Mountain.

God wrote commandments upon tablets which could, thereafter, be kept in a box as in a noun, and then the people could sinfully suppose that they controlled their God, controlling the box. They needn't trouble any more with fire and fury, risky dealings at the least. Rather, they needed only to return to the box and bear that box wherever they desired— into battle, if they desired—in order to place the power of God against their enemies. This is *faith* as a noun. They lost both the battle and the box to the Philistines.

But two things happened on the Holy Mountain. God did a yet more terrible thing.

God revealed himself to Moses, his glory and the thunder of his speaking—*to Moses*. And the man died at the sight; yet the man continued to live; which paradox is to say, the man was changed, having been called into a relationship with the Holy One. Changed, indeed, and continued to change thereafter, as fire is not a frozen thing; for he continued in conversation with God, says the Torah, "face to face."

Exodus 19:16–22

April 13

His Faith Was a Verb

And the virtue of that relationship was, in Moses, so real, so intense, so otherly (motion always abstracts itself from fixed things and shows itself so dreadfully different), so holy, that the prosaic people of Israel could not bear to look on him. The unnameable terrified them. Fire and fury *are* destructive of securities. So the people pleaded that Moses cover his face in a veil. In other words, Paul's words, they hid the glory, the direct perceiving of God and the free and furious blowing of his Spirit, in the law. In other words yet again, they named the unnameable after all; they nouned it, fixing the unfixable; and though they felt they rose to control it, they did in fact no more than sink their hearts in gloom. But Moses, by whom the Lord performed his signs and wonders, terrors in the sight of Israel; Moses, meekest of men in the presence of the Almighty, lost and living still; Moses, who himself regarded, yea, precipitated changings in the Deity—Moses was a man of faith in deed, in *deed,* in union, in relationship. And his *faith* was a verb. *Exodus 20:18–21*

April 14

Dancing With God

Who can say when, in any child, the dance with God begins? No one. Not even the child can later look back and remember the beginning of it, because it is as natural an experience (as early and as universally received) as the child's relationship with the sun or with his bedroom. And the beginning, specifically, cannot be remembered because in the beginning there are no words for it. The language to name, contain, and to explain the experience comes afterward. The dance, then, the relationship with God, faithing, begins in a mist.

In the beginning words talk; they merely talk; and language *is* encounter. Only later does language acquire the secondary function of containing the experience.

And so faithing begins. And because it begins in children, regardless of their cultures, regardless of what languages shall later contain, explain and edit reality for them—because it begins, in fact, *apart from* the interpretive function of language—faithing, we may say, is not unique to a few people: it is at least initiated in all. It is a universal human experience. We all have danced one round with God. But we danced it in the mists. *Genesis 12:1–5*

April 15
Christian Poets

Listen: There is a busy chorus of most extraordinary voices among us, talented people, poets in the company of God. But they go unpraised—unknown even—by most of us. And this is an irony, since most of us cache and carry and communicate our faith in words, words, *words*. But these are the experts of words. Their tensile language bears ten times the load of a weaker prose. Their sharper word is the point of the probe of faith. *Proverbs 1:1–7*

April 16
My Verses, My Obedience

Why obedience?

—Because, sir, the ability
To will and then to do belongs

To God; and nothing else I know
(A branch divides upon its tree,
The thrush is busy with her songs,
Sir, when she will) is peace below—

Psalm 127:1, 2

April 17

Stories and Reality

When my father bought a thick, pictureless book containing all the tales of Hans Christian Andersen and began to read them to his children, he did me a kindness more profound that mere entertainment. He began to weave a world which genuinely acknowledged all the monsters in mine, as well as all the ridiculous situations and silly asides which I as a child found significant. Andersen was my whispering, laughing, wise companion when I most needed companionship.

Night after night my father would read a story in an articulate, baritone voice. Gently the voice invited me. Slowly I accepted the invitation and delivered myself to a wonderful world, and I looked around, and lo, it was confident with solutions, and I was a citizen of some authority and reputation. I was no longer alone, no longer helpless. Even my foolishness seemed canny here. I could, with the soldier and his tinderbox, marry the princess, become a king—or, with the Little Match Girl, enter heaven.

Hans Andersen's stories, though simple on the surface, contain a precise and tender perception of personal development. They are honest about the hard encounter with the "real world"—honest about evil and the tendency to evil in each of us. Andersen did not coddle me, the "me" who was revealed within his fairy tales. He didn't sweeten the bitter facts which I already knew regarding myself. But he offered

me hope, for in his tales even when evil has been chosen, forgiveness may follow—therein lies extraordinary hope.

Ecclesiastes 12:1–7

April 18

Ugly Ducklings

But here appears the outrageous grace that we never antici-
pated: all along, while we were ugly indeed, another mercy
was working within us, uncaused by us but given to us purely
as a gift. What was this mercy? What sort of gift is given now
to us? Why, it is we ourselves, transfigured!

"Kill me," whispered the poor creature, and bent his head
humbly while he waited for his death. So goes the story, and
thus do we deny ourselves, surrender ourselves completely.
"Humbly . . . " writes Andersen. "Humbly," my father reads,
and I more than hear it; I experience it: I feel fully such humility in my heart. I am the one who cannot run. But what
does such humility reveal to me?

In Andersen's words: "But what was that he saw in the
water? It was his own reflection; and he was no longer an
awkward, clumsy, gray bird, so ungainly and so ugly. He was
a swan! It does not matter that one is born in the henyard as
long as one has lain in a swan's egg." And Andersen goes on
to name the goodness that has existed in all our sorrow, the
duckling's and mine. Andersen names the grace upon grace
that we have received, and the graciousness that we shall
show hereafter. "He was thankful that he had known so much
want, and gone through so much suffering, for it made him
appreciate his present happiness and loveliness of everything
about him all the more. . . . Everyone agreed that the new
swan was the most beautiful of them all. The older swans
bowed toward him."

But does sinful pride or vengeance then rear up in him, or in me? No, and that is much the point: for the suffering transfigures us even to the soul. Humility showed us our new selves; humility remains in our hearts to keep these selves both beautiful and virtuous: "He felt so shy that he hid his head beneath his wing. He was too happy, but not proud, for a kind heart can never be proud."

So then, there is hope—not only that there may emerge from my ugly self a beauty, but also that the suffering which my ugliness has caused is ultimately valuable, making my beautiful self also a good and sympathetic self. In the end I shall love the world the more; and even the people who once did me dishonor, I shall honor.

Can any child receive a better impress on his person, a subtler, more spiritual shape than this, that he be taught grace and to be gracious? And what is more fortified than the self-esteem that comes as a gift from God?   *1 Corinthians 15:45–50*

April 19

The Shape of the Story

Mercy! It never was what we might do that could save us. It never was our work, our penitence, our goodness that would forgive us and bring us back to God again. We can do nothing! It always was the pure love and mercy of God—God's doing, given us freely as a gift. When finally we quit trying, then God could take over. When we murmured in perfect helplessness the perfect truth of our relationship, "O God, help me," then God was no longer hindered by our spiritual pride. God was God, and not ourselves—and God was our God too.

Mercy. Mercy is the healing that had waited for us all along. Love. Pure, holy love, unpurchased, undeserved.

When my father reads the final sentences of this story, I am crying. I am tingling. For I am not learning, but rather I am experiencing the highest truth of our faith. Not in doctrine, but in fact it is releasing me from the sins against my mother, even as it is imprinting me for adulthood, to show in what I speak, to shine through what I write forever.

But I don't know that yet. I'm just a child, reshaped and borne outside to ride the north wind warmly to a home I shall never, never forget:

"The great organ played," my father reads, his dear head bowed above a tattered book of stories, "and the voices of the children in the choir mingled sweetly with it. The clear, warm sunshine streamed through the window. The sunshine filled Karen's heart till it so swelled with peace and happiness that it broke. Her soul flew on a sunbeam up to God; and up there no one asked her about the red shoes."

In the deeps of my bones I know and believe in forgiveness, for I have lived it. By Andersen's stories I was shaped in it—and the shape remains, forever.   *Matthew 20:29–34*

April 20

His Story Is the City's Story

The city? Hot with human enmity, cold with old mortality, the city? Busy and fatigued; kissing below back alley stairs, lips as limp as rotten violets; and children cursing like their parents, parents careless; parties for wasted wealth on Saturday night, exhausted Sunday morning; cars and lights and sirens; ointments, rouges, polishes, colognes and coin—the city? Turning to the city, do I turn from you?

No, my Lord, for you are in the city. In all the affairs of humankind, you are there. You were not ashamed to be born of a woman, flesh like hers and mine, troubled as she and I by all the bruises of that flesh. You emptied yourself to enter the city, and though your coming may not make it good, it makes you cry, and there you are. In the oily streets, damp with rain and human sin, lit by a single light, I see your face reflected. O God, your incarnation's in the streets. I see the city, and I cannot help but see you.

And I love you.

They ask me, "Whom do you love?" And I tell them I love you.

They ask, "But whom do you love?" I point to the city.

They insist, "But *whom* do you love?"

And since they cannot see you for themselves, I do the next best thing: I tell them stories. I tell them a thousand stories, Lord. For the city is active, and you are acting in it, always; and activity's a story. I tell them about you by telling them the story. *Matthew 23:37–39*

April 21

Jesus on a Bicycle

Jesus rides a bicycle through the city.

He wears neither robe nor sandals nor beard—and in this instance he's a he whose eyes are blue. They're my eyes. It's my bicycle. He's a 44-year-old cyclist with unkempt hair, a pain in his shoulder and a manner of pedaling most grim. He doesn't look holy. Neither is his mission holy. He is merely an incidental figure on the right side of the road.

"When, Lord? When did I see you on a bicycle and smile at you?"

And Jesus says, "When you did it to the least of these my sisters. Or to Walt."

"But when, Lord? Oh, Lord, this feels ridiculous! *When* did I mock you on a bike? When did I insult you by sexual harassment? When did my little fun belittle you?"

"When you did it to the least—"

"Well, why didn't you *tell* me it was you?"

And Jesus says, "I did. You weren't listening."

Matthew 25:31–40

April 22

God in the Preacher's Mouth

The preacher is not a mouth alone, self-effacing that God alone show through. (When that is the case, then God is a mouth alone, and that is *all* of him which shall show through.) The preacher in all of his parts is the proclaimer of God: his wonder, his humor, his faith, his body, the tone of his voice as well as its words, his *experience!* The entire drama of his own relationship with God, both in sinful enmity and in holy forgiveness! Her husband, if she be a woman, is part of that proclamation, and her children. His parents, his wife, the leaks in his roof, his surgery, his pains and his pleasures, his troubles and their resolutions. Three times in Acts the story of Paul's conversion appears, twice in his own mouth. It comes again in Galatians. His aggrieved experience threads the letters to the Corinthians: the message of Christ is proclaimed not only by Paul's intellect or teachings, but by his very being and in wholeness! He may be embarrassed by boastfulness; but he does it anyway, and so God is seen in lashes, in prison, on a ship, in dreams—everywhere immanent.   *2 Corinthians 11:21–30*

April 23

Relationship

Broadly, there are four areas for the borning:

1. The first was the first from the beginning of things—when God breathed life into nostrils of a cold, gray clay, and this poor standing dirt became a living soul. Every breath I take is a token, a sign of the First Breath: for God was the Source of our lives, and God continues to be the Source of all life, the *Primal Relationship.*

2. And then the Creator provided a context for life and for the living of individual lives: time and space, forms whose voids he filled with light and land and seas; and these he dressed in growing things; these he crowded with swimming things and flying things, beasts and cattle and creeping things, *Natural Relationships.*

3. Again, from God came people for people. Adam had nothing to do with Eve's creation: his "deep sleep" proves him passive and no partner in the divine act. And his "deep sleep" is also ours in this, that no human caused another; no human owns another; all are gifts to one another from the love of the Father of all, *Communal Relationships.*

4. But then, each human being individually is an astonishing complex of relationships, systems fitted together, parts in dialogue with other parts.

But Adam was different. Adam knew Adam! He was the thinker *and* he was the thing he thought about—and from the beginning he liked what he saw. He knew his potential. He knew his purpose. And he was given, by God, to govern himself, since God gave him free will.   *Genesis 3:8–10*

April 24

Why Fig Leaves?

God had intended humanity to be both "naked and not ashamed," completely open to one another, completely available, each the very completion of the other. Our wholeness, personally and communally, was in trust, maintained by the law of harmonious love.

But when we chose each to become our own autonomous gods, our "eyes were opened and we knew that we were naked." Nakedness, suddenly, was a problem. Complete openness to one another (when any other might be an opposing god) became vulnerability. Complete disclosure seemed rash and dangerous. So we covered the nakedness. We put on clothes. That is, sin persuaded us to hide the truth of ourselves—to conceal ourselves from one another!

The self-centeredness of sin made us fear the differences between us, for one might use his strength to rule another, or one felt threatened by her natural need. Differences became weapons or occasions of scorn; differences, among people striving for private advantages, became divisions. The survival of the fittest required those unfit to fake it, to lie, to pretend and scheme and manipulate. And the best of the people, those who did not seek to elevate themselves, did nevertheless cover themselves: merely to exist, they kept secrets, locked their doors, maintained a healthy suspicion regarding strangers. *Genesis 3:8–13, 21*

April 25

What Is Her Name?

There was a period when we feared that our tiny adopted daughter was deaf. We could clap behind her head and she wouldn't turn, would not so much as blink, so unresponsive was she to the stimulus. But that's all it was, after all: a pattern of unresponsive behavior, deep passivity. Little relationship to anything.

But she was so beautiful. A porcelain child with wide eyes and a smooth expanse of forehead, eyebrows dark as raven's wings, lashes that put me in mind of Egypt. I gazed always from a distance, my heart recoiling within me. Well, she was changing: she grew the softest tangle of ringlet hair. Her eyes shed forth an amber light. And her lips developed a delicate Negroid ridge.

Africa was in this child, the noble bone, the extravagant color, the generous blood of Africa. Now, to me this was an unspeakable richness. To her, of course, it was yet nothing, since she could not know it. But to the world around us, still criminal in its racism, this was going to be a problem.

When Thanne and this infant went forth into public, people shot them quizzical looks. Some turned a bold-faced loathing upon them. No matter that the child was beautiful: she was Black. No matter that she was also white: a little black is Black. And the mother is white? Here was a riddle whose answer the people detested: the husband and father must be Black! Unnatural!

Soon, soon the child would need to have a name, and to know her name, and by the name to know herself. For if we did not name her, the world would—and its name would wound her. Its name could kill her. *Psalm 11:1–7*

April 26

Eyebrow-Speech

I gazed always from a distance. I sat at one end of the dinner table, enacting fatherhood with three of my children, watching the fourth at the far end. Watching. If Joseph rocked back on his chair, I warned him of dangers and brought him down. If Matthew hid beans beneath his plate so that it rose on a small green mountain, I dropped the mountain and the boy together. If Mary sneezed, I wiped her nose and the right side of my face. If Talitha turned an entire bowl of oatmeal upside down on her beautiful head, I watched.

But during one such supper, in the darkness of winter, under a yellow kitchen light, oatmeal rolling in dollops all down her cheeks, the child glanced at me and, in meaningless spontaneity (I'm sure), flicked her eyebrows once, up and down, in my direction.

It looked as if the raven's wings had fluttered. It looked as if the sharp black brows had asked a question.

Immediately, compulsively—thoughtlessly, in fact, with no wisdom nor deep intent on my part—I flicked my eyebrows in return, up and down.

The child was transfixed, staring at me.

Slowly, slowly she raised her eyebrows so that both eyes widened.

And slowly I did exactly the same.

She popped her eyebrows, up and down, up and down.

So did I.

She giggled! Talitha giggled.

I leaned forward with an intense expression on my face. I pursed my lips as if thinking a most solemn thought. And then I arched one eyebrow, all by itself, half-way up my forehead—

And my daughter burst out laughing.

I had just told a joke, and she got it.

Precious Jesus, I had discovered her tongue! The baby talked with eyebrows, a sort of sign-language, eyebrow-speech!

Bingo! In that instant we came to be, she and I, Talitha and me: life flowed warm and real and good between us. I screwed my eyebrows into a hundred configurations, and she answered, twitch for twitch. I said, *Pass the salt,* and my daughter laughed exactly as daughters do laugh at stupid daddies. I said, *You're covered with oatmeal, kid,* and she reached to rub the stuff with her fingers. I said, *I love you, Talitha.*

She said, *I know. I love you too.*   *1 John 3:18–20*

April 27

Winning

After a night out, we, bland parents, entered the kitchen to find Talitha sweating, Talitha rolling out the most enormous hunk of dough I've ever seen: it drooped down all four sides of the butcher's block.

Casually Thanne said, "What are you making?"

Talitha, laboring: "Coffee cake."

Thanne, smiling with genuine humor, unaware of the importance of the conversation: "Oh! Well, that's three coffee cakes for sure."

She said, "Three."

And Talitha, freezing above a blob of dough the size of a bean-bag chair, said: "The recipe says *one* cake. This is *one* coffee cake."

If Thanne had said nothing, that much dough would certainly have become three cakes. But the single maternal word, *three,* made it *one,* one absolutely, one as a statement of teenage independence. One!

Talitha (*ain't nothing I can't handle*) covered her dough with butter and sugar and cinnamon. She turned it over on itself, then brought the ends around in the shape of a croissant as huge as a human hug. She removed all the grates but the lowest one from the stove, and stuffed the oven with her cake. She baked it at low heat for nearly two hours, grimly, with a droop to her eye that declared a magnificent self-assurance and contempt for mothers, generally.

And it worked.

That is to say, the coffee cake—greater and grander, more glorious than the thrones of many parents—baked clear through. Now, finally, Talitha cut it in three parts. With one she fed the marching band of her high school. With one she fed her family through a month of breakfasts. And one she froze—which we have since eaten in various manifestations. We have had french-toast-coffee-cake by Talitha, a victor who gloats long in victory.   *Proverbs 16:3, 9*

April 28

His Daughter's Difference

O my daughter, I do feel sad at your growing independence, even as I marvel and thank the Lord that it should be—for how would you survive without such strength? But you, like adolescents everywhere and every-when, use the differences between us as if they were knives to cut us apart. And you get one more knife than most teens do: color. "You don't understand, Dad," you say. "It's a Black thing." It's a Black *thang,* you say, insisting on the Blacker vowel.

But my love leaps over the differences, girl, applauding in you what is *not* like me. My love embraces our differences, genders, colors, ages. It is my love, therefore, that suffers the separation you force in these places.

This is what I think: if I weren't hurting to lose you, neither would I love you. It is a sign: my grief reveals my love, dear daughter. The one is equal to the other.   *Proverbs 21:21*

April 29

Are Children a Gift?

I saw a woman pick at her child, no more than 2 years old—pick at him, pinch him, push him and prod him ahead of her down the mall. She was scarcely aware of her behavior. She was enjoying conversation with a friend who was walking beside her. But the kid could not maintain their pace.

So she was pushing him forward at his shoulders while his eyes grew huge with the fear he might fall; her eyes stayed fastened on her friend. She was interrupting (though never losing) the thread of her conversation: "Tad!" she said. *Poke!* "Go!" she snapped. *Poke!* "Move it!" *Poke, poke.* Finally she stopped, put her hand on her hip, and actually looked at him. "Tad, what is the matter with you?" He had sprawled face-forward on the ground.

But he had gone down in perfect silence, because there was no one to call to for safety or support. His mother was making her own golden days at the expense of her son's. No one was laughing.

Sorrows like these shall surely come—but surely, parents, not through us! Haven't we ourselves suffered such abuses? Even as adults? And weren't they more than misery could stand? Isn't that motive enough to stop our tongues and stay our hands when we might hurt our children? Do we need more?

Then hear this: Children do not exist to please us. They are not for us at all, but rather we exist for them, to protect them now and to prepare them for the future. Who is given unto whom? Are children a gift to their elders? No—not till children are grown and elders are older indeed. Till then it is we who are given, by God's parental mercy, to the children! And it is we who must give to the children, by lovely laughter, the lasting memory: *You are, you are, you are, my child, a marvelous work of God!*   *Proverbs 24:13, 14*

April 30

Joy of Life

Oh, Felix! There was nothing wiser in all the world to do, than to follow the Phoenix eastward. Nobody asked, "Is this right?" They simply did it.

They? They, by the thousands. Birds by the tens of thousands, singing the songs that Potter had heard at a distance. Potter had company!

Out of the green, across the wilderness they came in a rushing multitude, every family and feather, a great cloud of witnesses, a skyborne jubilation! Pigeons and eagles and sparrows flitting; hawks and swallows and geese; thrashers, kingfishers, terns, the shrikes and the crow; tanagers, warblers, larks and the loon, and here and there a dumpy chicken given flight; starlings in overwhelming population; robins, wrens, and cuckoos; pheasant, partridge, turkeys, buzzards, vultures and the owl—a wonderful company, so thick as to darken the earth, and laughing all as Potter laughed, delighted by their holiday, and no one pecking another one. No, these were at noisy peace together. They flew with the joy of life, life not overcome by death. The story had happened again: the Phoenix was their hope, and all their song was "Hallelujah!"   *Psalm 47:1–9*

May

May 1

Mary's Words

O dear Mary, my sister, how I love you. I watch you lift your skirt the better to run, to run from the tomb into the city, to run without weariness but in the joy of an endless energy and with supernal purpose. I watch you burst into the disciples' hiding place, and I love you. I see the very radiance of your face as you touch the poor men, one by one, with your eyes. I see the eagerness with which you gaze at them, yearning for them to believe the thing you are about to say, so that they, too, might come to life and be blood brothers to you. I hear you draw breath to speak—and I love you, dear, because it is my Jesus bright in you, and because you are now hidden perfectly in him, and I cannot understand the mystery of that new relationship, but shan't I love you deeply, deeply, completely and innocently on *his* account? I shall. I do. It is the sole response that I can have to the wonder before me, the thing you are and are about to do: that I love you.

No! No, Mary. No, there is one other response in me when I hear the laughing music of your language, the Truth particular and universal in your speech to the disciples, the Word in your words, the Confession, now, of Faith. It is to beg you, my sister, my saint so far ahead of me:

Won't you tell me of the raw thing itself, of the thing made primal and eternal, of Life? Won't you tell me how it felt to say,

I have seen the Lord!   John 20:11–18

May 2

Agnes Brill, I

This selection and the next describe what Wangerin calls the patience and kindness of love.

When we sought a piano teacher for me, Brian Lank suggested Agnes Brill.

"I visit her Sundays," he said. "She knows piano, and she needs pupils."

Brian was a college student who sometimes played the organ in our church. Lean, long-fingered, a somber and steadfast gaze, so unassuming that he scarcely moved his lips when he talked, Brian persuaded us. He had perfect pitch and a tiny wrench. Every Sunday he would tune Agnes Brill's piano because she suffered a perfect anguish at the slightest dissonance. In return, she served him a Sunday meal. They talked. She lived alone.

"Listen," he told me, "be patient with her. She's suspicious of young people. She hates waste, and she thinks the young waste everything. Just be patient, and she'll make you a musician. Oh—and she has allergies."

At my first lesson, Agnes Brill sat on a small stool to my right. She let me labor through several pieces, then stopped me. "Walter," she said, "you're wearing woolen socks."

I pulled up my pant cuff and beheld a woolen sock. "I guess so," I said.

"Please," she said, "wear cotton. I'm allergic to wool."

Agnes Brill was thin and brittle as a stick. The flesh of her face was drawn so tight that it went white on the bridge of her nose. Her fingers were red and spidery—but the woman could play the piano with a pounding power and then with such a sweetness that it made me want to cry.

Oh—and she has allergies.

Throughout the autumn she moved her stool farther and farther away from me. "It's not just wool," she explained. "I'm allergic to animal lanolin. You have a cat? No? Then the mice must run up your leg."

I laughed. I know now that she meant no joke; she was growing fearful because the allergies were multiplying.

She was allergic to synthetic fabrics, to color dyes, to living creatures, to animal lanolin which, she was convinced, the wind blew in through cracks in her house. Courageous woman, she fought back. By Halloween she'd draped her windows with white cotton sheets. She hung sheets over every interior doorway and covered her carpeting with them. She herself wore white. I tiptoed in this ghost's abode feeling big, rude, clumsy and nervous.

Once in November I wore a checkered flannel shirt. Agnes Brill said absolutely nothing for 15 minutes. Then she snapped, "I cancel this lesson. Go home." I looked surprised. "You could have worn a white shirt," she said.

I didn't wipe the surprise from my face, and she grew furious. "You don't believe me? You think I exaggerate?" She strode toward me, grabbed my arm and rubbed the flannel across her wrist. Within a minute I saw red welts rise up. Agnes Brill was bitterly triumphant. "Go home. Next week wear white."

So then I decided to quit piano lessons. But Brian Lank said, "Please be patient. She's losing all her pupils just when she needs them most." I stayed. I returned to the soundless house all swaddled in white.   I Corinthians 13:1–8

May 3

Agnes Brill, II

When Agnes Brill played Chopin, I could forget the strangeness—or else, what was strange received a universal name and a tragic consecration, and I seemed to understand.

One day the woman met me at the door, panic cracking her face. "Walter," she whispered, "there's a mouse in the kitchen.

Get it out!" I entered the kitchen and saw nothing; but she cried from the front door, "In the refrigerator!" I opened the refrigerator but saw nothing.

"In the tureen!" she cried. There was a covered bowl. As I reached for it, the woman cried through the house, "Don't lift the lid! The mouse will escape!" I carried the bowl outside to the garbage and left it there. I never lifted the lid.

My final vision of Agnes Brill that winter has her sitting by the window staring at snow, erect and formal and desolated. All the world is white. She has ignored my piano lesson altogether. When I prepare to leave, she speaks with an almost pleading intimacy.

"I have another allergy," she whispers toward the snow. "I don't know what to do. There's nothing I can do." She falls silent and begins to weep. "I'm allergic," she whispers, "to my own body."

So then, I quit piano lessons for good.

The following spring I met Agnes Brill on the street. She was wearing a paisley dress. I was glad for her recovery; but when I spoke, she answered icily.

"It was Brian Lank who visited me," she said. "Brian was the only one."

Ah, Brian! Steadfast student, what did you do? "Nothing," he said when I asked. "I tuned her piano. I ate her food."

Nothing? No, something of infinite mercy. She always served potatoes, beef and gravy. They'd talk for hours, then she would wrap the leftover food for him, saying, "Waste not, want not." But you can't wrap gravy, however stiff the grease has gone. Therefore, Agnes Brill would get a spoon and feed the grease to Brian Lank.

"I knew she hated waste," he said. "I didn't want to upset her." So what did he do? Every Sunday, gratefully, uncritically and patiently, he ate cold grease from the hand of Agnes Brill. What did he do? He loved her.

This, in the sinful confusion of our world, is the love of the Lord Jesus Christ, palpable, powerful and therapeutic. Brian ministered to the woman as no injection could. He honored her. He ate cold grease until she healed. Love is patient and kind. Let all the people say: *Amen!*   Matthew 5:38–42

May 4

The Church Our Mother

They made the Divinity male, and according unto that gender I experienced him. But when they spoke of the creating and the re-creating love of that Deity, their words slipped to the abstract and degenerated into thin, analytic theologizing. *That* love was left to my intellect, but my heart could find no handles for to hold, and my heart hung helpless in a void. I thought of a potter, and I was a pot. I thought of the dust of the earth, and I was still a pot. It is hard to imagine life as a pot, impossible to experience it.

On the other hand, they allowed the Church to be the Holy Mother—and there they struck a chord, and there they found warm-blooded memory. This story I know very well by experience—   Revelation 12:1–6

May 5

Before the Sky

In the beginning of time, even before this world was created, there was no sky. No sky—yes, that's a frightful thing to think about. It's like a room with no ceiling, like a house with no roof. If you had been here then, child, and if you had looked up in the daytime, you would have seen no clouds, no blue, just nothing at all. If you had looked up in the nighttime, you would have seen no stars, no moon, just empty spaces forever and forever.

No sky! What would protect you, my child, from the terrible emptiness of the universe when there was no sky above? Why, it would be like living in a nightmare all day long. Anything could happen. Creatures as strange as grasshoppers with human heads could swoop down to chase you, because there was no sky to stop them. And then you would be scared for sure, and no one would have blamed you if you cried.

But God knew that you'd be scared without a sky. And even in the beginning of time, the dear God was in love with you.

Therefore, after he made light and looked at the universe without a sky, the Lord God spoke. "No! No!" he cried in a voice like the clap of thunder. "This will never do," he said. "Soon I'm going to make a child. But first I must make a safe, protected space where my little child can live." And right away he went to work.

The great, good God stepped out on the rim of the universe, where only God can stand. Mighty was he, and unafraid of anything, and deep in love with you. He had a voice of tremendous power—and he was God.

"Nothing shall harm the child that I am going to make," he declared. "Nothing!" Then the Lord God raised his arm and swept it round from one side of the world to the other. "Let there be a roof here," he commanded. "Let there be a firm, blue dome to keep all frightful things from the world below." And God said, "Let there be a sky!"

And so it was: God made the sky as it is today, huge and high and comforting. He pricked its dark with tiny lights. He told the moon to ride at night, and the sun he sent to burn there in the daytime. He blew it full of wind and cloud. And he whispered, "For my child, to tell my child what time it is, and to guard my child at any time, day or night. Yes," said God as he looked up at his sky, "this is a good thing."

Genesis 1:1–8

May 6

Created for Love

Now the mighty God came down and touched the soil, the dirt itself. He whispered, "Swarm," and the good earth heard him. It trembled and squeezed, and it bore its children. The caterpillars began to crawl, and ants and bugs and beetles.

Then animals came forth, my child, that walk the way you walk, on their feet; animals with hair like your hair, with noses, ears, and mouths that smile. They came two by two. They came in the thousands, and they filled the whole garden of the earth.

But every creature, as soon as it came, began to search for something.

The caterpillar twisted left and right, looking. The wolf cubs tumbled about sniffing for something. The lions and the leopards ran with smooth grace through the forests and the plains, looking, looking. The great bear stood on her legs and raised her nostrils to the wind, trying to find the scent of something important. But then she sat down sadly, because she couldn't find it. Something was missing! Lambs and goats, cows and oxen, birds and fish and all the beasts went wandering everywhere throughout the world, crying, "Where is it? Has anyone seen it?"

But no one found the thing that everyone desired, the thing which would finish creation, the most beautiful creature of all.

So the animals said, "Ask God." And that is exactly what they did.

Oh, child! This once in the whole history of the world all the living creatures came together in a single place. Ten thousand, thousand animals gathered at the mountains of God. They covered the hills and the valleys with life.

"Where?" they cried to the mighty God. "Where?" they pleaded in a million voices. "Where is the little child that shall lead us?"

God answered them quietly, "That child is not yet here."

And then it seemed that the mountains themselves burst into tears. But it was the sound of animals. Great and small, the animals were crying, child, exactly as I heard you crying yesterday, lonely and afraid—because without this child they could not even know their own names.

"Listen to me!" God made his voice sound like a trumpet, louder and clearer than their crying. "Listen to me," he called until the animals fell silent. Then he said, "Creation is ready now. The time is right. I have made the spaces. I have made a garden. I've filled my garden with goodness and music and friends. Now I shall make a child."

And then, dear child of mine, whom I love more than I can say—then God made you.   *Genesis 1:20–27*

May 7

Confirmation

I remember my confirmation. It felt that it happened wrong. In fact, it happened right for me; but the feeling of personal terror was a measure of the personal, important and public step this infant took into adulthood. Spiritual and communal independence is, when it is real, a scary thing.

I think my terror in that moment had its holy purpose. Our society has few real rites of initiation, by which children leave childhood and, through the valiant accomplishment of a significant task, enter adulthood with all its rights and responsibilities. The task must be a personal *experience,* relying on self and God alone, so that the self can feel—and be persuaded of—change. The task must be *significant,* not a safe parody of adult tasks, so that passing the test is a genuine entrance into adulthood. And it must be *public,* so that the whole society might honor the change and receive the new adult as a responsible citizen.   *Luke 2:41–50*

May 8

A Maturity of Faith

Confirmation was my initiation. I can conceive of nothing more significant than that I should, of my own heart and strength and mind, declare that God is God, and is my Lord. This was not some childish entertainment for the church. This was a matter of life and death: I was crossing into a maturity of faith. In baptism Jesus had made me his. But now, of my own soul, *I* was announcing the same to be so; and I, a long time saved, was now embarking on discipleship. The presence of people both sharpened the terror and heightened the consequence of what I was doing.

The pastor said, "Wally, what does this mean?" I stood up. My mouth was dry. In that instant my competitive classmate whispered, "I-believe-that-Jesus-Christ-true—"

And a marvelous thing occurred. I thought, *I can do this myself!* And I began to bellow, "No! *I* believe that Jesus Christ, true God—" "—and that Jesus Christ, true man—" While I roared forth my affirmation, I forgot my father, my pastor, or anyone whom I was supposed to represent except my God and myself. And was my mother proud of me? O let her be proud of this: "—that Jesus Christ is my Lord!"

Matthew 16:13–20

May 9

Poets = Makers

Only God performs this function purely. Yet dimly, and in a mimic, we too may be poets [of creation.] The poet is *poiētēs:* in Greek, "the maker." Though not from nothing, the poet causes to be what had not been before. He sings, and there gathers under the heart of his hearer the pressure of his music, the swelling of a new word, like an infant. It isn't that the hearer learns a new teaching, but rather that she *has* a new being in her, complete and suddenly. The poet makes a story, peoples the story with characters, sends the characters through twisting histories, and behold: the hearer believes his story to be true—if not historically true, then the *Truth.* And the hearer truly grieves for characters whom the poet merely made.

Proverbs 8:22–31

May 10

Boxed in Doctrine

The differences among us and in our faithing occur, however, because of our various uses of the functions of language.

No child escapes the first passage of faithing, wherein he experiences, undefined, the Deity; and dialogue takes place within that relationship.

Some children (they may be adults by now) receive the benefit of the naming language at the right time, and the relationship is preserved by a fine and timely confession of faith. At this point many others cease the *passi*, the passages, for lack of language.

But then many of those confessors stop too, right where they are. They presume that this confession, this clear commitment ("I have accepted Jesus in my heart; I am saved!") is the full accomplishment of faith. They have arrived. They have found their place in the bosom of Jesus. They are done. All that is left, they believe, is to go forth boldly with the Gospel, themselves examples of—and witnesses to—its finished product, since for them the heavenly marriage is fixed. For them the fluidity of a living relationship has been boxed in doctrine; dialogue has hardened into litany (or hymns repeated, or repeated prayers), and the creating word would horrify them, could they hear it. Their words from the Creator are laminated on the pages of their Bibles, unchanged, unchanging, unalterable forever. *Luke 20:9–19*

May 11

Death Changes Our Knowledge

As long as death, however many words we spend on the subject, remains an indistinct eventuality, so long will resurrection from the dead seem nothing more than mild insurance—however many words we spend on it. Resurrection is only as good as death is bad, as easily believed, as easily dismissed. We call it a miracle, but we don't really mean that, because we don't really need it. We call it a miracle, but in fact—until death is experienced and proves it otherwise—we don't think resurrection all that impossible or even unlikely, and this is because life itself is so persuasive: we can hardly conceive of there *not* being life. So resurrection is simply life's extension. What should be, what *should* survive the nuisance Death, is no wonder nor miracle. Miracles are things that simply cannot be.   *John 11:1–16*

May 12

The Cause of All Our Sadness

"Why art thou cast down, O my soul?"

The psalmist (Psalm 42) knows his sadness. When we are sad, we all know *that* we are sad. But we do not always know the source of the sorrow, and like the psalmist we have to ask, Why?

"Why art thou cast down, O my soul? And why are thou disquieted in me?"

What causes the sadness—even in seemingly good times?

Why, for example, does the mother of the bride, who truly desires best things for her daughter and who genuinely loves this son-in-law, weep at the wedding as though it were a funeral?

Well, because it is, in a sense, a funeral.

Or why, when a man has finally achieved the freedom of retirement and now can putter to his heart's content at things that give him greatest pleasure, does he sigh and descend to a sorrowful silence, as though his dearest friend had died?

Because a dear one *did* die.

Almost all our sadness has the same cause, though its forms are various in the actual events that we experience. Sometimes the form is outrageously evil, and then we forget it, if we do, only by severe and necessary effort: certain abuses in childhood, the beatings humans deliver to those they promised to love. But sometimes its form is that of the natural changes in human life, and so we scarcely recognize the cause at all. Yet all these, the causes of sadness, are at the core the same: the leave-taking of the children; the failure of one's soul-sustaining dream; betrayal, whether grand or gossipy, by a trusted friend; the surgery that took a breast; marital divorce; the loss of some beloved possession, the loss of a house by fire, or the invasion of thieves; the loss of a human function or of a significant role in society; the increasing loss of liberty with advancing age; the loss (and this is the paradigm of all our losses) of my dear one to the casket and the grave.

The details change, but the cause and the sorrow are always the same. The experience is universal. No one born to human flesh is ever exempt. Not one.

The cause of all our sadness is Death. *John 11:17–31*

May 13

Losing a Role

When elders slip toward senility and children must assume the role of parent to their parents, no one should be shocked by feelings of a sudden and tremendous sorrow. Nor by feelings (oddly) of anger, or depression thereafter. Even though the elder is physically present to be honored and nursed, the old relationship (that of adult to respected adult) has cracked and can't be mended. This is, though without corpses, a death. Sorrow, anger, depression are grief, right and natural and good.

The first response is human compassion. The second is our private dying. The first we suffer in common—as a gift to the one we love. The second we suffer alone. It is critical to recognize the difference between these two, since the former must be kind, while the latter might take the form of anger. Now, anger can rightly be directed at the change we both must undergo—that is, at the impersonal circumstance, the cause of our friend's crippling. But anger must never be directed at the invalid! If our anger should be misdirected, death multiplies, and a new relationship might never develop again.   *John 11:32–44*

May 14

Retirement: Tasting the Dust

That which used to authenticate his being, and his being *here,* has been torn from him. He has been sundered from his reason to be, his worth, his purpose, his name, his repute, his glory. Can we stress enough the separation that is death to him? He is like "Adam," whose name means "soil," who was sundered from the *soil,* the stuff of his work and his identity.

Grandpa is not suddenly peculiar. It doesn't have to be Alzheimer's disease. Don't dismiss him as senile and cantankerous. First seek causes not in his mind but in his spirit: he has died. He is grieving.

Then I considered all that my hands had done and the toil I had spent in doing it, and behold, all was vanity and a striving after wind, and there was nothing to be gained under the sun.

When that thought—the "Why" without an answer—seizes us, it doesn't matter what disturbance had caused it: we taste the dust in any motivating purpose and all our goals seem fatuous.

The curse upon our willful estrangement from God is a lonely estrangement from his fields and all their fruitfulness. That which we dress and till, the weeds will steal as soon as we cease. That which we do, it dies with us.   *Genesis 2:10–15*

May 15

Broken Trust

Every communal relationship has a covenant, a code of behavior that gives form to the relationship and to which each partner is committed. This code is mostly unspoken, but both partners know it; and as long as both obey it, the relationship is protected and nourished as a living thing. Likewise, it serves each partner, who can drop defenses and trust the other, who can enjoy the stability, strength, and fulfillment of mutual exchange—who live therein and thereby.

Trust permits life to flow among people in relationship.

Trust is as precious as the arteries of a physical body: they carry the blood.

The rupture of such trust, then, causes life itself to hemorrhage.

And with sadness I note that this particular Secondary Dying, the killing of people by people in covenant with them, is likely more common than any other. Those who love us most are also most vulnerable to us. Daily we kill and are being killed.

[Among those capable of this deep betrayal of trust] are pastors. Their position receives relationships of such complete need and tenderness—the bodies *and* souls of communicants—that a sin in this place is tantamount to blasphemy. Yet pastors do abuse the vulnerability of those in covenant with them. Ah, it is murderous. Moreover, even a pastor's private sin (seeming to involve no one but himself and perhaps one other) can destroy a people's credence. Can kill. And then an entire parish grieves. I have seen churches spiritually silenced by the act of a pastor, complete congregations withdrawing into sadness and depression, or else falling apart in recriminations—and no one knew that this was the manifestation of grief because something dear had died.

Such grieving among a people, once the cause is recognized and the consequence named as "grief," is *natural!*

John 21:15–18

May 16
The Reason We Will Live

The new covenant is Grace.

This relationship can endure even when I am helpless. Especially then. *This* relationship endures though I am nothing in a nowhere—because I remain a something in the heart of God! *This* relationship endures in spite of the flat reality of the grave and my own dissolution, my crumbling into dust, because my side of the covenant is not fulfilled by *my* flesh and blood but by Christ's—who continues to live, yes, even while they bury me and the worms translate my subtle brains to soil.

"My sheep," says Jesus, "hear my voice, and I know them, and they follow me; and I give them eternal life, and they shall never perish and no one shall snatch them out of my hand."

I will die. All my resources will exhaust themselves. In myself and on my own, I will not be.

But the Shepherd remembers my name.

The Shepherd will whisper, "Walter"—and though I have no ears to hear, yet the whispering Lord will give me the hearing.

The Savior will cry across the divisions: "Walter Wangerin, Junior!"—and though I have no tongue at all, the calling will give me voice. The Word of God has always contained my own capacity to answer it.

"Walter Wangerin, *come forth!*"

And straightway I will rise up, laughing and loving and leaping, alive: "Here I am! For you have called me."

John 10:1–5

May 17

The Days of Our Humility

The highest joy of the fourth act [of our grieving] is beyond a secular comprehension.

It is this, that God does not impose the sentence we know we deserve. The seemingly indifferent God is a Father after all, who hugs us, who slips rings on our fingers and shoes on our feet and food in our mouths, who kills the calf and throws a party—the dance to which Death never shall come.

In the days of our personal majesty, we would not have seen a Father. We could see nothing but an enemy and cosmic hostility.

But in the days of our humility, any gesture from God is dear. Any gesture. How stunning is love, then. And how unspeakably glorious is life everlasting, relationship with the Source of Life even beyond our Corporeal Dyings and into eternity.

This drama of grieving, able so to transform us and lay us like children upon the bosom of God again—this grief rightly we call good. *John 12:23–27*

May 18

A Cold Wedge of Intellect

In fact, shock may depersonalize the experience of dying, may generalize it into a phenomenon to be observed: anybody's house, anybody's fire. That which is too great immediately to be grieved is not perceived as one's *own*. The personal and passionate participation is stalled for a while. Distance is established.

The "disinterested" intellect can drive a cold wedge between the griever and the event. Thus, many people protect themselves *from* the death by a very precise scrutiny *of* it, perhaps by describing it in a journal or a letter.

An ironic (even a cynical) humor, likewise, causes distance between the griever and the thing to be grieved. Imagine how little this behavior is appreciated. Understand how much it is needed by the one who is laughing.

Even a sort of philosophizing—a cool generalization of this death as the fate of all human flesh—forestalls the sense of a personal blow. The griever takes an Olympian view, a godly superiority, abstracting his own experience, making it but one illustration of many such in the cosmos. "Ah, me," sighs the divorcée. "How many people divorce these days! It's a characteristic of the age." Civil tears for the culture at large are easier than the anguished and helpless howl for a personal devastation.   *John 12:28–32*

May 19

Socks Are Fixable

But in shock we return to strategies of our childhood.

If a hundred relationships break all at once, shock shuts down awareness of all but a manageable few. These we suffer consciously. These alone we seem to mourn. But these are symbols for the whole. Childish? Yes. Silly? Of course not.

I know a woman for whom the greatest outrage of her husband's death was that he died with a hole in his sock. His big toe stuck out that hole. The man was a farmer. He was mowing ditches in front of the house when the tractor turned over on him. She ran and arrived just as others did. There was much to grieve a widow in such an accident; but his boots were removed, and there was her husband's exposed big toe, and that's all she could think of: she spent endless energies explaining to people that he didn't need to wear torn socks. She wept for his socks.

Some neighbors wondered why laundry should bother her much at that moment. Grist for gossip. She seemed more concerned for her reputation that for her husband's life. In fact, humiliation was an easier emotion than the woe that must sooner or later follow. Socks are fixable. Death is not.

John 12:33–36

May 20

Something Should Be Different!

Gloria's father, Sonny Boy, has just died, and Gloria is on her way home from the hospital.

Gloria's enormous Buick LeSabre sits at the intersection facing east but going nowhere. The light is green. No matter. Her car is not moving. In the street on the driver's side a long-legged, high-backed, goose-necked youth is jumping and screaming. He throws back his head as if cocking a gun and pours vituperation toward the skies. Then suddenly he tucks his head, spreads his arms, and flies at the car. He bangs the roof with the heels of his hands, which bounce up like rubber—BOOM! BOOM!—and which open into a gesture of outraged supplication. Then the whole boy springs high into the air, absolutely taut with fury, screaming, screaming:

"You gon' kill me, Bitch! You *aimed* to kill me. You done it on *puh-puss!* Murderer!"—BOOM! "Murderer!"—BOOM!

On the other side of the car, scarcely able to see over it because "all us Hopsons is short," Marie Landers has emerged to challenge evil face to face. She too bellows, making gestures of potency and wrath. But she is a grandmother and a great-grandmother with access to different authority:

"BOY!" she booms, rattling windows, "BOY, AH KNOW YO MAMMA. AN' IF YOU DON' SHOW SOME RESPECK, AH'M GON' *TELL* YO MAMMA, AN' SHE GON' *WHALE* THE RESPECK INTO YO SITTIN'-DOWN, TILL YOU *CAIN'T* SIT THAT SWEET BROWN SMILE DOWN AGAIN!"

And so forth.

A truly memorable scene. Marie in church, rocking to a strong song, can raise her hands and roar glory to God. Well, the voice that reaches heaven with praise can also meet wickedness with weaponry, in this case the marvelous cannon, YO MAMMA!

Just as I arrive, Marie decides to hobble around the nose of the Buick—so the furious boy (taller than either of us) is flanked on two sides, and neither the old woman nor the white pastor is impressed by his cursing.

Cursing still, then, and vowing monstrous vengeances, he backs up, turns, and retreats with his slickery-fingered, loop-necked, knee-popping pride.

Gloria sits in the driver's seat, staring straight ahead. No expression whatsoever. Her hands are locked to the rim of the wheel, her small mouth pinched. I lean through the window beside her.

"Gloria, how are you? What happened?"

Without the slightest motion, scarcely parting her lips, she whispers, "He's right, Pastor. Somethin' in me wanted to run that poor boy down." Her face is ashen, drained of its blood.

"Gloria, do you want me to drive you home?"

Her hands are locked to the wheel. "God help me," she whispers with awful quietude: "He was eatin' an apple. He was amblin' 'cross the road. An' then he up an' grinned at me, an' he winked, an' my car just jumped forward like my foot slipped. But it didn't."

Traffic is creeping around the Buick now, grazing me behind.

"Come, Gloria, come—we've got to get out of the way. Move over. I'll drive you home."

She doesn't move.

But she turns her head and looks up into my eyes, her face a mask of amazement. "How can they jus' go on an' do, Pastor?" she begs with piteous appeal. "Sonny Boy *died* today. Sonny Boy *died*. But folks don' notice. They walkin' 'round, gettin' on buses, goin' 'bout their business. Something should be different. Something should . . . Pastor," she whispers with slow astonishment: "Nobody's crying. Nobody's holding his hat for sorrow. Nobody's even walking slower. An' here comes a boy, strutting and smirking and eating an *apple* an' spittin' the *seeds*—"

Abruptly she faces forward again.

She whispers, "I almost killed him."

And then, again, she whispers, "I am so scared—"

John 12:37–40

May 21

Anger in the Face of Death

The failure of the will leads to, and intensifies, the effort of emotion. Simply, the obduracy of death frustrates us. It angers us. Anger is the reaction of the unreconciled.

And it is often characteristic of anger to believe that one has been dealt a personal injustice. Anger feels righteous in the face of our foe's unrighteousness. Moral law seems on our side, giving us the right to even greater rages: *out*-rage!

With the opposition of our will we tried to be the Creator and failed. We are not God.

With the opposition of emotion, now, we admit as much; but then we take up an adversarial position against the Deity (for the fact that he *is* the Deity and we are not) and attack him—as though we might be equal to God in our fury if not in our nature. Moreover, like Job we believe that our case is just in the courts of the cosmos: anger indicts God for our particular pain and then for the misery of all flesh. No: we do not always name God in the indictment. Rather, we may depersonalize it and "rage against the dying of the light," or complain about "the way things are," or fly in the face of a human authority, or accuse the impassive skies. But these are symbols or dodges. God is responsible. God is our opposite. Jacob is striving with God.

There is a grandeur in the expression of emotion, here at the limits of existence. Humans confronting the Deity, whether in the assizes or with swords, do always seem heroic. And for a while the poetry of the thing, the epic stature, swells us. And we are strong.

For a while. *Genesis 32:23–33*

May 22

Why Blame God?

First because we *think* God is responsible. Even when we fear to admit it, God is our final antagonist. God the Omnipotent, Sheer Infinitude, the Holy Other, by his mere being and by the contrast to ourselves, teaches us our tiny-ness. It is plain honesty, then, that carries the anger to God.

But second, because God can take it! God, who understands us better than we understand ourselves, will not be destroyed by our most passionate rages. In fact, he sees already the fury and its intended object before we confess either one. And it hurts the Lord when our anger hurts his people.

Better, then, to give it to God.

It doesn't matter that we are wrong to accuse him for our sorrows. God will not give tit for tat. Instead, he is glad for the chance to communicate. When we speak, we are also inclined to listen. When we confront the Lord we open ourselves to divine response—and then the Lord can engage us in dialogue, and *then* he can heal us.

Even so did he do for Martha when Lazarus died. She berated Jesus for that death: "Lord, if you had been here my brother would not have died." She was wrong in the accusation but right to take it to Jesus, because no one else could do what he did. First, he named himself before her: *I am the resurrection and the life.* Next he required from her the confession that could both change and save her: *Do you believe this?* And only then did Martha answer with faith, "Yes, Lord, I believe that you are the Christ, the Son of God, he who is coming into the world." In this way Martha's wrong was made right, and she was brought into relationship with her Lord again. *John 11:17–27*

May 23

Struggling from the Husk

Exactly at eye level on the bark of the cherry tree in my backyard, I saw one cicada all alone. *Katy-bird?* I was seven years old that summer and happy. *Katy-bird, hello.*

She stood six legs tight to the tree-bark. She was the size of my mother's big toe, thick and blunt. An insect, surely—but I called her "bird" in my mind. Her face, aimed upward, looked like the front of a truck, the eyes set wide apart and separated by a sort of grillwork grimace. Her whole body was dull brown and hard as a husk.

But she had popped her skin like a pea pod and was slowly, slowly crawling from the shell of her old self. One cicada, but two cicadas, and the new cicada wasn't ugly at all, but soft and moist and sweetly green. Listen to me: a self emerging from itself. This was amazing. *REE-rrr-REE-rrr-REE-rrr:* the woodsaw song of enormous cicadas higher in the summer air. They were cheering her on, and so did I.

I watched while she struggled to climb from the hard brown husk, which kept the perfect image of herself, except that the face was empty now, its eye-windows like plastic bubbles clear and thoughtless. Her new face was attentive, sober. I gazed as she felt for a grip with her new front legs on the neck of old armor, and pulled. By degrees she dragged her green body through the crack in the casement. She rested. She twiddled her forelegs in fresh air. Then she pushed with the hinder legs, still inside. *Go! Go!* I helped her out with my desiring: *Be born, beautiful Katy-bird! Be!* Oh, what a summer's day! *John 12:12–15*

May 24

In That Day . . .

The truth is in us; there we hear it. But this is because we have always been within the Truth, like the chrysalis being shaped unto our birth. There is no tighter relationship, than that each entwines within the other, causing one another being. Jesus is the Truth. "In that day you will know that I am in my Father, and you in me, and I in you." Such a statement is the interpenetrating conundrum of being. Holy being. The sinner's existence was a solitude. But the existence of the resurrected being is symbiotic, one life in two. This infant is not lifted into being until it has touched another being, realizing at once the face it touched and the fingers with which it touched. For us, that face is Jesus, smiling, permitting our baby pats on his most lovely eyes.   *John 14:18–21*

May 25

On the Other Side of Grieving, I

Moreover, "rising" and "healing" do not mean that sorrow is finally abolished. Wounds leave scars, and deep wounds scar the soul.

Whatever the death, if it has caused a drama of grief as complex as the full four acts, it shall never be forgotten—nor shall the grieving ever altogether pass away. Something lingers. Gloria will always miss Sonny Boy. Always. Missing him has now become a part of her person.

But grievers do not, in the end, return to their "old selves." The "old life," "that old sparkle" are gone.

Resurrection blots out neither death nor the long sorrow it caused.

Resurrection is not the sweetening of bitter truth.

Nor is it a pious sentimentalizing of disaster, as if one suddenly surrendered common sense by saying: "Well, it was the will of God. I've learned to accept that now. I'm a better person for it"—or some such simplification.

Resurrection is this: that though she was sure she would die, she lives. And though she *knew* she'd never feel again, she feels. Against all reason, against all evidence—a consequence that was impossible to any who entered the Pit—she is alive, breathing, feeling, thinking, making decisions again, again!

She lives *in spite of death*. Now, if death were forgotten at the end of grief, the preposterous nature of life would likewise be lost, the flat miracle of the thing, the miracle of her own being: she is the miracle! *John 16:20–22*

May 26

On the Other Side of Grieving, II

To whom does the griever, now rising, give thanks? Like anger, gratitude seeks an object. Its nature is outward; its yearning is to identify a Someone Responsible for this conundrum of life in spite of death; and (if gratitude is genuine) that One must be Someone Greater Than the Griever's Self, must be the Source of Life, Creator, Deity—

The transcendent God.

But God comes near to us in the Word made flesh.

Gratitude seeks the Christ. Even if she knows not his name or his story, the griever now seeks the Lord's Messiah.

Humbled as never before (not abjectly so, not beaten down, but full of astonished thanksgiving and praise) the griever is ready to see his glory now.

In small things. In common things. In the persisting, daily things.

It is precisely because the Lord inhabits ordinary things that she did not see him there before; but she has changed, and absolutely everything (since anything now is undeserved and all is unexpected) seems extraordinary in her sight. Simple sunrise is like the solo of God at the dawn of creation, a splendid *Fiat lux!*

Holy! Holy! Holy is the Lord of Hosts: the whole earth is filled with his glory!

The whole earth: each piece of creation. Now the griever may see divinity in any common thing, and so renew relationship with the Almighty Creator even as she renews relationships with the bits and pieces, the handiwork of God.

Romans 11:33–36

May 27

On the Other Side of Grieving, III

One day you're hungry. You eat. And while you eat, a remarkable thing occurs: you taste exquisitely—you do thoroughly appreciate—the food. It's just a french fry! But you think, "I've never had a better french fry! Oh, I've been missing french fries." And you find yourself chewing with something more than mere pleasure; you are chewing with a distinct feeling of gratitude. You want to thank someone.

But it's just a french fry! Isn't it silly to be moved to tears by a french fry?

Not silly at all. The goodness of this moment (of the spasms of renewal) is not to be measured by the material thing that caused it, but rather by the passion in you that receives it, and then by the glory of him who gives it. If you are compelled by a french fry to give thanks, by all means—give thanks to God.

Of course, by tomorrow your heart may be cast down again. And then you may feel the worse for a moment of gladness that didn't last. No matter: the rise is always fitful at first, with fallings again when sadness returns, and fallings when you doubt the signs of life. Be patient. Wait. The gift will come again; and again—despite setbacks—you will feel the rush of thanksgiving.

Romans 16:25–27

May 28

What It Means to Follow

Follow me meant "Suffer the abandonment of God. Suffer to know him as he is, unmediated—which is not to know him at all. Suffer *his* complete control of the relationship: trust absolutely." This, too, was a death—not to the world, nor to ourselves, but *into* a fullness of relationship with God. Ironically, we felt that this death we could most easily die, since it consisted in our doing nothing. And some of us did—and these, then; were done. But for Peter and for the most of us, this was the death we could not die. Instead, our inability to die it has finally raised into our consciousness the very truth of our natures, and it has prepared us for the death we *shall* die—

One more time the dear Lord Jesus whispers (but we do not hear him, and we would not believe him if we could; he does this thing, not we) *Follow me.*   *John 1:43–51*

May 29

Possessing Nothing, Possessing All

I truly honor the little monk St. John of the Cross, even as I do that more bemisted figure whom I cannot see but who teaches me, the author of *The Cloud of Unknowing*. These are mentors to me, together with others of the long mystic tradition. It moves me, how peacefully they name and recount the most relentless torments, assuring me that the darknesses are of the Light and that the anxieties are of God. They dwell in paradox with a dancer's ease and lightly. They make the moves of faith which Kierkegaard described as a balletic leap so perfect that, on landing, the dancer seems never to have leapt at all, but perpetually to be standing still.

By him I accept (I do not say I understand; it is beyond reasonable understanding; I stand in awe of, I see as true and
trust, I accept) this divine irony: that only when finally I have
nothing do I possess anything, may I possess all things; that
"having nothing" means, in its extreme, not even having the
self to act as owner or possessor, and makes *impossible,* then,
the possession of anything, for I am not there to say, "It's
mine"; but that Jesus *may,* then, dwell in me, in *my* name saying, "All is mine, all is thine," and I say, without saying it,
"Then all is mine as well." That irony. I accept that irony.

John 17:5–10

May 30

I Have Promised

Listen: marriage begins when two people make the clear, unqualified promise to be faithful, each to the other, until the
end of their days. That spoken promise makes the difference.
A new relationship is initiated. Marriage begins when each
vows to commit herself, himself, unto the other and to no
other human in this world: "I promise you my faithfulness,
until death parts us." That vow, once spoken, once heard,
permits a new, enduring trust: each one may trust the vow of
the other one. And that vow forms the foundation of the relationship to be built upon it hereafter.

A promise made, a promise witnessed, a promise heard, remembered, and trusted—this is the groundwork of marriage.
Not emotions. No, not even love. Not physical desires or personal needs or sexuality. Not the practical fact of living together. Not even the piercing foresight or some peculiar
miracle of All-seeing God. Rather, a promise, a vow, makes
the marriage.

"I promise you my faithfulness, until death parts us."

Here is a marvelous work, performed by those who are made in the image of God—for we create, in this promise, a new thing, a changeless stability in an ever-changing world. We do the thing that God does, establishing a covenant with another human being: we ask faith in our faithfulness *to* that covenant. We transfigure the relationship thereafter, transfiguring ourselves, for we shape our behaviors by the covenant. A new ethic has begun for each of us. We have called forth a spiritual house in which each of us may dwell securely. Whether we know it or not, it is a divine thing we do, and it is holy.

Ephesians 5:21–33

May 31

The Husband Knows His Wife's Love

Slowly Pertelote returned his hug. He felt the warmth coming to him as a gift. He felt her cheek upon his neck, caressing him, and now the tears did run from his eyes, for she had chosen; he had not demanded.

"You are my husband," she whispered. "I am your wife. I love you, Chauntecleer. *That* is not madness."

"O mighty God!" the Rooster cried. "Watch over this woman! Never, never let her go!"

And then, while they clung to one another on the Liverbrook, their backs to the weather, he said, "You sang to me once in my desolation. Do you remember?"

"I remember," she said.

"Do you think that you could sing to me again?"

That night Compline was a tender shock for all the Animals. It woke them, gently, then composed them for a yet more blessed sleep.

It was sung in a woman's voice.

Pertelote did not crow or cry out or lift up her voice in the treetops. It was crystal, ringing clearly of its own accord, completely clean. Her soul was a crystal bell.

> "—For safety I commend my friends,
> Their spirits, sleep, and all their ends,
>   To God;
> And him whose life myself I live,
> His name Sweet Singer, most I give
>   To God—"

Chauntecleer inclined his ear and swallowed. It was an exquisite benediction, to hear his name within her prayer, as though he were eavesdropping upon her love for him.

Song of Songs 1:1–4

June

June 1

Graduation

That church had been my school, that man my teacher, and here was the ceremony of endings and beginnings, with music and preaching, lights, flowers, rites, noise, my seat center-front, my self the single excuse for the gathering. "Walt's excited—"

But I knew even then that the excitement of the ceremony was not cause enough for the fire in my face. This was more than mere blush.

Rather, the burning came of this: for once in my long and vigorous struggle with the Lord Jesus Christ, the struggle itself had ceased. For a moment, the relationship had reached a certain purity. At that instant my faith was not being ripped between yes-and-no, nor my calling ripped between yes-and-no, as both had been for years. My Lord was Lord and Mine, my calling exquisitely clear—

My faith, you see, was the flame in my face.

2 Timothy 1:6–11

June 2

The Early Invitation

In the beginning, "Follow me" was a delightful if difficult invitation: "Come unto me." *Come* not yet unto what Jesus would perform, but *come* unto who he was, a teacher above the picayunish teachers of the Pharisees, a rabbi whose laws were few, supernal and comprehensive, the which he would himself accomplish. To *come* was therefore to be relieved of a hurly-burly of responsibility, of heavy burdens hard to bear, weighing on our shoulders. When we took his yoke, why, he took it too: it was a double yoke, and we were yoked together. And love was not only allowed, but empowered: we loved him with his own love back again. Likewise, he loved us unto the full flowering of our own beings and not to the flattering of his own. Certainly he sought to see his image in ourselves; but behold: his image *was* our personal selves made perfect, the *imago dei,* clean as at creation! *Matthew 4:18–22*

June 3

Detachable Body?

Sometimes I wish I could define myself as soul alone. When this body gives me trouble, I want to say, "It's detachable. Ignore it. The real me is purely spirit, caught in the cage of this corpus." But I can't. My self is (as Adam's self was) as much the clay of the earth as the spirit/breath of God. My visible and evident *self* is shaped by this (square-jawed, blue-eyed) face, this frame (six-foot-one), this particular slouch, this brain, these physiologic capacities. My body is more than the "cage" in which my soul lives. It is in fact my material substance and much my *self*: both how I live and who I am.

My body is that part of me that Thanne embraces, however much she likes my mind. It's my body that lies abed with her at night.

Of course, then: when this body begins to suffer internal separations (even of the physical kind, radical changes now and forever), so do I!

When pieces are cut from the body, when the body itself diminishes, I do too.

I die a little.

Sitting in my study the night before the surgery, then, I began to suffer a sadness of separations. For when the things of one's deepest affections seem suddenly more beautiful because they are suddenly more remote and possibly untouchable, that is grief. *Psalm 94:18–23*

June 4

Losing the Self—in Pieces

When the body breaks and separates, so does the person.

—It is the grief of bereavement that an amputee of any sort experiences, sad for the lack of a leg or a larynx.

—The pain of a paraplegic is more than physical torment, as great as that is, and more than the mighty frustrations of incapacity; it is grief in the extreme, and it is likely to present all the stages of grief, and it will require the consolation we give the bereaved—because this one has died a terrible death, a severe internal separation.

—Clearly, a mastectomy is more than removal of cancerous tissue. With her breast has gone a significant part of the woman's self, though just how significant only she can determine. She will measure it by the depth of the grief that follows, sorrow and anger and a thumping gloom. She will measure it by the feelings the hugs of her children cause in her, the touch of a beloved man.

One dear friend of mine told me how fearful she was of her grown children's touch—not that they might hurt her delicate balance, but that they would sense the radical change in her even through their fingers' tips.

She expressed this fear curiously, by "hagging," she said, "the children," making herself so cantankerous and difficult they wouldn't *want* to touch her.

Then she would weep in secret because no one touched her. She pitied herself and infuriated herself, both at once, thinking that she herself was the cause of all her woes.

And then one morning the visiting nurse neglected to visit. But Kathy's bandage absolutely required changing.

Her son happened to drop by.

Necessity overcame her reluctance. "Would you—?" she whispered to her son, embarrassed to be asking such a thing.

"Would you, um—?"

Kathy tells to me now that his response raised her to life again; the gentle touch of her son as he cut the old bandage, the unchanging expression of kindness in his face as he washed the wound where her breast had been, the slow bindings with clean cloth her whole upper torso—all this proved that though she had changed, his love had not; and though she had died indeed, yet she could live again.

Psalm 103:8–14

June 5

Facing Faith's Dark Times

But how does the passage actually unfold?

In the beginning, despite all warnings and the announcement of the interdict, the faithing one thinks, "I can do it." He comes encouraged by his burning love for Jesus and flushed with the success of that love's accomplishments. "What is it after all?" he thinks when time has taken the vision away. "A little waiting. With the promise still inside of me to give me hope. I can do that," he thinks. "I can be still a while. Better to wait in the foxhole than to endanger myself on the battlefield," he thinks, unaware that the foxhole *is* the battlefield of the soul, and infinitely more lonely. In the foxhole one is one's own foe, and thinking is the weapon. And, unaware (because he hasn't yet experienced it) of the completeness of the occlusion, the darkness of this night, he thinks, "How bad can it be?"

I can do it: this is the attitude exactly which will be excised. Graver still, this is the declaration which later will cause spasms of an even more horrible pain: guilt. Guilt is the pain of a pride cut away. Darkness is the scalpel. *Psalm 130:1–8*

June 6

The Aftermath of "Spiritual High"

Jesus had had his own celestial experience, sweet and good and signifying. He had heard himself named as "beloved" and "my son," the Son of God: the divine relationship had been divinely validated, and with it, his identity; and to make the validation an objective experience and not the dreams of a fervid mind, he *saw* the invisible Spirit descending visibly like a dove; he *felt* it to alight on him.

But straightway the experience devolved into a memory, and the dove became his drover; for he had, by the will of God and the urgency of the Spirit, been led (passive voice) into the wilderness, whose nature is privation, to experience which is to experience want. He did not eat for a generation of days (as Israel was denied, for a generation of years, the milk and honey of the promised land, living with the promise only, itself repeatedly jeopardized). And now he was hungry. And now the tempter came to him.

What did Jesus have then? He had the memory of the voice of God, but the voice of God was silent now. *Matthew 3:13–17*

June 7

Not Seeing Jesus

Here is an anomaly: we took up the cross to follow Jesus; and so we do, when we are nailed to it—we follow Jesus. But following him, repeating in our own experience his, we suffer the question of whether *he* is following *us!*

Jesus? Are you there?

For at noon, by the same divine fiat that made light, God makes darkness, and we hang in it. And the cross to which we are affixed, why, it is the hard, unbending command not to turn and see. We hang *on* that command, and the silence torments us. Were we only thieves, one of two criminals, we would hang to the left or to the right of Jesus, clearly in his company and in sight of him. But we are not mere sinners, either mocking him (persisting in sin) or else pleading his forgiveness. We are the faithing ones, called to believe on him; and so we hang precisely where we cannot see him at all.

Jesus? Jesus? Matthew 15:29–36

June 8
An Unusable Storehouse

The Joseph here is the Wangerins' oldest son.

Ah, Joseph. Here is my fear at your chrysalid growing: that I can help you in this labor less and less until I help you not at all. I've no choice in the matter; and sometimes you will understand and demand that I let you alone (when independence will hurt me). Other times you will cry for a father to catch you, but I *will* let you alone (then independence will hurt you). No choice! This is the very index of the act. This *is* the act. Your "growing up" means needing to need me less, dear Joseph; and until you need me not at all, the labor remains unfinished, and my son remains merely my child.

It is this backing-off that scares me, this letting you into yourself. For neither of us knows what shape shall arise from private change. Will he, Heavenly God? Will my son succeed?

More than that, I choke, being all unable to share with you the storehouse of my own wisdom and experience, do choke, seeing you make the mistakes which I by a word could prevent.   *1 Thessalonians 2:17–20*

June 9

Coming of Age

Too often the parents make absolutely nothing of their children's coming-of-age. They let it happen, as it were, by accident. Ho! They took more time over potty training than they take over training toward adulthood. They imply, then, that it is nothing, this "growing up"—or else that it is a distinct hazard in the household, a problem, a sin, a sickness, something that wants correcting. In consequence, the adolescent, unprepared, is shocked by the maelstrom which he has entered. Next, he feels an abiding, unspoken guilt at the changes occurring in him. And when he most needs resources to fight this good fight, he least has them. Indeed, the fight seems anything but good and heroic when his voice breaks, her cramps come, but the family (neither parents nor society) has given no dignified name or place to these profound and exhausting efforts.   *1 Samuel 16:1–13*

June 10

Idealization

Love lies a little. Love, the desire to like and to be liked, feels so good when it is satisfied, that it never wants to stop. Therefore, love edits the facts in order to continue to feel good. Love allows me an innocent misperception of my fiancée, while it encourages in her a favorable misperception of myself. If it isn't blind, it does squint a bit. Love idealizes both of us.

No marriage is the perfect union of perfect people. But if we saw only imperfections before we married (however true they are), marriage itself would seem too great a risk for anyone to take. On the other hand, for those who have the tool of forgiveness, imperfections are rightly dealt with *inside* the marriage bond, after marrying. (This is one reason many who live together before marriage do not marry: they discover their partners' faults without the motive or the means to redeem those faults; so they merely escape; they separate.) The time and the tool for repairing imperfections will come with the marriage. During courtship, then, we compulsively pretend perfection. Idealization is more than natural. It is necessary. *Song of Songs 5:9–16*

June 11

Lonely

And how does he feel then? Why, lonely. They are spiritually separated, as though each had put on clothes to hide from the other. The marriage, meant to abolish loneliness, makes him even lonelier than before. "She thinks only of herself."

More subtle still, the husband may be right, but not in the way he thinks. It could be that the wife who breaks her back to please her husband has deep within her the selfish motive that she cannot live in a tense household, that she is trying to relieve the tension for her own sake. Therefore, she tells him what he wants to hear and shows him what he wants to see: she mirrors to him not his true self, but his own false picture of himself. And of herself she reveals nothing, hiding both anguish and her private motives in the clothing of smiles, a (sometimes manipulative) servitude, and Christian goodness. How does she feel? Well, when she cares to admit it, lonely. Together—but separate—they suffer the selfsame dying. *Song of Songs 5:6–8*

June 12

The "Home" of Marriage

Far from Indiana, Wangerin and his choir experience ugly racism in the church where they are scheduled to sing.

And then Thanne came in, carrying a plate of supper for me.

I saw her familiar face in this alien place. I saw her kindness in the midst of enmity and criticism—and I burst into tears.

I stood and put my arms around her and hung with all my weight on her thin shoulders and sobbed so hard I couldn't speak. I was weaker than Herman. Neither did Thanne speak. But this precisely is the point of my story: I *could* cling to her, and she didn't *have* to speak.

For five minutes we stood wordless together, saying nothing, doing nothing, accomplishing miracles. This wife of mine had through the years assured her husband—for whom tears were an embarrassing difficulty—that tears were a fine, acceptable release, that she did not love him the less for them, that they were no shame at all. This wife had so patiently done the marriage task of comforting that she had created in me the *expectation* of comfort. She had caused to surround us the very atmosphere of "home," so that however far we traveled, however strange the territory, I was "home" as long as I was with her.

It was in the city of Dallas that I wept. But that says nothing significant. Rather, it was within the "home" of our marriage that I was given the right to weep; here I could safely reveal my tears, my exhaustion, my brokenness: I could be true. And from the spirit of our marriage I could be assured that I would receive comfort and healing and strength again. I could heal. I could be empowered.   *Psalm 142:1–6*

June 13
Tasks

"Times past" are not so very long ago. Do you remember how at harvesting the men worked field-to-field and farm-to-farm, while the women gathered to cook and feed them as they went, to boil the jellies, to preserve the fruits and vegetables? Do you remember, at slaughtering, the natural division of labor that put the men nearest the bloody beast and put the meats in the hands of the women? Even so did our grandparents allow the expectations of the community to teach them their tasks.

But things (so suddenly) have changed today. The immediate survival of any one family does not depend upon a close association with the community. Industry has taken the basic labor out of the family's hands. As our contemporary culture has chosen to survive by mechanization, it has less right or reason to demand similarity of our various households. We do not farm together; we do not hunt, slaughter, and salt meats together; we do not, in fact, depend upon our neighbors to perform, together with us, the labors of survival. Therefore, it no longer matters to us or to the community what tasks our neighbor or her husband have chosen for themselves. Families can and do survive alone. As a result, the old distinction between "women's work" and "men's" has lost its purpose and its force.

But cultural habits run very deep in us; so parents and grandparents, and even the marrying partners themselves, maintain unconscious expectations of what shall be the wife's tasks in the marriage, and what shall be the husband's. The old pattern, the old division of labor which sent a man into the world while it kept the woman with her children, still exerts great pressure on our consciences. Is it wrong? No, it need not be an improper pattern to follow—so long as the spouses realize that they are free, now, *not so much to obey it as to choose it.*   *Genesis 3:14–19*

June 14
Sharing Tasks

As your spouse accomplishes her tasks and as you experience the benefits of them, you praise her very character—for she is actively essential to your common survival and cannot be replaced by someone else. She did not shape herself to fit the tasks; rather, you together shaped the tasks to fit her being. That makes all you do a sharing. Moreover, she will be much more motivated to do that work which suits her, which manifests her value, work which is critical to your existence— and which is no drudge, therefore.

Can we now dispense with such demeaning epithets as "the little woman" and "woman's work" and "behind every successful man there is—"? I hope so. I pray God we do. Because the division of tasks in every marriage ought finally to be specific to each marriage, dictated by the faculties and aptitudes of the partners themselves. That the survival-work be done by someone—that is the only law. That it be wisely divided between you—that is your freedom. *1 Peter 1:13–21*

June 15

A Way of Life

[One of the continuing tasks of marriage is healing, which] recognizes that the spouse will suffer, and that intrinsic in your promise to be faithful is your promise to heal his suffering, always to be her first physician—to "keep" your spouse in sickness as well as you keep him in health. Healing, too, is essential to marriage work.

But the name is broad because suffering is not restricted to bodily ailments alone. Your spouse will suffer both physically and emotionally, will suffer both diseases and dis-ease. The world will surely batter his self-esteem, and he may grow uncertain regarding himself. Her duties outside the house and inside of it will surely try her fortitude, drain her energy, and leave her weary. Sadness wants healing as much as a flu. Fearfulness wants comforting as much as convalescence after surgery. Grief and bewilderment need careful ministrations as much as does diabetes, or incontinence, or high blood pressure, or any of the hundred handicaps that come with old age. And to care for your spouse in this way requires more than a medicine chest. You are married. Healing is not a profession but a way of life. Your spouse is not your patient but your flesh. Healing, then, is a task for your heart as well as your head and your hand. And it cannot wait for some disease to strike before it acts; it prepares for all dis-eases even before they come.

This task is performed at all times, with all your being, by three miraculous acts: nursing, building a house of mercy, and sympathizing. *2 Peter 1:3–11*

June 16

Confession

To confess in your soul before God may be the beginning of goodness; but there you don't experience God's hearing you. The words become more real when someone of flesh and blood—someone who will have obvious feelings about what you say—hears and reacts to those words. It is this *hearing* which authenticates them, which places the secret deed clearly in the open and in the community where you dwell. When it is no longer hidden in your heart, then it can be dealt with. *1 John 1:8–22*

June 17

Matthew Teaches

Well, I'd been a father one bare year; Joseph was the first, but you were the first we adopted, so I had little experience at the job and no knowledge at all whether a parent loves the ready-made child as much as the child that comes from his own loins. I wondered if we missed some mysterious ingredient since you arrived of a mental decision and not of the physical love of your parents; and you were brown and I was white. Where was the love to come from?

Here is the miracle: my love for you came out of you! You came with printed directions. You trained me.

At first it was foolish love, aggressive, fierce, protective. When we carried you to the grocery stores, we gathered the stares of the people. Our family was a riddle they couldn't solve. My ears would burn at their ill restraint; I'd grab you to my heart and stare back to shame their eyes. My face said, "*Mine!* He's mine, you little minds!" And so you were.

There was a neighbor, in those early days, who said that you couldn't play with her daughter. She'd seen the two of you holding hands, and she said, "Black and white don't marry." Nip it, I suppose, in the bud: you were four years old. I sat in that woman's kitchen and in a low, choked voice declared you were my son and she should think of me precisely as she thought of you. Curiously, she acted as though she and I were the buddies and you the odd-boy-out, since she and I were white together. But to me her kitchen was alien territory, and she the foreigner, and I despised her stainless steel complacency; I hated her hatreds, and I hugged you hard when I went home again, but you didn't understand that nor the burning love begun in me, half angry, half apologetic.

You took my love for granted. You were the wiser, and you trained me. *Psalm 145:8–11*

June 18

Dependable

Do you see, then, that dependability is, first of all, a personal and spiritual labor? It is a struggle, in fact, against self-centeredness, against thinking you have the right to follow your own immediate moods, to satisfy your own feelings. Now your previous pledges must shape your activities, your schedules, your priorities, and your labor. Dependability requires that you will sometimes sacrifice the unforeseen opportunity, that you will decline certain personal advantages, that you will not be blown about by every whim or new event. Rather, you yourself will control the day's events according to the marriage's expectations upon your promises—not because your spouse commands you, but because those promises do. Is this submission in marriage? Obedience? Yes. Is it the submission of wives to husbands, or of husbands to wives, so that one might dominate the other? No—but of either partner to the pledges which he or she made both to and for the sake of the spouse. *It is the purer submission: submission to relationship.*

And this is the blessing it provides: that when one is dependable even in the small things (making a bed every morning, for example), the spouse is inspired to trust in all things. So a whole world may be foundationed on the head of a little deed—and cosmic peace upon a little promise kept. What an astonishing return upon a penny's investment!

Matthew 7:21–27

June 19

I Call It Righteousness

O God, speak to me.

I think I've lost charity. *Caritas.* I am not kind or merciful. Speak to me!

I think my love is no longer generous. It narrows. I dole it out in pennies and make my people pay for it—as though it were a precious thing because it's *mine.* This isn't love.

Please speak to me.

For want of charity to everyone, for want of love for even a few, my manner has stiffened to civility. I comfort myself with hauteur. But I call it righteousness, and I grow grimly glad that I find no wrong in me.

But this rightness isn't good. Sweet Jesus, speak to me.

1 Corinthians 13:4–7

June 20

Clergy Burnout

The generations are changing, confusing the social stability that our churches once enjoyed but reducing none of the duties that must be done. Duties are heaping on the pastor's desk. And if they are not done, criticism is curling at the pastor's door. It would be good, I think, for the church at large to know what a goodly number of our clergy are suffering.

It is both holy and possible for the laity to serve its precious crew of servants, now as before. I fear we've ceased this service somewhat. And then we've blamed the pastor for the consequences.

Not all pastors are at a critical stage of loneliness. But many are. Not all are burned out with overwork, with relationships (in an age that extols the empathetic relationship) which are all one-way, with private problems for which there is neither counsel nor kindness. Not all of them feel a dead-end desperation. But far too many do. And I think their spiritual weariness will tell too soon upon our church.

2 Corinthians 10:12–18

June 21

Pastoring the Pastors

No one is pastoring the pastors. But in the past of our own memory, the parish *as a body* did it. Unconscious custom (in steadfast, unchanging communities) used to divide ministerial duty between pastor and parish.

Members used to know by instinct and tradition what duties they could shoulder in the church. They didn't propose and vote and worry about turf or sensibilities. They acted. They were bequeathed their spiritual positions in the church.

Grandma and grandpa shared the ministry by spontaneous wisdom, by visiting the sick unasked, by feeding the bereaved as well as consoling them, by noticing leaks in the roof and fixing them, by scolding and loving anyone's child at any time, by shoveling snow, by foreseeing financial distress, by preparing potlucks without the long discussion of some committee, by paying the pastor in potatoes and eggs.

Grandma and grandpa have passed away, and their roles have vanished with them. And we wait around to be elected or appointed.

There are pastors operating now purely by habit, with little sense of success or worth. And no one knows.

People, first we confess. Then, by God, we combine again into whole communities. *We* are the body of Christ. And then we learn the selfless service of our grandparents. We are the pastor of our pastor. We, together in holiness.

2 Corinthians 10:1–5

June 22

The Pastor Visits the Jail

The jail caused in him a miserable confusion of emotions, and he hated it.

He confessed his feelings of relief as one confesses a sin. He prayed for a holier, happier attitude. He prayed, "God, make me hungry to serve. Make me content in service." He prayed his prayer passionately because he truly suffered the sharpness of his conscience. But the prayer was never answered. He loathed the jail until the end, suspecting that his loathing came of pride. He hated what it did to him, because he was a near nonentity within its walls, subject to the moods of the guard. He hated what it did to the prisoners whom he visited (which hatred he counted worthy, since it indicated human sympathy). But he also sometimes hated the prisoners themselves and feared them (which hatred was clearly unworthy and caused him Davidic spasms of contrition: shouldn't he feel tenderness for those he served?) Harder and harder he prayed the prayer which God refused to answer. The turbulence persisted in his spirit—

—but he persisted in his work.   *2 Corinthians 4:7–15*

June 23

The Pastor Prays for the Prisoner

So Pastor Orpheus prayed aloud: "Dear God, I'm begging you for Corie Jones. *I have the right!* You must hear me, because of the need, because he is dying, because he shouldn't die, because I have done everything you asked of me, because I am not praying for myself, but for him, and he is your child after all. Tell him you love him! Prove your mercy for him. Let him be at peace, and talk with me, and live. O God almighty, let Corie Jones live again. Do you see that I pray out of my suffering? Is that nothing to you? And do you see that I suffer because of my love for you and for Corie Jones, both? *I have earned the right!* You must, by expressions of your own love, persuade my Corie Jones that he is worth something in your sight, and that he can live—"

In these and other words Pastor Orpheus prayed a desperate prayer, all his ministry balanced on the scaffold—nay, ministry itself thrown into the wager, and waiting the hand of the almighty God.   *1 Timothy 2:1–7*

June 24

The Pastors Prepare

We were preparing the place for the annual picnic of Grace Lutheran Church. And since our picnics, always scheduled on a Sunday, began with worship, we were preparing for worship. Cheri and I were dressed alike, both wearing black shirts with clerical collars; or else you might say we both wore black blouses with clerical collars. Pastor Cheri Johnson. Pastor Walt Wangerin. The ministers of Grace. We shuffled furniture. We gathered old Coke cups from windowsills and paper trash from corners. We pushed brooms and wiped tables and broke ice into a cooler and measured grounds into a coffeepot and chose a board for potluck dishes and generally attended to matters most sacred, as ministers of minor parishes are called to do.

And then the people began to come.

"Mornin', mornin'!"

Cheri was bowed at a small stove, fingering water in a pot and finding it warm. Now she poured the water into a glass salad bowl. And now she carried the bowl to a pedestal in front of our makeshift altar. Her face was long and as solemn as an icon.

But I wondered whether her heart wasn't beating harder than normal as she bore the water altarward. I think so. Her face is long by nature, a slender nose, an even brow, a contemplative, slow-blinking eyelid, a nunnish droop to the corner of her mouth: she has a face composed against such excitements as the harder beating of the heart. And she has a long and slender body, calm, unrevealing of heartbeats. Nevertheless, I'll bet she felt a shiver as she set the water on its pedestal—because this water was meant for a baptism.

In this particular worship service, on this particular Sunday morning, Pastor Cheri Johnson was going to baptize her baby, her firstborn child, her Hannah.   *1 Samuel 1:19–28*

June 25
Visiting the (Difficult) Sick

From the beginning, I did not like to visit Arthur Forte.

Nor did he make my job (My ministry! you cry. My service! My discipleship! No—just my job) any easier. He did not wish a quick psalm, a professional prayer, devotions. Rather, he wanted acutely to dispute a young clergyman's faith. Seventy years a churchgoer, the old man narrowed his eye at me and debated the goodness of God. With incontrovertible proofs, he delivered shattering damnations of hospitals (at which he had worked) and doctors (whom he had closely observed): "Twenty dollars a strolling visit when they come to a patient's room," he said. "For what? Two minutes' time, is what, and no particular news to the patient. A squeeze, a punch, a scribble on their charts, and they leave that sucker feeling low and worthless." *Wuhthless,* he said, hollowing the word at the center. "God-in-a-smock had listened to their heart, then didn't even tell them what he heard. Ho, ho!" said Arthur, "I'll never go to a hospital. That cock-a-roach is more truthful of what he's about. Ho, ho! I'll never lie in a hospital bed, ho, ho!" And then, somehow, the failure of doctors he wove into his intense argument against the goodness of the Deity, and he slammed me with facts, and I was a fumbling, lubberly sort to be defending the Almighty—

When I left him, I was empty in my soul and close to tears, and testy, my own faith seeming most stale, flat, unprofitable at the moment. I didn't like to visit Arthur.   *1 Timothy 6:3–10*

The Gestures of Loving

I do not suppose that Arthur consciously gave me the last year of his life, nor that he chose to teach me. Yet, by his mere being; by forcing me to *take* that life, real, unsweetened, bare-naked, hurting and critical; by demanding that I serve him altogether unrewarded; by wringing from me first mere gestures of loving and then the love itself—but a sacrificial love, a Christ-like love, being love for one so indisputably unlovable—he did prepare me for my ministry.

My tears were my diploma, his death my benediction, and failure my ordination. For the Lord did not say, "Blessed are you if you know" or "teach" or "preach these things." He said, rather, "Blessed are you if you *do* these things."

1 Timothy 6:11–14

Climbing the Stairs

She had begun. She was not done. From that day forward Mrs. Story determined to climb her stairs to the top and to make her house her own again.

And she did not mind if [the pastor] stood by, praying.

Day after day she approached the low steps of the staircase and gripped her leg at the joint. She bent it, lifted it, and placed a foot one step up. Then she dragged hard on the banister, hoisting herself body and soul upward. It was an exhausting trial: she leaned, breathing, on the banister before she attempted the next.

It was exhausting, and it put her into awkward, unflattering positions; therefore, [the pastor] took it as a pure kindness that she allowed him to witness her weakness. But she wanted his prayers, now, and he prayed them.

With the stony, horned forehead of a Moses, in Deuteronomic language, he prayed, "Jesus, strengthen this woman!" He prayed with the excitement of an outrageous hope. Oh, they labored together, that old black lady and her pastor, one grunting and the other shouting prayers. They made noises in the silences. They streaked the darkness with their laughter.

"Allouise," said [the pastor], "he's a merciful God after all, isn't he?"

And Mrs. Story, struggling one step upward, muttered, "Well," said, "let's say that he's keeping the banister from breaking, but it's me that's doing the pulling."

Hebrews 10:32–39

June 28

Sacred Sawdust

Potter's father said nothing at all. But, smelling of wood, his strong arms covered with sawdust, he lifted his son into the air and bore him from the room.

Potter remembered forever the smell of wood as the smell of the nearness of God; and the feel of sawdust on his cheek was the stuff of love. Whenever thereafter the saws would cut to the heart of the white pine, Potter would fall silent and whisper in his soul, "Ah, this is sacred."   *1 Peter 1:3–5*

June 29

And God's Name?

How we speak the name of a thing reveals how we feel—at deepest levels—about that thing.

Our plain, public pronunciation of a name witnesses not only (1) to the nature of that thing, but also (2) to us who speak, to our attitude regarding that thing and (3) to the nature of the relationship between us and that thing.

The power and the value of a name, then, depends upon these three things. For the name of one who is powerful is a powerful name; but if our attitude (and so our tone) is nasty or cheap, the name is cheapened. And if our relationship is at bottom selfish or cynical or silly or empty, the name is rendered powerless—or else, if powerful still, it becomes a power that endangers us.   *Revelation 19:11–16*

June 30

Sleep

Night. The night descends, and the streetlights string a lace of beads down the streets of the city, and the drivers switch on their headlights. In the city the cars are slick with reflected light; in the country one pair of headlights sweeps the road and splits the dark some 20 yards ahead. People go home and turn on their lamps. They sit in front of the blue-green glimmer of the TV screen. They murmur half-sentences to one another. They get up and lock their doors. They stop in the kitchen, the bathroom. They darken the house, room by room. They retire. They sleep.

Night. Midnight. A dog barks. Another dog sends up its howl and joins the warning. But the alleys are empty. The two dogs woof; they clear their throats and themselves of duty, and are still.

Night. The small hours after midnight. All the world is bedded. All the world's asleep—

—But you, my child. You.

You sit on your bed with your knees drawn up, gripping them with your arms. Why do you tremble? Why do you start at the shapes the occasional car will flash through the window on your walls? Why do you peer around you?

"I'm afraid."

It's your bedroom. What can you be afraid of?

"I'm afraid of the dark."

But the dark's no enemy—

"I'm blind in the dark! I'm lost. I can't see what's in front of me, nor what could attack from behind, nor what I am, nor how protected, nor *who* I might be—"

Faith, child! Even in darkness it is God whose hand is leading you, God whose right hand holds you. For the dark is not dark to the Lord, but the night is as bright as the day.

Be still. Be very still, and listen. Silence your hectic mind. The night itself was made for the lonely, for the Spirit breathes in silences and in the dark, and two might chatter too much to hear it, but one Elijah all alone can hear the silence *in* the silences.

Make little of yourself, my child, and nothing of all your need. Sleep is the self gone small, and the Lord shall swell around you. Thou art a grain of sand, and God the sea.

Oh child, I love you. Know that the night is holy, and the darkness a gift of God. Rest in a refuge and in a bosom of strength. Rest, and afterward—sleep.   *John 1:4–10*

July

July 1

For The Healing of All

Listen: In *Stride Toward Freedom* Dr. Martin Luther King Jr. wrote of the bombing of his home: *At home I addressed the crowd from my porch, where the mark of the bomb was clear. "We must not return violence under any condition. I know this is difficult advice to follow. But this is the way of Christ; it is the way of the cross. We must somehow believe that unearned suffering is redemptive."*

King was a public anomaly. He did not react to suffering as the world expected. He neither blustered nor broke. He was different from the world. He declared aloud the disease of the whole society. Then he acted for the healing of all by offering himself, by personally refusing the will of evil and bigoted powers.

I say, "for the healing of all," including the powerful, because everyone suffers so long as oppression continues: Hatred imprisons the body of one but the heart of the other, and I don't know which is the worse.   Matthew 5:43–48

July 2

A Confession and Forgiveness

Lord God, will you hear us in our sorrow?

Congregation:

This is our sin: we have not always discerned the Lord's body, nor loved and nourished all of its members. Therefore, we have wounded it.

We've judged our neighbors harsher than we judge ourselves—and then, self-righteously, we've severed ourselves from them.

The powerless among us we've abused—for we scorned them, or forgot them, or patronized them, or manipulated them for our own sole satisfaction.

And those who were different earned our suspicion.

And some who sinned we chose not to forgive.

Yet all of these—these people, these parishioners, these relatives of ours, these churches, these races and colors and classes—they are members of your body, dear Lord Jesus. It is you whom we have wounded.

We preached love, but we did not love.

O God of fire and forgiveness, have mercy on us.

Pastor:

This is the grace of God: the crucified, the wounded body of Jesus died; but in three days he was raised again, whole and holy, wholly one, that we who die in separation might also be made alive.

People, you are forgiven; the wounds are healed. You are forgiven; the body grows one again. You are by God entirely forgiven!

Stand, then, O Body of Christ, in joy and in the singular name of God, Father, Son, and Holy Spirit.

Congregation:
Amen!   *Matthew 18:23–35*

July 3

A Thanksgiving Hymn

It is suggested that the names of this light, happy, dancing melody be replaced with the names of those who actually do come forward out of the congregation, in order to personalize the thanksgiving. This hymn is suitable for a children's choir.

1. *Mary comes with money, Lord:*
Herman brings you meat;
Paul sets all he can afford
Before your feet.

2. *Peter has a hand can make*
Nearly anything;
Sarah has a little cake,
Dear Beth can sing.

3. *Bread was baked and wine was poured.*
Cups and platters placed:
Supper's set before you, Lord,
And waits your grace.

4. *Things and people, talents, food:*
These are we in few;
But anything of any good
First came from you.

5. *Give the Giver, happy hearts,*
All he gave to you:
All you are in all your parts,
And all you do.

6. *Take from us, O goodly God,*
All that we return;
All we have is all we should:
We've nothing earned.

7. *Amen, amen, let us pray,*
Now that we're prepared.
Amen, Jesus deign this day
To answer prayer.   *Matthew 6:25–34*

July 4

A Prayer for Good Government

Allow the Holy Spirit now, O Lord, its pouring forth,
its smooth anointing of your holy people, their
    empowerment:
Where nations still neglect your will,
    disturbing good order,
    distressing each other,
    destroying their citizens in every manner of war,
empower us to preach peace, to be the very spirit of
    peace among them.
For governors and presidents and counselors and all
    in leadership.
Hear our prayer.   *Romans 13:1–7*

July 5

A Recessional Hymn

The Latin refrain Ite, missa est *is the ancient phrase announcing the ending of the worship service.*

Now snuff the candles; make a lesser smoke,
And scent the air with wax; the room divest;
Bring down the cross; unstole yourselves, uncloak
Your shoulders, Ministers, another yoke
You must put on, now. Ite, missa est.

You mortal chorus, do you plan to stay
Forever on the mountain? Down were best:
Down from your flight, down from your Kyrie;
Come down the aisle, at once an alleyway
Into the city. Ite, missa est.

And we will follow you, now we are done,
Now we've seen Jesus, now that we've been blest.
He's bound us each to each and all to one,
Not one of us could leave alone, and none
Can choose to linger. Ite, missa est.

One body we go forth with one command,
One Spirit to empower one behest:
To love, To love, To love, so that the land
May see our Lord's own love and understand
Who sent him sends us. Ite! *This is best!*

Hebrews 13:20–21

July 6

The Black Parish

One by one they knelt before [the pastor], filling the rail from wall to wall, bowing shoulder to shoulder. The rest of the people were singing: "—drink wine together on our knees, / Let us drink—" They were singing from memory, rocking unconsciously left and right in their pews, sixty, seventy of them, a goodly number in a sanctuary which could hold a hundred comfortably. It was a small congregation. It was a celebration in the colors of human complexion, since the parish was black and situated in the inner city and "black" meant walnut and chocolate and umber and sepia and cream and ash and parchment and gold and coal. "When I fall on my knees / With my face to the rising sun—" they sang, their faces forward, watching the familiar ceremony, waiting their turns to line the aisle and to move into the chancel and to kneel.   *1 Corinthians 11:28–34*

July 7

Only the Oppressed

"For the healing of all," because in Martin Luther King's vision we are one, and none is free till all are. And who has the subtler power to inaugurate this freedom of all? The oppressor? No. The oppressed! That is the mystery which you must never forget, even if you do not understand it. The oppressor cannot and will not change a thing. Only through the oppressed can essential change begin; and through suffering, redemption.

"If I respond to hate with a reciprocal hate," King said, "I do nothing but intensify the cleavage in broken community. I can only close the gap in broken community by meeting hate with love." And the love he returned to a bomber gave that one the opportunity (whether he took it or not) to confess a sin, to accept forgiveness, and so to be changed. For unearned suffering declares the sin to be the sole responsibility of the oppressor. And love despite the sin—why, love redeems him.

There is no other changing under the sun but that. Everything else is vanity. *Galatians 5:1–12*

July 8

Manifesting Christ

When people of genuine goodness suffer, they can comprehend the suffering of any who are oppressed. By deep pain they see deeply into all pain. By their own imprisonment they know the imprisonment of all, and so the prison doesn't hold them any more, nor their wandering souls.

But if the spirit of Christ dwells in them, they can take the next step, the astonishing step, of comprehending even the internal torment of their oppressors (for none can persecute another unless his spirit is severely crippled). This is the sympathy of the cross. This is knowledge into the oppressor which is deeper and truer than the oppressor himself possesses. It sees all humankind as one.

The third step must be considered miraculous. It is willfully *not* to return evil for evil, physically *not* to reduplicate cruelty in any way—not bullet for bullet, nor bitterness for brute oppression—but rather to swallow the cruelty in oneself, and then to annihilate it in forgiveness. This is the very gesture of the cross. This is the action of Christ within us (we cannot do it ourselves). And a new thing enters our world: The Spirit is blown abroad.

But how will the world know this material presence of Christ in the sufferer unless it is published? Preached? Spoken? Declared? The fourth step requires that the oppressed both announce their love aloud and, at the same time, resist the cruelty of the oppressor by showing no effect of it: lovingly *not* doing what the powerful demand, lovingly turning their power to impotence by refusing every expected response—not raging, not whimpering, but not obeying either, never obeying evil, loving only.

Even so is Christ made manifest among us. Such love can deflate oppression by confounding the oppressor.

Ephesians 2:11–18

July 9

My People

Force against force; death for death—what good can come of that? What can save a nation under hard apartheid? Well, this (but this I speak in wonder): that the nature of the dying it-self be changed; that Black southern Africa make its dying Christ's dying, a sacrifice, the divine ability to love the execu-tioner—not despite death but *by* that death. Who can under-stand the power, the paradox of such love? I can't. But this is the dying that redeems.

This is the love I heard, marvelously, in the mouth of Black Africa, in the person of Dr. Zephania Kameeta, Namibian Christian. Standing here in America—humble, soft-spoken, admitting his fears—he told me that he must go home again for the sake of his people. "For the liberation of my people," he said. Who are his people? "Botha," he said, "is bound in a dreary prison, heart and soul. Botha cannot see for darkness. Botha," he said, taking my breath away, "is my brother. *Brahthah,*" he said.

But why should I be astonished? This is the very evidence of Christian love, the source of change in our world, that one might love an enemy even unto death.   Matthew 5:38–42

July 10

Sham Love

Genuine love is defined by this, that it is prepared to sacrifice itself for the sake of the beloved.

Sham love, on the other hand, makes *itself* the motive, the "sacrifice," but only as a means to reach some goal of its own. It says, "Since I've given up so much for you, now you owe me. . . ." There is no giving without some getting, even if that which is gotten is merely public praise, or the sweet internal feeling, *What a good person am I!*

Genuine love serves. Neither requiring nor expecting something in return, its character is, simply, to serve—and those who stumble against these twin axioms of sacrifice and service will likewise stumble against the cross. They will fall down, crying, "Scandal!" Sham love stumbles.

Sham love may *think* it desires to serve the beloved; in fact, it desires only that beloved! It desires his company, her person—an answering love. Its service is not an end in itself. Sham love may perform difficult services, things its beloved shall absolutely need—until she becomes dependent upon them and bound unto her "servant." Do you see? Sham love fulfills itself in the end, by possessing the other. *Luke 6:36–38*

July 11

Rachel Asks for the Pastor's Voice

This and the following two selections are from "Rachel."

"I'm jus' lookin' for my grandbabies. And maybe you seen my grandbabies?"

The old woman's voice whines in my mind at odd times, grieving me, urging me, who can do nothing, to do some little thing after all. Oh, the humble supplications are the most horrible, since they enlist the conscience, and it is the conscience that echoes forever until I bend and put it to rest. "Woman! What, what between me and thee?" Conscience. Common humanity. The heart's language commonly spoken, and you speak it, and I understand it, though I do not always choose to understand, but we are members of the same Body, various extremities, and I am commanded to understand—

Woman, hush!

I will do something.

I will name you Rachel; and I will magnify your cry by writing it; and with it I will fill the ears of the people.

Luke 18:1–8

July 12

Helping to Find Them

Street-light glinted on her face, gnarled, wrinkled, deep-dark and harder than black walnut. She wore a man's vest and a man's shoes. Her eyes jerked left and right, so intent on the search that she didn't see me. She was a tiny bit of woman.

"It ain't no time," she said full reasonably, "it ain't no place for them to be about. And it's a dirty, weathery night. Hoo-ooo! Hoo-ooo!"

Who was she speaking to? God? The eyeless night? But her purpose was so inarguably right that I couldn't leave her now; and it was clear that love and yearning together had driven her into the rain.

I coughed.

"Hey, Mon!" She saw me. "I'm jus' lookin' for my grandbabies."

"How old are they?"

"Oh, they be strapping big boys," she nodded, holding my eye. "Each of him could give a head to you, Mon." I'm six one. So they were big, these boys. They didn't need me.

My wish to assist her melted in the chilly drizzle.

But the lady was earnest. Her fingers had sunk between muscle and arm-bone. "How long," I asked, "have they been missing?"

"You gonna look?" she demanded, bright old eyes drilling mine. She reached her other hand to my cheek.

"Well," I said lamely—she was buying me by touching my cheek—"yes—"

"Ooo, God bless you, child!" she said. "They been gone two lonely years, now, and I'm thinkin' they hurt, Mon, and

I'm feared they be troubled. Oh, Mon, you help me to find them!"

Two years! I spluttered in the manner of educated people whose education is meaningless before the bare, forked animal.

"Mon?" She drew down my face so that I had to look at her. "Yes, ma'am?"

"It's a promise? You use the powers Jesus given you? You be helpin' me to find them?"

She had no teeth. Gums black and a darting red tongue and lines at her eyes that enfolded the soul.

I said, "Okay."

Immediately she released me, forgot me standing there, and limped down Gum to Governor, a tiny and tinier bit of woman: "Hoo-ooo! Hoo-ooo!"   *Matthew 2:16–18*

July 13

Still Looking for You

Mad, I thought driving home and dripping in the cab of my truck. Ho, ho, crazy lady! Midnight's citizen!

And despite my vow I tried to forget her desperate, patient, weary search for grandbabies.

But I can't, you see, forget it. It's a moral memory.

Listen, and I'll tell you when I hear the pleading song, "Hoo-ooo."

When I see young strapping men slouch into Bayard Park beside my house—

They carry beer cans low at their sides, and bottles in packages. They drink, they laugh unmindful of anyone else, they gaze with vacant eyes to the void-blue skies, they leave a most unsocial mess behind. And compulsively I wonder with the crazy lady's sweet irrationality: Are these her grandbabies? These, the handsome, strong, and lost? Do they know what they have done to her? Can't they hear the old woman's call, "Hoo-ooo"?

"Is that old lady your grandma?" I want to say. "Don't you know that she still is looking, a singular figure in the night, still is looking for you? There are no private choices. There is no such thing as 'your own thing'! All selfish action damages those in love with you!"

No. The lady is not mad. She simply has a love that will not quit against reality—and that only looks like madness. She is Rachel.

"A voice was heard in Ramah, lamentation and bitter weeping. Rachel weeping for her children, and she would not be comforted, because they were not."

Oh, go home again, you strapping, slouching youth, so full of promise, so full of yourselves! Bow down before mad, merciful Rachel. Ask her forgiveness. Then give her love for love.

Matthew 23:37–39

July 14

Crying

This and the following two selections are one lesson in fighting and forgiving.

Behold the stiff-necked, the hard-hearted, the dummy!

Observe the camel, blind to one of the most useful gifts of the Lord God—which is that he arranges opportunities for confession and forgiveness between warring individuals, that they might smile and love again. He does so squarely in their day's experience. Yet note well how fierce can be the pride of this blockhead, and learn from him: it's a damnfool practice, to ignore the armistice which God keeps staging.

Behold me, when first my wife and I were married.

Lo! I am the dummy.

We used to fight, Thanne and I.

Well, it was always a "sort-of" fight, on account of, it was all one-sided. I did the talking. She did the not-talking. And then what she did was, she would cry.

I would say, "Thanne, what's the matter?" Real sympathy in my voice, you understand. And caring and gentleness in abundance, and great-hearted love. Dog-eyed solicitation: "Oh, Thanne, what is the matter?"

And she would only cry.

So then, I had my second stratagem. So then, I would sigh loudly in order to indicate that I have troubles, too, not the least of which is an uncommunicative wife—and how are we going to solve anything if we don't *say* anything? (I was skilled at the sophisticated sigh.) And I would ask again, allowing just a tad of aggravation to bite my voice, "What *is* the matter, Thanne?"

For all of which I might receive a head-shake from the woman—and crying. *John 13:1–5*

July 15

Silence

Now, silence is a saw-toothed tool of the devil. It's also excellent for self-righteous fighting, because it permits the other to imagine the myriad sins he must have committed to cause such tears. He stews in his own juice, as it were. It's the microwave stratagem of attack.

But I was intrepid. And despite the explosions of my imagination, despite paroxysms of guilt in my belly, I would move forward to my third maneuver, which was to *accept* her attack so willingly that it would throw her off balance. Guilty, was I? Guilty I would be.

"Okay, okay," I would cry with my hands up and my head down, the picture of remorse, "What did I do now?"

But all I got was crying.

Which left me mindless, frantic, and past control:

I would press her, and she would turn away.

I would touch her, and she would shrink from me.

I would stomp about the room to indicate immeasurable pain, cold loneliness, stark confusion, together with the fact that I had seventy pounds on her—

And finally she would cease her tears, finally look at me with blazing eyes and open her mouth—

And then poured forth such an ocean of wrongs, such a delineation of sins in such numbered and date detail (whether I had intended any of them or not!) that I would stand shocked before the passion in one so short, plain drowning in her venom, aware that things had gotten out of hand, but speechless myself and very weak.

Well, then there was no help for it. I was forced to my final weapon and unapologetic for its power, having been so iniquitously provoked. Without another word I'd jam my arms into my overcoat, bolt down the stairs of our little apartment, and pitch myself into the cold St. Louis night, there to roam the sidewalks three hours at a stretch, wondering whether our marriage would survive, but confident that I had dealt guilt to Thanne's solar plexus and had caused the desperate question in her heart of, Was I being mugged?

Take that. *John 13:6–11*

July 16

Laughter

But then it happened that the Lord intervened, and one night there should have been a different ending to the battle.

(But consider the camel.)

On that particular night (my birthday, as I remember, and Thanne had strung that fact in large letters from wall to wall of the living room, dear woman) we had followed the usual script of our non-fights letterly, through solicitation, tears, pressure, tears, stompings, undeserved accusations and the basset hound look on my face, and tears—

Indeed, all went well, right up to jamming of my arms in my overcoat, the running downstairs, and the dramatic leap into the night. But then God piddled on the affair.

When I slammed the front door, I caught my coat in it.

Mad and madder, I rifled my pockets for the key, to unlock the damn door, to complete this most crucial tactic against Thanne's peace of mind. Take—

But there was no key. My tail was truly in the door, and the door was made of oak.

I had two alternatives. Either I could shed the coat and pace the night unhoused, unprotected. There was real drama in that, a tremendous statement of my heart's hurt—except that Thanne wouldn't know it, and the temperature was below freezing.

Or else I could ring the doorbell.

Ten minutes of blue shivering convinced me which was the more expedient measure. I rang the doorbell.

So then, my wife came down the stairs. So then, my wife peeped out. So then, my wife unlocked the door—and what was she doing? Laughing! Oh, she laughed so hard the tears streamed down her face and she had to put her hand on my shoulder, to hold her up.

And I could have smiled a little bit, too. I could have chuckled a tiny chuckle; for this was the gift of God, arranging armistice, staging reconciliation between a wife and her husband, a gift more sweet than all the rains of heaven. Laughter! extraordinary forgiveness!

But what did the dummy do? Well, he batted her hand away, cried "Hmph!" and bolted to stalk the night more grimly than before. *Then* he should have worried about the survival of his marriage, not by fights distressed, but by his stupid, blind, inordinate and all-consuming pride.

For he had denied the manipulations of the Deity.

Oh, learn from the dummy, ye husbands and wives, ye children and parents, ye politicians so often so unbending from your former policies. Learn, all ye who suffer fallings-out with one another and ye whose inclination is to lick your wounds in cold proud isolation. God doth constantly prepare the way for reconciliation, even by his gimmickry, if only pride don't blind you to the opportunity. *John 13:12–15*

July 17

God Will Love You Forever

Brandon Michael Piper.

That's a sober name for a 2-year-old. Senatorial. An executive's name. But you can bear the name, my godson. You've a stalwart constitution and a sweetness of spirit that softens me when I hold you. The name is not too big for you. Rather, you make the name foursquare and strong.

Dear Brandon: Perhaps you won't remember in the years to come (but I will remember) that I am the one who holds you these Sundays during Bible class. Your mother and your father both have duties, but I have two arms free and a large heart, and I am your godfather, and I love you.

You cling to me, child. Stump-arms soft on a pliable bone, you grip my neck. You lock your legs around my body. I couch your butt on my forearm and press you to my chest and feel the deep warmth of a trusting infancy. Oh, Brandon! You hallow me with such trust! You make me noble and kind.

They call you "B," don't they? "Baby B." I remember when I happened to draw that letter, and you read it. "Beee," you murmured with wonder, gazing at yourself. "Ef," you said when I made an F. And "Ay" and "Eeeee." The kid's a prodigy, reading at 2. This kid is my godson.

Brandon Michael, there will be much that you do not remember in later years, but never forget this: God loves you.

I was there, my godson, when they signed the love of God on you. I was there when they gave you that sober, senatorial name; and I will remind you of this forever: That they washed you thrice with a purging water, and I heard them say, "Brandon Michael Piper, I baptize you in the name of the Father, and of the Son, and of the Holy Spirit."

That's how I became your godfather. That's how the mighty God became your God. And that's how the name of Brandon Michael was written in the book of life. That, sir, was a healing to conquer all hurts and even death itself! Whatever occurs for you in the future, hold to that God. Pray as your parents prayed for you. Cling to the body of God more closely than you do to mine on Sunday. And God will love you infinitely, finer than I do now.

And I will continue, Brandon Michael Piper, a little longer to let you sleep on my shoulder in church. You will grow, of course. Even then I will continue to pray for you, my god-son, my Baby B. But God shall be your God forever.

Matthew 3:13–17

July 18
What Can I See?

This and the following two passages are from a chapter about attending a dying friend and experiencing angels.

"You shall see greater things than these," says Jesus. "Truly, truly, I say to you, you will see heaven opened, and the angels of God ascending and descending upon the Son of Man."

It's a marvelous prediction. It echoes Jacob's experience at Bethel. And since it places the Son of Man at the bottom, while we remember that the Presence of the Lord God was at the top of the ladder of messengers, it seems to be a characterizing promise—one solely directed to Jesus, identifying him and given to us for our instruction, but *not* one given to us as actual beneficiaries of the promise. It seems to say, "By this you will know," and not, "you will yourselves receive." Thus, it seems a closed-circuit sort of promise between the Father and the First-born, and we get to look on. That's all. The image of ascending and descending angels is so symbolic—so much a backward allusion—that I could apprehend no reality for it in my own experience and in my future. It could be a doctrine of mine. But how ever could it be for me a breathless expectation, with these two eyes to see it?

Why couldn't I expect, then, to "see" these angels, if not in my experience, then *behind* it? Ah, but how, how, with a promise so vague?

Genesis 28:10–18

July 19

Do You See Them Yet?

Does he promise the Holy Spirit? Well, and then he gives the Holy Spirit by the experiential event of a resurrection appearance, and a breathing upon disciples, and a clearly evidential *changing* of them. A spiritual occurrence, to be sure; but not one invisible to the eyes of flesh.

Does he promise peace unlike the giving of the world's peace? Well, and then in the same appearing he makes good his promise and delivers unto them his peace.

Likewise, joy.

Likewise, "I will come to you."

In John, promises find their fulfillment, are *not* forgotten. And in John that fulfillment is inclusive (not just between the Father and the Son, but also involving the disciples) as well as transfiguringly real (and not just spiritualized to a teachment).

So: then where did I come in? And how would *I* see the angels?

A friend of mine, an exegete named Robert Smith, helped me. He pointed to a possible remembrance of this first promise of Jesus, one that followed the same pattern of promise-keeping as I've touched above, because it came post-resurrection, was inclusive, and was fleshy sight on its way to spiritual insight. And when I looked at this keeping of the promise, I found not just the backward allusions to Jacob, but the configurations of experience which I myself knew and could know in the future; I saw the fleshy objects of seeing, common details, through which, by the grace of God, I might hereafter "see" angels!

Bob pointed to what Mary Magdalene saw, but could not yet see *through:*

"But Mary stood weeping outside the tomb, and as she wept she stooped to look into the tomb; and she saw two angels in white, sitting where the body of Jesus had lain, one at the head and one at the feet."   *John 1:47–51*

July 20

I Have Seen the Angels

No knowledge, yet, that these are angels. No, not until Jesus himself calls her by name and sight turns to insight, flesh *through* flesh to spiritual truth, and death to resurrection, desolation unto joy.

But listen: whereas I hardly know Jacob's experience, I do most certainly know the experience of Mary Magdalene! And though I've never slept with my head upon a stone, I *have,* dear God, stood in places of death and have myself been riven with sorrow, blinded by it, broken by the loss. These details I know by the bone. Now, don't you see, the promise takes on the flesh it must have ever before it reveals unto me its Truth, its spirit. Now it finds focus in *my* future, too. O Mary Magdalene, you are my sister; I know where to look!

Bob Smith, dear friend of mine, I have a good thing to tell you.

Though not at the head and the foot, but rather on the left side and the right, I have seen the angels. Seen them, and after that, "seen" them deeply, and I was blessed.

John 20:11–18

July 21

Jesus Loved Like a Woman!

From instructions for a Holy Week liturgy:

There is a dancer. She is female. She alone takes the chancel, in which no furniture is but the rail and the altar. Nor does she enter the rail and approach the altar until that moment when Jesus is crucified—and then her feet are rooted and motion appears in her upper body only. At death her head and body sag. At burial she crumples altogether. Before then she may use the passages of music—particularly when the congregation sings—for sweeping steps and speed. But she will also vary her presentation so that sometimes it closes in on mime; for example, during the words of the Last Supper, "This is my body," she will seem to draw from her very abdomen the invisible gift which then she proffers; and at the right moments she will turn her head through sad degrees to look at Judas, to gaze upon the Peter figure.

The congregation, as it busies itself in reading and singing, shall catch fleeting images of this dancer—and so shall she effect a metaphorical communication. Since they shall not see her whole and lineal, they will find themselves unconsciously filling in the blanks; and what they give to her by imagination shall be diverse among them and mighty indeed.

Please note that she does not play Christ. Rather, she represents, as best as possible, the moods, the changes he must have passed through. She represents both his suffering and his love. That is why she is female. For whatever is right or wrong about our society's perception, in love we understand the woman to be sacrificial, the man to be aggressive and a threat. In his passion, Jesus loved like a woman!

John 20:19–23

July 22

What Private Wars?

This and the following three selections are titled "To a Lady with Whom I've Been Intimate, Whose Name I Do Not Know."

You. I saw you in the Great Scot Supermarket tonight, and now I can't sleep on account of you—thinking that, perhaps, you're not sleeping either.

Ah, you! You count your coins with bitten nails, not once but again and again. This is the way you avoid the checker's eyes, as though ashamed of the goods you buy, as though they declare your loneliness at midnight:

Two six-packs of Tab, because your buttocks, sheathed in shorts, are enormous and hump up your back as you shift your weight from foot to foot. You sigh. I think that you do not know how deeply you sigh, nor yet that I am behind you in the line.

Four frozen dinners whose cartons assure you that there is an apple dessert inside. Swiss steak, roast beef in gravy, chicken drumsticks, shrimp. Which one will you save for Sunday dinner? Do you dress up for Sunday dinner? Do you set the table neatly when the dinner thaws? Or do you eat alone, frowning?

Liquid breakfasts, a carton of Marlboros, five Hershey bars, Tampax, vitamins with iron, a *People* magazine, Ayds to fight an appetite, two large bags of potato chips. At the very last minute you toss a Harlequin paperback on the counter. Is this what you read at Sunday dinner? Is this your company?

What private wars are waged between your kitchen and your bathroom? Here I see an arsenal for both sides: the *She* who would lose weight against the *She* who asks, "Why?" and "So what?"—the *She* whose desires are fed too much, even while they're hardly fed at all. "It's your own fault," the first accuses; "two tons were never tons of love." But the other cries, "If I were loved I would not need to eat."

Ah, you.   *Lamentations 1:1–4*

July 23

How Are You?

Rubber thongs on your feet. The polish on your toenails has grown a quarter inch above the cuticle. I notice this because when the checker rings your bill, you drop a quarter which rolls behind me in the line. I stoop to pick it up. When I rise, your hand is already out and you are saying, "Thanks," even before I have returned it to you.

But I do a foolish thing, suddenly, for which I now ask your forgiveness. I didn't know how dreadfully it would complicate your night.

I hold the quarter an instant in my hand; I look you in the eyes—gray eyes of an honest, charcoal emotion—and I say, "Hello." And then I say, "How are you?" I truly meant that question. I'm sorry.

Shock hits your face. For one second you search my eyes; your cheeks slacken, then, as though they lost their restraint and might cry. That frightens me: what will I do if you cry? But then your lips curl inward; your nostrils flare; the gray eyes flash; and all at once you are very, very angry.

Like a snake your left hand strikes my wrist and holds it, while the right scrapes the quarter from my hand. I am astonished, both by your strength and by your passion.

You hissed when you hurt me. I heard it and remember it still. Then you paid, crunched the sacks against your breast, and walked out into the night, the thongs sadly slapping at your heels.

Ah, you. You.   *Lamentations 1:5–8*

July 24

The Only Gulf that Matters

How much I must have hurt you by my question. Was that mild commonplace too much a probe, too lethal, too threatening for the delicate balance your life has created for itself? Does kindness terrify you because then, perhaps, you would have to do more than dream, more than imagine the Harlequin, but then would have to *be?*

I think so.

To cross the gulf from Life Alone to Life Beloved—truly to be real, truly to be worthy in the eyes of another—means that you are no more your own possession. You give yourself away, and then games all come to an end. No longer can you pretend excuses or accusations against the world; nor can you imagine lies concerning your beauty, your gifts and possibilities. Everything becomes what it really is, for you are *seen* and you know it. "How are you?" triggers "Who are you?" And it wasn't so much that I said it, but rather that I *meant* it and that I awaited an answer, too—this caused the lonely *She* to know her loneliness, even in the moment when I offered you the other thing: friendship.

It's frightening, isn't it?

To be loved, dear lady, you must let all illusions die. And since, between the bathroom and the kitchen, between *People* magazine and the Harlequin, your Self was mostly illusion—at least the acceptable self—then to be loved meant that your very Self had to die—at least the acceptable self.

Instead, you attacked, and my wrist is still bruised tonight. Ah, you.   *Lamentations 1:11–17*

July 25

Crossing the Gulf

A rich young ruler came to Jesus, desiring eternal life. He announced that he had kept all the commandments and wondered whether that weren't enough. But Jesus told him he lacked one thing. He ought, said Jesus, to sell all that he had and give the money to the poor. Upon these words, two were made sorrowful: the rich, because he could not lose his riches, which were his identity and his Self; he turned away. And Jesus, because he loved and would not love this man; but the man turned away.

Riches. O my dear and lonely lady, how rich are you in your illusions. Ironically, you cling to the very loneliness which you despise. It feels safe. But love—God's love—always comes in light. That's what scares you. Light illumines truth: obesity, the foolish game between Ayds and potato chips, between cigarettes and vitamins. These things are the truth. These you hide. Yet it is only truth that Jesus can love. He cannot love your imaginings, your riches. Sell all that you have. Undress—

Not me, after all. It is Jesus who asks, "How are you?" And if you would then sell the false self by which you sustain the contemptible Self and die; if you would answer truly, "I'm fat, helpless and alone, unlovely," then he would love you. No: then you would *know* that he has loved you all along. To see one truth is to discover the other—which is that he loves you not because you are lovable, but because he is love. And here is the power of his love, that it makes ugliness beautiful! To be loved of God is to be lovely indeed.

All night long I keep a quarter back and ask, "How are you?" I can't sleep, waiting for the truth: "I'm just terrible." For then I would cry, "Good! Now there's a confession I can love!"

And the mighty God, the trumpet-voiced, cries, "I love a child. But she is afraid of me. Then how can I come to her, to feed and to heal her by my love?—" *Lamentations 1:20–22*

July 26

Creepin'

This selection and the next tell how Gloria and Mary deal with fear.

One evening in a city of the South, Gloria Ferguson was rushing to church: "Creepin'," she said, "in the turrible dark in the strangest o' places."

Our choir had reached its southern-most stop on a very long tour; neither the city nor the church were familiar to her; she was late. She was alone on impoverished streets.

Twilight: The telephone poles and the sagging wires were black against a deep green sky.

Suddenly there sprang from an alley a tense and skinny man. Gloria uttered a tiny shriek but kept on "creepin'," she said, "fast as my pistons could go." The man was old "an' so black," she said, "he was blue." He fell in step beside her, rolling his eyes, waving huge hands and roaring warnings.

Now, Gloria is a mother and a grandmother, for years her family's sole support, a citizen of inner cities. By nature and necessity she's an independent woman; I should not have worried.

But Mary Moore, her cousin, noticed the absence just before the program began. Did I know where Gloria was?

No, I didn't.

Could we go looking?

Too late! This particular parish was black and Baptist. The preacher had said, "Our choir will sing first. Render an A and a B selection. Warm the folks up, y'know. Then you can take 'em hot."

Well, though we were black, we were also Lutheran—we didn't usually take things "hot." But all at once the Baptists burst into song, and it was too late to look for Gloria.

Two songs—A and B, with refrains that grew louder and louder, with clappings increasing, with swayings and sweatings and solos emotional—stretched to 20 minutes.

Three women "fell out." Slain in the Spirit. That is, they fainted dead away, to be fanned by their sisters in pure white dresses. One of our own went whooping and stomping. The Baptists, in other words, were beating the Lutherans; but the triumph was lost on me.

I kept searching the back of the room for my sister.

She has a pouty mouth, small and bitten by long labor, a skein of gray in her pure-black hair, eyes smoky with human sympathy, a complexion darker than bark of the walnut, a spirit sweet and true. I have loved Gloria since the day she told me of her decision to raise her children without a husband—and without the satisfactions of the flesh. I was her pastor then. I am her friend forever.

And I worried. Night descended outside. The program inside lengthened to three hours because one of our members now was singing countless verses of a spiritual, "gettin' down," as it were, and causing a glad commotion among the Baptists, who felt they'd made a convert.

There was much joy that night, truly. Two peoples, two races, two strong denominations fusing. I saw a large lady fly straight up from her high-heeled shoes, leaving them neatly side by side and undisturbed. Music and laughter joined, and God was not just praised. God was PRAISED! ALLELUIA! AMEN!

Isaiah 26:12–15

July 27

Creepin' Home

But Gloria was missing.

Only later did I find her sitting in the basement, her eyes as wide as boiled eggs. I thought it was some lingering fright. But then she began to tell the story, lowly, slowly, grim: A man so black, she said, he was blue came warning an Indiana woman about lizards exceedingly great. A crazy man. Beware! Beware!

Gloria never cracked a smile, her mouth as solemn as the ancient that had accosted her. But Mary Moore began to giggle and then to laugh and then to howl till the tears streamed down her cheeks.

For this is how these women survive! They transfigure the difficult things, shocks, disasters, the labors of living, into art. Into story and humor. Into a music fully equal to any human experience.

Thus the spirituals, and the gospel music, and the stomping and clapping—and songs as soft as baby's breath.

And thus this poem, which Mary Moore composed in laughter and gratitude for her cousin come safely home again:

Got lizzuts ya no,
Bout dat big.
Runnin o'va dere . . .
N'eath dat twig.
 Why you tellin me
Bout lizzuts sir?
So's ya'll won't be sceered
Wen dey stir.

 Cat's gonna eat em,
Dem lizzuts, ret up—
Jest to de nec doe,
Wit one big gup.

 Dey no's deys head will
Make dem sick;
Oh, lizzuts no!
Dem midy slic.
 How you no bout
Lizzuts so?
Bo'n ret yere.
I no. I no.

 Ya'll go walkin,
Heer som scratchin,
Dat's dem lizzuts,
A pullin an'a snatchin.

 Got rats n' ro'ches
Weer ya'll liv?
Got som here . . . dat big
But TNT I sho nuff giv.
 Why you talkin bout
All dis stuff?
Go on home now,
Dat e'nuff.

Member now what
I sa' is ret.
Dem lizzuts sho is no'sy,
Spch'ly in de nite.

Isaiah 40:9–11

July 28

Wholly Human, Even in the Public Eye

The author waits at an airport departure gate.

Two young women were rooting through the enormous purse of a third, an older, bonier woman obviously nervous, obviously the traveler of the three.

"Where you *got* them Tums?" cried one of the younger women, her face and her full right arm deep inside the purse. "You know you need—*Whoop!*" she shouted. "Looka here!"

Laughing, laughing till tears streamed from her eyes, she drew forth and held up for inspection five magazines, a sandwich wrapped in waxed paper, earplugs, canned juice, an umbrella—and a new package of underwear titled *Three Briefs*.

"Mamma!" she cried. "Oh, Mamma! What you want with these?" The older woman looked baffled. The younger one laughed with a flashing, outrageous affection. "You got plans you ain' tol' us about?" Maybe she and the other were daughters, or nieces, of their more solemn elder.

"Honey, it's the Tums'll do you the most good. Where you got—Oh, Mamma, Mamma, look."

This young woman had a magnificent expanse of hip and the freedom of spirit to cover it in a bright red skirt, tight at the waist, wide behind, and tight at the knee again. She stood on spiky heels. Fashion forced her to walk by short, precarious steps—oddly opposite her amplitude of hip and cheek and laughter.

"Oh, Mamma." Suddenly suffused with gentleness, she pulled from the purse a worn leather-bound New Testament and Psalms. "Mamma, what? What you think?" The two women exchanged a silent gazing, each full of the knowledge of the other. Generations did not divide them.

"Well," said the older, bony woman, "you found the nourishment. But you ain't found the Tums." With a bark, Young Woman in Red dived into the depths of the purse again—tottering on her tiny heels.

Now down the concourse came an old man, so gaunt in his cheek as to be toothless, bald and blotched on his skull, meatless arm and thigh. He sat in a wheelchair, listing to the right. The chair was driven swiftly by an attendant oblivious of this wispy, thin and ancient passenger.

The old man's eyes were milky, mildly worried by the speed; but the old man's mouth, sucked inward, was mute. His nose gave him the appearance of a hawk caught in a wire trap, helpless and resigned.

Now the attendant turned into our gate area, jerked the chair to a stop (bouncing the skeletal soul therein), and reached down to set the brake. He left. But the brake was not altogether set, nor had the chair altogether stopped. It was creeping by degrees toward the generous red hips of the woman whose face was buried in the generous purse of her elder, laughing.

The old man's eyes—the closer he rolled to this rear as wide as Texas—widened. He opened his mouth. He began to raise a claw. He croaked. And then he ran straight into the back of her knees.

"*Yow!*" Up flew the great purse, vomiting contents. Backward stumbled the young woman, a great disaster descending upon a crushable old man.

At the last instant, she whirled around and caught herself upon the armrests of the wheelchair, a hand to each rest. Her face was frozen one inch from the face of an astonished octogenarian. And so they stared at one another, so suddenly and intimately close that they must have felt heat and found the odor of the other.

Then the woman beamed. "Oh, honey!" she cried. "You somethin' handsome, ain't you?" She leaned forward and kissed him a noisy smack in the center of his bald head. "I didn't hurt you, did I?"

Strangers, no strangers at all: suddenly something more.

Slowly there spread over the features of this ghostly old man the most beatific smile. Oh, glory and heat and blood and love in a body dried to tinder.

And the young woman burst into thunderous laughter. "Look at you!" she cried. "What yo wife gon' say when she see my lipstick kiss on yo head? Ha ha ha!" He reached to touch the red, and she cried, "You gon' have some explainin' to do!"

That old man closed his eyes in soundless laughter with the woman: The two made one for a fleeting moment.

So also laughed the elderly woman, who still had not found her Tums. So did I, surprising myself. So did a host of travelers I had not known were watching the episode with me. We all laughed, gratefully. *We*, in the brief event and the silly joke of wives and kisses, were unified.

It wasn't the joke, of course. It was the good will. It was spontaneous affection. It was the willingness of a single woman, wholly human even in the public eye—in risk and under judgment—suddenly, swiftly to love another, to honor him, to give him something graceful without hesitation or fear, something free and sweet and durable.

But she gave it to us all. I won't forget her. I beg God, in such revealing moments, that I might be as generous and good as she. There was a sanctity in the kiss of that woman.

And in this: that the man was as white as the snows of Sweden, and the woman as black as the balmy nights of Africa.

Isaiah 43:1–7

July 29

Common Kindness

I miss you, Arthur Bias. Old man, enormous man, deep-voiced, large-jowled, slow-striding black man: You were a police officer in your day. That was—oh, my!—back in the '40s, the '50s and '60s. I came to know you when you had retired. But you hadn't retired the stories. You told them while we fished, your eyes gone thin in remembering, squinting above a Kentucky lake, talking and talking in tones that knew no guile or anger.

You bottom-fished. Therefore, we both bottom-fished. Took less energy letting a line hang down from its bobber, a grub on the point of the hook. Or an angle worm. Or a cricket. Caught catfish on bacon. Bullhead on cheese. Carp on anything.

Tossed the line. Sat down in a lawn chair. Lit a pipe. Slit the eye. Stayed silent a good long while. Let the droning flies soften our brains to drowsiness. Sighed at the goodness of an uncomplicated world. Thanked God for lazy afternoons.

You would doze, Arthur, making moist buzzings in your nose. Then you'd wake to the tug of a fish, twitch your brows, reel it in and start a story. Old man, I miss the benediction of your presence, your life constructed of common things. You desired no more than that. You were *more* than contented. You were *kind*.

Maybe you were, in your ordinariness, extraordinary—a cop who caused harmony! A friend who, in fishing, hooked God at the heart. A man of strength and love together. A man of law, but not of condemnation. Law doesn't require condemnation, does it? But grace requires kindness.

And grace is this, that an old black man took a young white pastor to his bosom, and told him stories and redeemed the time with kindness. I yearn for the kindness of common people. It seems so uncommon a quality lately.   *Isaiah 51:4–8*

July 30

Contemplating the Death Penalty, Post-Resurrection

Old Israel had almost no notion of heaven or hell or Judgment Day. If awful punishment was to be exacted, it had to occur right then, before the faces of the people, and by the people of God.

But through Judah's history, the critical concept of "the day of the Lord" evolved. First it had promised a time at the end of time when all existence would come under the rule of a Messiah. Finally, there grew up the teaching of a resurrection of the dead. In the "day of the Lord" (now Jesus speaks) the Son of Man would judge the world, imposing sentences precise and horrible—the eternal abandonment of God. Lo: *God himself shall act as judge and executioner* before all people.

That changes things. Judgment Day cancels our need to act in God's stead. If we still desire to impose ultimate penalties, are *we* then sitting in the judgment seat of the Almighty? I begin to think so.

"No!" say some. "We sentence only the body; God sees to the soul." But that argument divorces God from our judicial action. If you accept it, you've no right to appeal to the Old Testament code, whose purpose was to restore *God's* order!

Surely, the murderer must be removed physically from society—as he has removed himself spiritually—and so the social order is restored. Imprison him.

But since the Messiah has come, the restoration of God's order has not been by the imposition of law (life for life) but by the exposition of grace: forgiveness! This, too, is a divine change: the criminal, even in his prison cell, should hear the gospel—until, perchance, he confess and *be* changed and, in the mercy of God, be made God's own again. The abiding purpose of the Old Law is accomplished, but in the new covenant of the Christ: God is acknowledged as God again. God is *revealed* as God. Or so goes my struggling thought in these latter days. *Revelation 6:9–17*

July 31

I Am Growing Rich

Last night Matthew finished a term paper for English. A good paper. It took him a month of conscientious labor. *He* did it, and then before sleep he thanked me.

After catastrophe, even so minor a thing as a term paper indicates major survival: The boy's becoming an adult. Listen: A parent has the right to weep and to thank God. There are no small things in parenting. None. The tiniest change in a child is treasure pressed down, shaken together and running over.

And I am growing rich.

For my daughter Mary—whom I've offtimes caused to cry when discipline demolished the world around her—so easily puts her arms around me now and hugs me, *hugs* me, with uninhibited love. Quick to cry, so quick to give is Mary. And last night, formally, she brought a boyfriend home that I should meet him. Both Mary and the boy blazed with embarrassment, and my heart soared up to heaven that they would do the difficult thing for my sake. So today I'm sitting next to God, my own Supernal Parent, and grinning.

And Talitha has been plain nasty in the past. "I don't appreciate," she's yelled at me, "your piggy eyes and your red face when you come in my room and yell at me." She has cut me cold at high school when my parental appearing seemed to jeopardize her reputation, and we walked home together—a block apart.

But sweet Talitha just bought an outfit which is both subdued and stunning. She is utterly beautiful! And she cared for my opinion. I gasped to see her in this dress, and my gasp was exactly the approval she needed to prove her beautiful. In me she found her beauty reflected. "Thanks, Dad," she whispered—and straightway I carried her thanks to God. No, nothing in parenting is too small for jubilation, for killing the fatted calf and making merry.

For Joseph once considered me a fool. He asked my help exactly when my help was most contemptible to him—so he was setting me up for a fall. Halfway through my help, he'd turn on his heel and stalk away. He was exalting himself by debasing me.

But yesterday I picked him up from college. On the way home he (casually) revealed that he'd been reading my writings; and (casually) the young man offered steady, accurate insight into my novels. Equals! Adult to adult! That casual conversation nearly killed me, for who can praise me with profounder effect than my own son? *I have arrived! I have survived.*

Is it a small thing that today our children all are home, and healthy, and whole, each (by tiny signals) blossoming to normal adulthood? Of course it is. It's as common as sunrise or the spring. But no it isn't! It's as glorious as resurrection.

I am utterly fulfilled. I'm tasting a toast with my own most Holy Parent, whose love I understand now better than I did ten years ago. *Psalm 100:1–5*

August

Waiting for Judgment

Slowly, my father arose behind his desk. I didn't look at him. Just as slowly, he rounded the far side and came toward me—black suit, black hair, black spectacles. Judgment cometh. The multitudes are gone. There are two of us after all. Only two.

I was prepared for the spanking. The order of things would be righted in my punishment. I lowered my head.

But I was altogether unprepared for what my father did. I think I would not have cried if my father had spanked me. But he knelt down at my side, and he took me in his arms, and he hugged me, and then I began to cry, and I couldn't stop crying.

Love killed me. I hadn't expected love. I hadn't expected the most undeserved thing, to be forgiven. That fire of my father's love—it melted me altogether, reduced me to a little mess, to a child again, for sure.

Oh, how pitifully I loved my father then! How God-like his love for me.   *Isaiah 43:1–7*

Doncha Love It?

Shortly after my father's retirement from the ministry, the whole Wangerin family gathered in the Colorado Rockies for a reunion. Talitha was four. This was the trip when she drove her brothers crazy by her happiness, loving everything under the sun.

On Sunday the family worshiped outside, under a scrubbed sky, a light wind whistling the pine boughs. Dad climbed a crag in order to see and be seen—in order to preach. I imagine that he had bowed his head a long, long time, searching the words to give us. Precious words. I remember them exactly.

The man on his mountain, as oracular as the prophets, lifted his voice and called loudly: "I have thought of the best legacy that I could leave my family."

There was, of course, no money. Dad had spent his energies as a parish pastor, a college president, an editor of Christian educational materials, a foreign missionary. Who pays dearly for such dear labors? Mom probably made more money than he. Well, and there was little property: a house in Colorado, books, an excellent desk; I already had his Underwood typewriter. What sort of legacy, then?

The wind blew his hair into a morning halo, a sunlit cloud around the old man's skull.

"This I know," my father shouted, "and this I beg you to receive. Please! I can bequeath you with nothing richer or nobler than the Lord Jesus Christ and faith in him."

Little Talitha leaped to her feet, threw open her arms, and yelled as loud as her grandpa: "Doncha *love* it?"

Her grandpa loved it. He grinned then and hitched his jeans and finished his sermon with joy.   *Philippians 1:27–30*

August 3

Whose Laws?

We act as though God *needs* our support. The instant we answer Temptation with words *of our own* to strengthen the Word of God ("We may eat of the fruit of the trees") we have elevated ourselves to a level of some equality with God. And although this is not yet in itself a sin, it is dangerous.

Even as it increases our importance in this Primal Relationship, it focuses our attention a little less on God, a little more on our Self.

—*Self-pity:* And the more important we are, the more confining seem the rules imposed upon us. The equaler *we* are to God, the more equal we wish our circumstances to be.

And the evidence of this new discomfort within God's restrictions is that we exaggerate them. We ourselves (like the Temptor) lie a little about the laws, as though they chafed a little much. We say (piously), "We may eat of the fruit of the trees of the garden. But God said, 'You shall not eat of the fruit of the tree which is in the midst of the garden, neither shall you touch it, lest you die.'" Whoops! That new phrase is not God's, but purely our own, *Neither shall you touch it.* This is the whine of the child who says unto her father, "You never let me have anything." Never? Well, not never. It just feels like never because self-pity is increasing. *Isaiah 44:24–26*

August 4
Evidence of the Hard-Hearted

I have evidence of a meanness of soul: I feel sudden spurts of fury for small infractions of the law. (But I love the law!) Drivers too late for the green light, who race the amber and miss that too, who clip first seconds from the red that should have stopped them—they infuriate me. Shoppers who munch on peanuts they didn't pay for; litterers of every kind; children who giggle untended in church; pastors too loose with the doctrine—all of these anger me.

But for every anger I feel justified. I *delight* in the law to that extent. And to this, that it should crack the skulls of those who break it. I've calculated exactly what I deserve, and I will call to account those servants who don't deliver it.

Grocery clerks, I watch your beeping computer registers with a computer of my own. Ring one item twice, and I will not shout at you, but with cold articulation I will spotlight your stupidity. I leave a trail of the terrified behind me, but I haven't touched one of them, have killed by contrast rather.

My rightness is the death of them: garrulous dentists, ungrammatical teachers, weather reporters who speak of weather "on tap" as if it were a beer, cops whose English condemns them, postal employees who cannot find a house—doorknobs all!

Yet I have evidence of a hard heart.

I am lonely.

I *say,* "None can match me!"

I *say,* "What good to me is a self-indulgent community, malingerers, sinners, impious and rude?"

I *say,* "I'm solitary by choice.

But I *feel* lonely. *Matthew 13:12–15*

August 5

Purpose

Any job that anyone performs is justified by an ultimate goal. This final purpose encourages the worker while he works; more significantly, it also shapes his behavior and his attitudes on the job. Long before the goal is accomplished, it is there in anticipation. It dwells in his mind, and so he plans; it dwells in his heart, and so it guides his actions. If a carpenter crafts a chair for a rich stranger, he may do it well; but if he crafts it for his daughter, he will do it lovingly. Much, much is different between the first and the second crafting; and much is different between the two chairs, too, though only he and his daughter may see the difference. *Deuteronomy 32:1–4*

August 6

Evidence

The future is always cloaked in the darkness of our ignorance; we move into it by calculated guesswork and by faith; but the less we can guess by present evidence, and the less we can believe in those who move with us, the more fearful we are to move at all. In a sort of terror we may be paralyzed, unmoving—till we sit in a stony conservatism and wait for the future to come and get us. That is, we cease to risk, cease to make the significant decisions, cease in great measure to live.

And the world at large defrauds us, promising promises it never intends to keep. Advertising uses, but does not love, us. Friends disappoint. Governments propagandize for their own purposes. Economies rise and fall in mystery. Superiors walk on the heads and hearts of their inferiors as on rocks in a stream. This is a sad, familiar litany, but its very familiarity witnesses to the instability of the present, the treachery of the future. There must be something upon which we can depend in order to plan, to act, and to live.

You, loving husband; you, faithful wife: you may be the light which illuminates the future and frees your spouse confidently to enter it. But only insofar as you are dependable. Otherwise you *are* that world to him or her.

Psalm 33:13–22

August 7

A Crisis

In the days when Potter was a boy and sick, the doctors did not have penicillins for healing, no shots to shoot the fever down. Therefore, children had to fight fevers with the strength of their own small bodies, and often no one knew who'd be the stronger, the boy or the fever. If the boy, then the fever went away. But if the fever, then they both departed to the everlasting cold, "zero at the bone."

A boy could die.

And there was a name for the worst period of the disease. When the boy and the fever fought each other the hardest— when they wrestled desperately to death or to health again— that was called the "crisis." Parents agonized during the "crisis." They couldn't sleep. They sat by their child, praying, wiping his forehead in cool cloths, wishing that they could fight the fiery enemy for him and sad that they could not. Parents paced in their kitchens under yellow light bulbs, deep at night. They drank coffee. Sometimes they just stared at one another, as though someone might say something magical and their child would come downstairs yawning and asking for a drink of water. But no. They wouldn't say anything at all. There was nothing magical to say. What they did during the "crisis" was, they waited.   *Isaiah 38:10–16*

August 8

You're Killing Me!

This selection and the next form one essay on hatred.

There was a woman who had two sons and no husband. It was her joy, her labor and all her pain to raise them on her own. They were bright, likely lads of brown eyes and black, and she loved them equally with a yearning love.

Before she left for work, she stroked their cheeks and gazed into their eyes. When she returned, she cooked.

She watched in misty gratitude as her children enjoyed her cooking; she stole glances at them when they slept—her light-boned Brown, her Black so bold—and she wept.

Thus daily did she love them, but with a breaking heart and pain.

For they fought.

From the time they learned to talk, her sons made weapons of their words, knives of their tongues and fire both amber and jet of their eyes. They hated each other. They said so, loud and heartily.

But she mothered the both of them; she was the oneness and the blood between them. She loved them and as they together were her heart, their hatreds tore her heart in two.

"I'll *teach* them," she thought. "They have the gift of speech; surely they have the gift of hearing too. Surely a word of mine might change them."

In the evening, then, she spoke a wisdom to her sons.

"Blood shouldn't quarrel, nor families fight," she said. "It's as simple as that. Let the children love as their mother loves; and if the example alone is not enough, then use my love itself to give away. Oh, my children, I have twice too much for each of you, and if you share it I'll have double that again. I'll swell with loving to see you love, and all will be nourished and no one endangered, none."

She took their faces between her hands and wept upon them, and behold, they wept as well with eyes both brown and black, because they loved their mother after all—deeply, deeply.

But they didn't love each other. And they didn't stop fighting.

They grew stout lads. They grew sinewed youths, with muscles like traps and fists that didn't hesitate.

Now their fighting caused cuts in their lips, splits on their knuckles and broken noses—all of which wrung the blood from their mother's heart.

It hurt to see their wounded faces, for she loved them. It hurt to see their faces enraged, for she loved them. It hurt to see them divided, for they were together her fullness and all her heart.

So she thought, "I'll *show* them how much it hurts me, and then they'll stop. If not my words, my actions will change them surely."

So that is what she did. At dinner some minor insult between the lads turned looks to words, and words to deeds: a great grabbing of noses, ears and hair with punchings and bashings too.

Their mother didn't speak. She seized with two hands the hem of the tablecloth, all covered with the dinner she'd prepared; and uttering a loud cry, she yanked the linen backward.

Food and dishes swept crashing to the floor, and the eyes of her sons were astonished: glasses, milk and silverware, and heart's blood.

"You're killing me!" she screamed, her hands turned up in pleading. "The hate and the hurting are murder inside me. Stop it, my Brown, my Black. Oh, stop it, please. Because I can't stop loving you—and love in me, so long as you hate, is an acid, a fire."

Then the lads wept on her and for her. But each devised a method for turning guilt to blame, and they kept on fighting, justified.   *Genesis 25:19–28*

August 9

Mortal Hatred

It is useless to number the reasons for their fighting. There are always reasons (though reasons are more the pardoners of passions than their causes, and can therefore change with the weather).

There are always reasons on reserve, all of them unimpeachable, most of them asinine. Forget them. Hate's hate, however it is justified.

Know this alone: that as the lads grew into men, they found more manly ways to prosecute their injuries and means more modern, more efficient.

They bought guns.

"Oh God!" their mother prayed, "What can I do to change them soon, to save them for me and from themselves?"

For here was a wonder: She loved them still, and her love was so rooted in her nature that she could not lose one and live. Yet she was losing both to their hatreds.

Thus she prayed. And in the end she found a way, a terrible way. She would herself *take* their hate, and hope to take it away.

And so it happened. Late on a Friday, late in a Lenten gloom, late, late in the life of a mother, when one son Brown spun round with his gun, discharging more than a word—a bullet—at one son Black, the mother of both was found between them.

Mortal hatred cut her crosswise through the chest, and she fell.

"Mama! Mama!" they shrieked. "Mama! Are you all right?"

"No," she murmured. "Not all right."

They bellowed, "I didn't mean to hurt you."

"Yes, you did," she whispered. "You meant to drop whoever was in your way. It was me, son. Till now you did not know, but it was always, always me."

And she died.

Sons Brown and Black—what burning tears they wept at this final effort of their mother to preserve them good and whole and holy.

They raised the faces she once had stroked, and they wailed like babies again, unable to think of tomorrow, unable to think, unable—

Which things, my blood, my family, are a parable. Before the Sunday of the Resurrection there is a Friday. There always was the Friday. On Friday I am your brother Brown. And you—?   *Genesis 33:1–11*

August 10

Can You Do It, Wodenstag?

This and the next four selections, through August 14, are Chapter 40 in The Book of Sorrows, *the story of the mice who do more than their duty to comfort the Lady Pertelote, the Hen.*

So it was first of all Wodenstag Mouse who crept out of the hole and across the snow like a thief. Next, Donnerstag Mouse. Then one after the other, Sonntag, Montag, Dienstag, Freitag, and last of all the youngest of all, Samstag.

Not that Pertelote recognized each tiny face. It was midnight. They looked like nothing so much as purposeful hairballs. But she'd known Wodenstag by his manner and had counted the rest. Besides, the thieves were gathering at the root of her Hemlock, and as their number grew, so did the noises of one telling another to shut up.

Mice and a midnight raid.

Pertelote had nearly tucked her head beneath her wing again when a change in the noises drew her attention and a curious activity held it. No, it was a very daring activity—for Mice. While six stood semicircle, staring straight up with their noses, their mouths hanging open, the seventh Mouse had begun to climb a tree. He had all four legs extended as wide as they would go, like a daddy-longlegs on the wall;

each paw had its little nip of bark; and he was trembling so furiously he looked like a plucked rubber band. But his expression was earnest. And somewhere inside of him was the conviction that he could climb a tree, and somewhere, too, the notion that he *should* climb a tree.

Pertelote forgot, for the moment, the torments of the day in watching this tiny test of fortitude: *Well, can you do it, Wodenstag?* Psalm 23:1–6

August 11

Thinking of Her

The Brothers whispered upward, "Are you going to fall? Should we get out of the way?"

But grand efforts are always performed in solitude. Wodenstag answered them nothing. What he did, stuck to the trunk of a tree: he trembled. His chin drummed the bark like a woodpecker—and lo! His eye lit up. It must have been the chin-drumming that imparted him a flash of insight, because he suddenly called, "Bite the bark!" And Pertelote felt a little cheer in her throat. "*Bite* the bark. There's the ticket!" Wodenstag bit the bark. So then he could let go successive paws to move them higher up—and what is that if it is not climbing? Why, it's climbing of the finest sort! Pertelote wasn't tired. She was enjoying a miniature triumph. *Bite* the bark! What a breakthrough.

So then up the tree trunk, one by one, with instructions from Wodenstag on a branch above, and encouragement from Brothers on the snow below, a constant buzzing of grunts and information, Mice climbed the tree. A string of thieves up a tree. And how they patted Samstag, and how they praised that youngest Brother when he had gained the branch with them. How they congratulated one another all around—and then!

Then they turned in unison to look down the branch itself, and the Hen at the end of it. So that stilled their jubilations.

"She's probably sleeping," they said in dreadful quiet.

"So much the better," said Wodenstag. "She needs to sleep."

Pertelote experienced a true softening in her breast, and her head inclined for gladness. Why, the Tags were thinking of her!   *Ezekiel 34:11–16*

August 12

Why Does a Mouse Roost in a Tree?

So Wodenstag came balancing along the branch, picking his inches with monumental care. And after him, frowning severely, Donnerstag. And Sonntag, and so forth, all staring at the wood in front of them as if the staring itself were gripping. And then this is what they did: they lined up next to Pertelote, side by side, sitting on two legs (aye, *there* was the peril: two legs) and facing south the same as she. And then they were done. This was it. This is what they came for. As solemnly as worship they sat still.

Rather, they tried to sit still. In fact, they had all begun independently of one another to rock. Forward and backward, in an effort to keep their balances, like round-bottom peppershakers. Too far forward ("Whoa!"), too far backward ("Whoa! Whoa!"), but all done with the greatest solemnity and an air that it was right to be here; no other place to be, amen.

Pertelote the Hen for whom they had come, she could only shake her head. There was a pressure in her heart that might have been laughter or might have been tears, either one.

"Tags," said Pertelote.

"Ah, Lady. Ah, Lady, we didn't mean to wake you up," whispered Wodenstag as though she were still sleeping. He began to pat her side.

"But here you are," she said.

"Yes," he said, simply because it was the fact. "All of us."

"What a remarkable thing for you to do."

"It isn't easy to climb a tree," said Wodenstag.

"Whoa!" said Montag. And Sonntag said, "Whoa!" spinning his forepaws like whirligigs.

"But it's night," said Pertelote.

"Yes," said Wodenstag, patting her, patting her. "And a very dark night, too, I think."

"Aren't you going back to sleep?"

"Whoa!" said Dienstag. "Whoa!"

"Maybe we could sleep right here," said Wodenstag. "We thought that this would be a very good spot for a sleep."

"Whoa! *Whoa!*" It was Freitag who tipped too far backward, too far altogether. Up shot his hind legs, and down went the whole mouse, plump into a snowbank.

Pertelote seemed the only one to notice his departure. "I don't suppose," she said, "that it's easy for a Mouse to sit this way?"

"Roosting," Wodenstag explained.   *Jeremiah 23:1–4*

August 13

To Keep the Dear Lady Company

Samstag went over head first—"*Whoa!*"—and plopped into snow.

"We talked it over," said Wodenstag. "We agreed that this would be an excellent way to sleep sometimes."

Donnerstag dropped.

Freitag had begun to climb the tree trunk again, whispering, "Bite the bark."

"Whoa! Whoa!" said Montag and Sonntag together. They had locked arms.

Wodenstag himself still patted Pertelote. Sometimes he clung to one little feather; but then he patted her again.

"Why, Wodenstag?" said Pertelote. "Could you tell me why you decided all these things?"

Samstag was on his way up the trunk again, and Freitag on his way out the branch.

"Yes," said Wodenstag.

"Whoa!" roared Montag and Sonntag together. Together they hit the snow.

Wodenstag kept his earnest composure. "To keep the dear Lady company," he said. "She's got no easy day of it, and at night she's lonely—don't we know that? So we said—Whoa!"

Wodenstag's turn. He flew out to emptiness. But he caught a feather and so was left dangling from her breast. "So," said Wodenstag, gazing down at the ground, "we said, 'Let's keep her company.' We have us. But she has no one special just now. We thought that we would give her a little bit of us, and since she can't fit in the hole, we came to roost—"

Pertelote sobbed. It was *both* tears and laughter in her heart: she sobbed through an absolutely dazzling grin. And the sob felt good, but did no good for Wodenstag, who lost his grip and punctured the snow beside his brothers.

John 10:1–5

August 14

She Was Not Alone

"The carefullest, kindest friends I know," sighed Pertelote, "so special to me indeed." She spread her wings and sank to the snow herself. Instantly all the ascending Mice became descending Mice, and Pertelote purely laughed.

"Don't you think," she said, "that you could sleep on the ground tonight, if I sat with you?"

"Oh, Lady!" cried Wodenstag. "What a fine idea!"

"Well, and what if you nestled beneath my wings? What about that?"

Little Samstag couldn't stand it. He began to laugh at the top of his lungs because his gladness was so great.

And Freitag said, "Just like the old days!"

And Pertelote whispered the nearly unspeakable profundity of Freitag's words. "Just like the old days," she sighed.

Then under her wings seven separate paws took to patting the down of her heart and her love, and she was not alone. Wodenstag popped his head out with an afterthought: "Don't feel bad you sobbed and I fell," he told her. "It's okay if you cry."

It was okay. She did cry. Pertelote bowed her head that night and wept the blessed tears of consolation.   *John 10:7–11*

August 15

The Proud Pray–er

I want to arise in your Spirit, with your Spirit. Please! I want to come home, dear Jesus. I want to be home with you. There is no other Lord but you.

Take me beneath your breast as a hen protects her chicks: thou art Lord! Blessed is he who comes in the name of the Lord. Blessed is she, my wife, in whom the Lord does dwell. Blessed are all the laborers whom I called fools, who neither heard nor concerned themselves with what I called them. They were free. They knew nothing of me. Blessed are these sheep, these lambs of a perfect thoughtlessness. Blessed are the children underneath your wings. Please: before the day, receive me too, a child . . .

So prays the proud man, dying in his pride, or the woman, or a whole church body.

The rest belongs to the Lord. But the Lord is good. It is the Lord who whispers to the breaking prayer: AMEN.

John 10:16–18

August 16

Living Despite Hatred

Young Wangerin, working a summer job packing peas among a rough lot of workmen, has found a nest of three baby hawks in a field and has taken them to the bunkhouse to raise.

Three times a day the crew stopped to eat. But so long as the peas were running, they worked from dark to the dark of midnight. Always after sleeping, the boy's knuckles had swollen so large that they cracked when he closed a fist.

Three and four times a day he fed his baby hawks. They crunched the grasshoppers. Field mice infested the loads of pea-vines, and the boy discovered that the hawks liked livers and viscera, which he served on the tips of his fingers. Gluttonous creatures! They took whole fingers in their mouths, so the boy felt the intimacy of their swallowing. The boy rejoiced in their trust and their life and loved them. They fledged at the wings. They grew. He worked a wire cage above the nest.

Now there appeared one day at Station 16 a grim, reclusive man whom the others called "Tex" because he worked in a dude cowboy outfit, hat and boots, perfectly new. Tex had extraordinary eyes, burning blue. He never spoke. In time it became evident that his habit was to wear his clothes to rags in two weeks, to take his paycheck to town and to blow it totally on new clothes and a solitary drunk.

A conflict arose between the boy and Tex of the blue-eyed morosity.

One Saturday night the timekeeper woke the boy and told him to dress. "You're the biggest man I got," he said. "Tex took a cab to Station 6. He swears it's his station and won't leave the bunkhouse." At 2 a.m. they drove to Station 6 and found it lit. Tex lay in vomit on a lower bunk, dressed in new clothes, seeming to sleep. Men stood back from him in their underwear. The boy didn't understand their hesitation. He went straight to Tex and shook his shoulder.

Immediately the man opened eyes fire-red around the blue, drew a knife from his pillow and rose up slashing at the boy. Spontaneously the boy slapped Tex's wrist. The knife dropped, and the timekeeper grabbed the drunk from behind. In that moment, Tex began to hate the boy.

Tex must have brooded for several days thereafter. He conceived a plan.

At supper break one day the boy heard a scraping noise outside the bunkhouse, and a certain fear clutched his stomach. He ran outside in time to see Tex at a distance, at the edge of a deep ravine, lifting and heaving the nest of his hawks—box and rags and cage and birds—into the air and over the bank. There was a splintering crash at impact. "My hawks!" the boy wailed. In panic he stumbled forward, envisioning bloody death. "My hawks!"

As the man remembers that moment now, it seems a long race he ran to the edge of the ravine to see the destruction of his birds. A terrible desolation seizes the boy's heart: "You killed my hawks!"

But suddenly there rises up from the ravine a miracle—one after the other, three beautiful hawks thrashing upward in the air, sweeping the wind with new wings, wheeling in astonished glory, flying, flying, flying! They are not dead. They are transfigured.

This miracle the man remembers even to this day. When those whom he loves have died (have died indeed a death as hateful as the blue-eyed Tex) and when in grief he races to the edge that denies him pursuit, he still can see the souls of his beloved rise up like hawks from the mortal ravine and fly, ascending the high supernal air in confidence to meet the Lord. He sees the resurrection. *John 6:53–58*

August 17

The Reason We Remember Orpheus

Who can endure to know this people not by its smiling face, but here, in the depths, at the core, according to its nature and its truth?

This is why the ancients remembered Orpheus and told his tale: no one chooses the horrors of the Kingdom of the Dead, its bitter revelations, the cold accusation it lays against the living. How could one trust even the living thereafter? To enter hell is to learn that hell has entered life above and is the darkness not only under the earth, but in the human heart. No one chooses such knowledge—except Orpheus alone, because he loved.

And down. Orpheus climbed all the way down—until, through the shadows of the condemned and past their personal and appropriate torments, he came at last to the thrones of the lord and the lady of horrible Tartarus.

Their glory was a lurid light, like pale smoke; and he could see. *John 8:23–30*

How to Deal with the "Doubting" Christian

And yet, all these convulsions of grief are a passage within the drama of faithing, very much a part *of* faith and not apart from it.

Be very clear about this, you who are discouraged by your suffering sister, you who would condemn her careless attitude as sloth, her anger as hard-hearted impudence, or her morbid depressions as signs of apostasy and a fall from faith. No, she has not left the faith. Job hadn't left the faith either, ye comforters. Rather, your sister is performing certain intensely necessary and painful acts *within* the faith. This is faith. This is faithing.

Therefore, do not cease to love her now; and surely never separate yourself from her.

She hasn't stopped loving Jesus. That is precisely the conflict and the anguish in her. Loving is the pain in her, because her loving's unrequited. Soon enough this difficult knowledge will surface; soon she will admit both the love and the death of her beloved; and then she will enter the third passage of the drama, wherein there is something to do. And she shall change again.

Until then, love her. Honor her for the depth of her suffering, if for nothing else.   *John 7:40–52*

Retiring into Doctrine

Our father's past is our Savior's present.

It is terrible to be in relationship with such a Jesus. How can we abide the maelstrom he releases around us? Why, we take up stones to throw at him. We assert our own authority. We grasp at personal control over our own lives and damn the dizzy horror of time let loose. This is what we do: we explain, interpret, theologize, create systems of balanced rationality in which there must be no ambiguity, each word meaning but one thing. We name, we name, we noun the thing until it is subject to our intelligences once again and teachable, until it is fixed in a writ, inert, and dead. Safe! We retire safely into our doctrines. *John 8:14–18*

August 20

Knowing Jesus' Death

In the beginning we love the Lord Jesus above all things. It is a good beginning. Then we learn to declare the death of this Jesus, and that too is right. It is the core of our preaching, whose theology is Christocentric, whose Christ is centered upon the cross. We *should* move step by step, dramatically, to Jerusalem from Galilee and to the cross. But so long as his death is theology, a proposition in a system of propositions, it is a pallid declaration after all since we do not experience the thing we speak about. Oh, it may move the more sentimental among us to sweet tears; but these are suspect, theology being a matter of the mind. And whether we are sentimental or coolly mental, this death too—this most momentous of deaths—we can file in some corner of our systematic understanding, and so it is lesser than us. We consume it; it does not consume us; therefore, it is never truly perceived by the heart as an ending absolute. What wonder, then? What sort of miracle can the resurrection be when next we come to declare that too? It is only words. *Acts 26:9–23*

August 21

The World Puts You to Death

Death shall come. In what arena shall it occur? In the world's arena. By whose hand shall you be put to death? By the world's hand—though God shall turn that evil thing to good. And why will the world kill you? Because you loved Jesus more than you loved it: it hated you. You severed yourself from its values. By not loving it, you became a curse upon all it loved— that is, upon itself, since it loved itself. And you loved Jesus in a way it could not tolerate: you loved him despairingly.

Had you loved him happily, the world might at least have been glad of your happiness, calling you silly, perhaps, but recognizing value in happiness for its own sake. But your persistent, undecipherable, isolating, and cursed despair is intolerable to its own merry romp to happiness, and it will preserve itself by killing you. *Luke 12:1–12*

August 22

Why We Do Not Scorn "Good Works"

On the other hand, when doctrine returns to its humble service, interpreting the acts of God unto our little intellects, both to explain what is and has been, and to prepare for what shall be, embracing the drama whole, though standing aside from it, as it were, the way a viewer humbly stands aside from the play, then doctrine will not issue condemnations upon a part as though that part were the whole, nor will it damn the young man simply because he is not wiser yet, nor criticize the older merely because he hasn't the energy of the young. In fact, doctrine will cease to sit in judgment at all. Even doctrine will say, "There is a glad, good time when it is right to believe in the holy effectuality of good works, disciplines, and acts of mortification." *Luke 10:23–28*

August 23

Sharing and Faithfulness

How, then, shall the worker "share" his labor with his spouse? By admitting that the single purpose of *all* his jobs and *all* his duties is the healthy survival of his household. Surely, other goals will encourage any given job; but this goal should justify them all. Then, whether he is at home or abroad, in the fields or in the factory, his marriage will continue to shape his behavior and his attitudes; it will be present *in his very actions*. Then his spouse indeed "shares" the work of survival.

In other words, "sharing" comes from faithfulness, which was the vow from the beginning. "I promise to be faithful to you till death" means that, except for God, "I commit myself first to you." I shall commit myself to no goal or purpose which denies you or neglects you—or contradicts my commitment to you. Sexually, I shall keep faith with you, yes. But in all other forms of relationship, and in my work, I shall keep faith with you. Ours is the contractual relationship which defines all others, which is finally served by all the others. What my job requires of me: can I do it lovingly, on your behalf? Is it a worthy offering to our marriage? Or would you be offended by it? Does it take me away from you, in spirit, in time commitments, in fact? Is everything I do at work open to your scrutiny? Is it in harmony with your image of me?

Philippians 2:12–18

August 24

Marriage Vows

I didn't think hard about the marriage vow before I made it. Neither was I unfamiliar with it. The words were common and seemed right enough; and I was sharp enough to know that, though I spoke them *before* the pastor, the witnesses, the people and God, I spoke *to* none of these. I made the promise *to* Thanne alone. I knew, too, that these words were not merely ceremonial, a sort of ritual formula to signal a solemn moment. They were supposed to mean something. I knew that I was communicating a particular thought to Thanne (and she to me) as a surety against the future. From this point on, until we die, I was going (I said) to do, or be (or not do, or not be) something—and she could count on that.

"Something." It's that *something* which I hardly considered—a shocking oversight, really, since this was one of the rare lifetime vows I would ever make to another human. This was intended, by my voluntary commitment, to qualify all my actions thereafter, shaping me, defining "Walt" in all things, not just "Walt" when he was with Thanne, because I wrapped my whole life into that vow. And if I didn't truly intend that vow so comprehensively, why then, all my vows and all my words are compromised. Who can trust anything I say, if neither Thanne nor our hand-picked witnesses could trust that?

And I know that I thought the vow to be mostly a negative one, a promise of what I would *not* do. If it was a positive vow (a promise of something I would do) this was only the vaguest, most ineffable sort of doing: "I give you me. It's you and me forever."

And that was meant to satisfy the woman? That shapeless-
ness was to shape our lives together forever? I did better than
that for every employer who ever hired me, promising with
bold clarity precisely *what* I intended to do for them, defining
the deeds they could count upon.

I promised her a positive thing after all. Yes, I would *do* certain things. And so did she to me. I promised to accept certain
responsibilities, to perform carefully, continually—*faithfully,*
so that she could count on it!—certain tasks on behalf of the
marriage, and so on her behalf as well. I promised to do work.
Specialized work. Relational, marital, practical work.

And the tasks I promised to do (whether knowingly or
not—that makes no difference) are not so mystic that they
cannot be defined.   *Galatians 3:15–18*

August 25

I Have Been Crucified with Christ

Finally, when all else has been burned away and when the
very self has fallen into dust and nothingness, doing and
being have become the same. If any should touch us now,
they touch the love of Jesus. And should we put forward,
now, our hands—which are not our hands but Jesus' hands—
and touch another, why, it is the love of Jesus that touches
that other. There is no identity left unto us but this: that we
love Jesus. There is no life in those who are individually
dead but this: that they love Jesus.

It is at this point that the words of St. Paul tremble on the
very edge of expression, though we cannot yet express them. It
is now that the experience which he declares has become our
experience, though we cannot yet declare it—speaks for us:

I have been crucified with Christ; it is no longer I who live, but Christ who lives in me; and the life I now live in the flesh I live by faith in the Son of God, who loved me and gave himself for me.

This is not parabolic language. It is not a symbolic utterance. Nor is it an effort to reproduce in the visible world invisible things. It is the plain report of a historical experience.

Galatians 2:17–21

August 26
Understanding the Impossible

But see the great love wherewith the Father has loved us!—that now he showers upon us blessings not only beyond our deserving, but also beyond our imagining. For as Paul came to know and so to express the wonder of the working of the Lord, so we too are raised again, *both* to experience *and* to understand the complete unqualified loving of Jesus. And since these two—to be the subject of an experience which is at the same time the object of our knowing, at once to be the actor within and the viewer without—are contraries incapable of occurring in the same singular being, but since they nevertheless *do* occur within and for us, this is a miracle. Resurrection is a miracle of God.

1 Corinthians 15:20–28

August 27
It Is Everything

Who can conceive of the love of Jesus, that it is not the mildy good whom finally he calls, but the abject and the dead? But resurrection never could be for the living. It is nothing for the living. It is only for the dead. Yet for the dead, it is everything.

And we are Peter: dead, so dead that we haven't even the existence wherefrom to repudiate our sinful natures: the whole of us died in the dying. "You will look for me tomorrow, and I shall not be."

Even so. But God created out of nothing. And into the lifeless dust he blew his breath, and into the mindless disciples he blew his spirit. It was precisely death and the dustiness that freed us to be the handiwork of God again.

1 Corinthians 15:54–58

August 28

Talking with the Sun

This selection and the next tell the story of "Lily."

Children, I'll tell you a story.

There were three sisters who lived far north, at the edge of the Boreal Forest where the sun in the summer shines a most marvelous light.

The oldest sister, named Bean Plant, was plain. Her flowers were tiny white purses, her stem both tall and skinny. But she was sensible and very busy. She turned the marvelous light of the sun into beans as long as sausages. She worked hard, and so she thought well of herself.

Marigold, the second sister, was beautiful. She said, "Hum," and "Yes, yes: I am a knockout." Her petals (which she was constantly combing) were as gold as the sun. In fact, she figured the marvelous sunlight had no other purpose than shining on her.

All summer long, life was fine for Bean Plant and Marigold. They had but one problem. Their youngest sister, Lily.

Lily, Lily, all leaf and no blossoms, no beauty, no brains, no nothing. She was just . . . green. She didn't even *make* anything.

And that's not the worst of the problem. Lily was "slow," a sort of an imbecile. She embarrassed her family. Well, what Lily did was, Lily talked with the sun. "Sister!" her sisters hissed. "The sun can't talk!" "Maybe not," said Lily, "and maybe so"—but she didn't stop talking with the sun. And this is how she did it. . . .

At dawn when the sun woke up in the east, it seemed to Lily that his marvelous, rosy light was a word; the word was "Good." So she cried, "Morning!" And together they said, "Good morning!"

At noon the sun gazed down from heaven, and the flood of his light said, "Good!" And Lily said, "Day!" So they said "Good day" together.

At night, the weary red sun lay down in the west, and just before he turned out the lights his smile said, "Good." But then Lily never, never said, "Bye." She was afraid of the word *goodbye*. For she loved the sun, and she wanted him to love her too, and to tell her so. Therefore, at the end of the day she said, "Night." And that's how they said, "Good night."

"Lily," said Bean Plant, "sunlight makes things grow! It doesn't *talk!*"

"Lily," said Marigold, "it shines so folks can see beautiful things. It doesn't *talk.*"

"Maybe not," said Lily. "And maybe so."

"Lily, you are impossible!"

All summer long she embarrassed her sisters. Then matters got even worse. Lily became sad. She started to cry, and she could not stop. "*Now* what, Lily?"

Lily said, "The sun is dying."

"You nincompoop!" cried Bean Plant. "The sun is a fire. It isn't alive!"

But Lily wasn't comforted. "Look how late he gets up in the morning," she said, "and how low he goes in the day, and how early he drops to bed at night." She sobbed and sobbed. "He's dying."   *Matthew 24:29–31*

August 29

I Come Again

Well, the sisters had to agree that the sun was declining. But Marigold said, "So what? The sun is a light. If the light goes out, *I'll* shine for the world."

Lily kept crying. She loved the sun, but he had never told her that he loved her too—and now he was dying.

Time passed. The days grew shorter. The winds blew colder. And lo: the sisters changed their tunes. For the winds brought news from the north. They tore through the forest screaming, "Killer! The killer is coming. No one is safe! He murders everyone!"

"Even me?" said Bean Plant.

"But not me," cried Marigold.

"Everyone," shrieked the winds. "And here is the terrible thing," they said, "this killer kills by kissing."

Poor, skinny, busy Bean Plant started to yell, "Not fair! I've worked hard! Hard! I don't deserve to die—"

All at once Lily was by her side—and Lily was not crying anymore. "Sister," she said, "it's OK! The sun has spoken another word, a promise. It's OK!"

Idiot Lily! Now that there's a good reason to cry, she's hopeful! "It's *not* OK!" snapped Bean Plant. "I like to live. I—"

But suddenly Bean Plant was silent. She stood on one foot, quivering in the middle of her field. The killer had kissed her.

The winter, cold and mortal, had come and killed her. She was dead.

Then a wailing arose, a grievous weeping. "Beauty shouldn't die!" cried Marigold. Lily said, "It's OK! The sun has said a new word—"

But Marigold's locks were blasted brown, and she'd broken her back to bury her head in the ground. "I'm too lovely to—" *Die,* she would have said, but winter can come through the earth as well as the air, and he kissed her to death.

So then Lily was the only one with guts. "I hate you!" she cursed the killer. "I hate you for killing my sisters! I hate you for killing me! And for killing the sun, I—"

Winter kissed her too. Lily was still. Lily was dead. But this is the reason why the dumbest sister was also the boldest: day after day, the sun's new word was, *"Again. Again. I come again."*

Dear children, when Easter returns this year, go with me north to the Boreal Forest. I'll show you a lily as white as the sun, in whose blossom trembles a drop of water. You will say the drop is dew. But I'll say, "No, it's a tear."

For the sun shall come through the air and the earth to kiss my Lily to life again. And that's how he shall say, "I love you too."

This is a true story, which I just made up. *Matthew 24:32–36*

August 30

Farmers and Reverence

This summer past I've thought about my father-in-law. He and the farmers like him are my hope. They preserve in their very beings the truth that we, in sinful ignorance, have forgotten: that we belong to the earth, and the earth belongs to

God. These are holy and living dependencies, as necessary as blood to flesh, as intimate as Martin Bohlmann and his horses. Surely I don't suppose that we shall live by the horse again; but I plead that we live on this earth with reverence.

Or what do we think it means that God gave us "dominion" over creation? That we possess it? That we can bend it to our own desires? That the earth is no more than a resource by which we support and satisfy ourselves? No! In the beginning, because we were created in God's image, our dominion was meant to image *God's* sovereignty over creation, *God's* personal and complete dominion, not our own. We were God's emblem within the universe, God's signature upon the work he had accomplished and then called "Good," God's stewards here below. We were placed here to serve God by serving the earth and so to be served by it. These are the intended relationships by the Lord of all. This is righteousness.

The earth is alive: thus Chief Seattle, Indian.

The living earth is holy: thus Martin Bohlmann, farmer.

And by his reverential stance the farmer calls again for honor to God and kindness to creation, that we dress and till and keep it rightly.   *Matthew 24:45–54*

August 31

Truth and Myth

Of the Icelandic myth of the fall of Yggdrasil, the world-tree:

Shall there never come such a day? Oh, but there shall. It is coming soon.

But isn't the Icelandic myth false in fact? Perhaps it is; but its instinct and its perception are better than our own. It is a language, at least, with which to interpret meanings in the world. We see the surface only and think that the surface is all. We see words and think they are nothing but stones. We see an entire story and think it is nothing but a white oak tree. We see prophecy and can read nothing there but firewood and kindling.

Some myth is better than no myth at all. Myth is convinced that Deity is greater than the world and can bring it to an end, but that Deity persists in writing legends in the clay of the world until the end should come.

Myth could read the fall of an oak tree.

But Truth is best of all (though our contemporary notions of reality have difficulty distinguishing Truth from myth). Truth does more than read the beginning and the endings of oak trees. Truth embraces both. Truth is there at every beginning and every ending, even at the beginning and the ending of the world—which shall indeed have its ending.

For: *I am Alpha and Omega,* says Truth, *the beginning and the end, the first and the last.*

Christ is Truth, which brackets and signatures Time, with which to read the world and the fall of a white oak tree—before which, stand in awe.   *Colossians 1:15–20*

September

September 1

Schooling: Law

Immanuel was a school that Walter attended as a child.

Of all the teachers at Immanuel, only Mr. Affeldt occupied an office of his own. Books rose up the walls of this room to the very ceiling, so that you had the sense, when you entered it, of entering the mind of Mr. Affeldt himself—each book a thought, each thought a silent eye inspecting you. To be surrounded thus by the cogitations of Mr. Affeldt (he was a man of cool rationality and legendary intelligence) could factor a child right out of existence.

On the books behind his desk (or else hanging from a hook when it was not in use), he kept a flat piece of wood, varnished and shapen with a handle, and burned across the face of it with the words: *The Board of Education.* I realized that these words constituted some sort of joke, because he lifted his lip when he spoke them and he showed his teeth.

Discipline. Regulations. The consequences of transgression. Nothing was hidden in those days. Nothing was particularly complicated. Principals and parents and teachers were not cryptic or tricky, but forthright and trustworthy. "Do this," they said, "and this will happen. Don't do this and the other thing will happen surely." And it did. It always did. They kept their promises. The world was orderly indeed, if a little severe. I knew what The Board of Education was for.

Proverbs 1:1–7

September 2

Schooling: Gospel

Miss Augustine, on the other hand, was mercy in my world; and I could abide the harshness of the whole world bravely for the sake of my third grade teacher, my Miss Augustine.

Early in the school year she had said, "Don't laugh in class. Please don't disturb the other children when I'm teaching them." It was a reasonable request, since she had to divide her time among three grades, all in the same room, and since at any given moment two-thirds of the students were working on their own. It was also a very persuasive plea, because Miss Augustine herself was a woman inclined to laugh—a pink-faced, musical laughter that stirred my soul when I heard it, a nearly killing benediction when I myself was the cause of that flush of delight in her face for something I had said—a persuasive plea, I say, because she controlled her laughter. She set us a good example. If she could get down to brass tacks, well, so could we.   *Proverbs 1:8–19*

September 3
Schooling: Independence

On my first day in the first grade, I panicked and cried and raced back to the car where my mother was, ran top speed before she drove away from me.

"Mama! Take me home!"

I thought she would be so happy to see me and to discover my undiminished need of her presence, her love and her protection. I sat smiling in the front seat and heard the car's ignition even before she turned the key. She never turned the key.

Only now do I understand her own tears as she took my hand and walked me back into the school again.

"Mama, do you hate me?"

"No! No, not at all. I love you—"

What she was saying was, "Go away from me—in order to *be*."

So here I am, all done with first grade and writing books like any independent adult, and it is done. My mother sorrowed in the separation; but I am, by miracle, her joy and her accomplishment. Both. It is an astonishing act of love.

Proverbs 1:20–28

September 4
Familiarity

Until the days I walked to school, my neighborhood *was* the world; nor did I shrink in that place, though it wasn't without dangers itself, because I knew precisely how I fit in it. The people of Overhill Street, they knew me. Therefore I knew me too. I wasn't a big person, but I was a whole one; and what I was, the strengths and the weaknesses together, remained unchanged from day to day. I didn't have to pay attention to identity, then: just be, because I belonged. Such being is freedom, although it is caused by the strictures of being known and by a thoughtless obedience to community.

These are the blessings of familiarity: being and freedom and confidence. *Proverbs 1:29–33*

September 5
Vanishing

Or how could I explain to him what happened to my person on the way? I shrank. The farther I went from my own familiar neighborhood, the littler I became. The houses around me, they grew huger, they swelled to tremendous sizes. The distance from corner to corner expanded, because my legs diminished like rubber bands. So I would run faster and faster, my lunch box flying at my hand, but I kept arriving at corners later and later. The whole world seemed vast and pitiless, because I was reduced to a dashing dot with a lunch box. And that's how I imagined I would die: *pop!* By vanishing.

Proverbs 2:1–9

September 6
Schooling: Power

Concordia is a prep school for Lutheran pastors.

Actually there were two systems of power at Concordia, one official, the other unofficial, unacknowledged, covert, and cruel. Both were alike in being unrelievedly male. Men and boys in loud community together tend less to mercy than to law; and if the law officially is the imposition of reasonable restraints upon disorder, unofficially it is merely brutal.

Proverbs 2:10–15

September 7
Schooling: Imagination

I used to cause myself sweats and panics by my daydreams, by the power of my imagination alone.

I would imagine that I was crouching on a high mountain ledge, on some lonely lip of stone projecting from sheer rock, the distance all dizzy below me and nothing above me to climb. I would, in the daydream, creep to the edge, peer over, and then begin to shake with fear. The height itself was not the problem, however high, however real I made it. I was the problem. For heights could always excite in me a perverse and nearly uncontrollable urge to jump; and I sincerely believed that if I relaxed my vigilance a whit, the wilder nature would prevail: I would leap, and I would fall. I would destroy myself.

Therefore even in my daydreams, I crept backward clutching at the ground; I curled with my face to the solid rock and shut my eyes and shut my ears—for the very air would murmur with a thousand sullen voices, "Come. Come. Jump." And my own spirit would answer, "What if—?" and "Why not—?"

So I would waken suddenly in the third grade classroom, trembling and sweating and hoping that nobody noticed the change in me.   *Proverbs 4:1–9*

September 8

Food and Compassion

In a little while his mother came back. Right behind her Mrs. Larson bustled in with the biggest bottom in all the world and great arms that could never hang straight down because, like the sides of pyramids, they had to make room for Mrs. Larson's bottom, seventeen feet from one side to the other. Mrs. Larson had enormous quantities of sympathy, had gallons of pity, whole oceans of compassion—and she kept it all inside her bottom. That's what Jonathan said.

When Mrs. Larson wanted to help the weak, the heavy laden, cumbered with a load of care, no man could stop her, and it didn't matter the time, night or midnight. Look out for Mrs. Larson, when she came to heal you! And how did she heal you? She cooked. She baked. She boiled and fried and diced. She measured and whipped and covered the kitchen in flour and generally caused food to happen everywhere.

Proverbs 23:6–8

September 9

Pew Places

*The seven selections, through September 15, comprise the story of
Jolanda Jones.*

Many of the faithful honored ritual and tradition by making
possession nearly an eleventh commandment—though no
one ever spoke of it: *Thou shalt stick to thine own pew.* Or,
since commandments generally take a negative turn: *Thou
shalt not trespass on thy neighbor's pew.* There was a practical-
ity in this, and a personal gratification as well, because you
could come late to worship without fear of lacking a seat.
Everyone had remembered you in your absence, had respected your position in the church, had preserved a place for
you. *Come up, come up, dear Joe and Selma Chapman, gentle-
folk honored among assemblies. See? We've saved your seat for
you. Come, though we've begun the feast. Occupy the pew, which
is your due.* Something like that. Even so do Christians, or
members of Grace at least, relish the trappings of reputation
together with a little modest praise.

And it were best unspoken; that's the Christian characteristic of this praise: its modesty, its pious restraint. Pew space
does it nicely, doing it mutely. It is simply, silently *known.*
And the less that has to be said about it, why, the deeper
strikes its root into the community: "These," no one says
unto another, because no one has to; everyone knows, "these
are people of repute. Give place to them."

Even ten minutes before the service was scheduled to
begin, there sat in Joe and Selma's pew a woman of uncon-
scionable beauty—and a kid of doubtful breeding. The kid

had an animal gleam in his eye, and canine teeth, I'd bet, if he
opened his mouth and grinned.   *John 4:1–6*

September 10

Beauty and Holiness

Her eyes had a catlike slant, a natural black line embordering
the lid, a shining white and a steadfast penetration as dark as
charcoal, lashes as long as luxury. She gazed at me with direct
watchfulness. This was a bit disturbing, to be so brazenly
stared at by a stranger—as though some question had been
asked and I had left it unanswered, but she was waiting, but I
didn't know what the question was. And this was the more disturbing, because she was so beautiful; I couldn't shut her out.
Her cheekbones formed an aristocratic V, and her mouth was
fine, so fine, *re*fined. Nor could I dismiss her gaze as admiration or curiosity. It was neither of those. It had some particular meaning. Some appeal in it.

And if Jolanda Jones caused confusion in me, what do you
think she did to the other good people of Grace?

Folks stood up to sing the first hymn, directing their attention to the front. But folks, when the hymn was done and
they sat down, quickly redirected their attention to one who
was slower at sitting, unused to the up-and-downing of
Lutheran ritual: to Jolanda Jones. And then their eyes popped
open and church got interesting, and I had a difficult time re-
minding folks that I was there, leading them in confession of
their sins.

Not only did Jolanda Jones possess an unreasonable beauty,
but she dressed it (so said their eyes) "like Satiday night on
Sunday mornin'!" No skirt, no blouse on her. A dress. But
even a pants suit would have been more sanctified than such

a dress: low in the back (and most of the folks apprised her from the back), loose on the shoulders, utterly missing below the knee, and as tight on the hips as taste on a minister's tongue. She wore a hat. Well, grant her that—she covered her head in church. But this hat swept left from the side of her head and brushed one bare shoulder with a black feather. Black. That hat was a midnight black. The dress, it was resplendent black. And black were the long Egyptian eyes she never removed from me. Devout were some of the eyes on her, and pious were other eyes; but I don't think it was the absolution which I was pronouncing that caused devotion in certain men and piety in certain women. *John 4:7–10*

September 11

A Place for Me?

It was severely noted by folks in the congregation that this woman, whoever she was, put no restraints upon her child— indeed, paid him no mind throughout the entire time that others were trying to worship God. The kid lacked discipline!

Smoke stood up on the pew while I preached. He grinned at me; then all at once he squatted and flung himself into the air. That child sailed into the aisle, landed belly-flop and loudly, then proceeded to swim a sort of breaststroke up the floor in my direction. Giggling insanely at himself. So we had three noises in the church: my preaching, Smoke's fun, and the hennish sound of clucking in the pews.

But Jolanda Jones did not remove her gaze from me. It grew sharper, more intense, increasingly an act of pure, dark will, a burning as beautiful and stinging as a scimitar.

And when the service had run its course and God had received what praise God could under the circumstances; when folks had arisen and filed out of the church (none speaking a criticism to the woman, such restraint also being characteristic of Christian piety); when that woman herself had finally, the last of all, come down the narthex steps with Smoke at her heels, I learned the question of her deep Egyptian eye.

"Good morning," I said. "Thank you for visiting—"

I don't think the woman even saw my hand extended. She prized me with her eye and straightway blurted her question:

"Is there a place for me in this church?" *John 4:11–19*

September 12

Need

Jolanda Jones did come back again. Not immediately. In fact, there was a longish period when we didn't see her at all; and then, when she did return, it wasn't our welcome but a particular urgency in her own life which persuaded her to come. But she came. And she had made changes which proved that the woman had not been unconscious of the feelings of the people of the church. (How courageous, I thought, to come full knowing! How deep her need must be!)

Changes: she dressed, as it were, down to Christian tastes, down to her shins and up to her neck. No hat. And she sat in the very back pew on the right-hand side facing Jesus (the pew the youth took for themselves). And she wore enormous sunglasses, covering a third of her face.

Suddenly, "I wanna show you somethin'," she said, and she took off the glasses, gazing at me.

"Oh! I'm sorry," I said. And I was.

The right corner of her brow was angry with swelling. Blood vessels had ruptured in her eyeball, which was a hot, crimson red.

"Jolanda? You hurt yourself?"

"No," she said. "It ain't because I hurt myself." Her language banged against her beauty. But it fit her injury. "I didn't earn it neither," she said. "It was give me."

My voice grew tentative and low. All at once we were entering private territory. "Someone," I said, "hit you?"

"Hit me? Beat me!" she said, almost belligerently.

But her level eyes were asking, *Is there a place for me—?*

John 4:20–26

September 13

Somebody Oughta Know

But then she said, "Somebody—" and her voice caught, and her face grew tight with appeal. She surrendered a tiny gasp. She was suddenly terribly young, and the rest of her words came out in the sad humility of need: "Somebody oughta know," she said. And for the first time, she dropped her eyes.

"Well," I said, a little breathless: so much she revealed to me; so moved was I by the intimacy and this sudden softness, the dropping of her eyes; at the same time, so stupid, so helpless! "Well, now I know," I said. "But what can I do for you?"

Immediately the street asserted itself. She popped the dark glasses back on, grew erect, and said, "C'mon, Smoke. We gotta go."

"Jolanda," I said, suddenly hasty, "you know that Jesus loves you, don't you?"

"Hey!" she said with a smirk. "Hey, what? Me *and* poor Smoke?"

"Of course, you and Smoke. Of course. This is Jesus."

"So, then." It was her mouth alone. Her eyes were concealed. "Me and Smoke can come to your church."

"Absolutely."

"And ain' nobody here goin' be tarred by that?"

"No."

"Smoke, he's bad. Smoke, he don' bother the people here?"

"No. Well—no. Well, I'll tell you what, Jolanda. Did you know there's a nursery where little kids might feel more at home?"

"C'mon, Smoke. We gotta go."

And she was gone.   *John 4:27–30*

September 14

So Sorry

Her eyes flew to mine, now, for the first time. They fixed on me, as though suddenly realizing that I was there. And then she began to shake her head left and right, and the fear that had sharpened her face turned into utter misery, and the poor face melted. "Jesus, Jesus, Jesus," she murmured. "I made such a mess of things, of everything. O Jesus, *I* am the mess—" but she was looking at me "—an' you can do to me what you want, but what about Smoke? It ain't none of it Smoke's own fault."

"Jolanda, talk to me."

"Is there a place for a baby in this church? Won't nobody laugh at Smoke, will they?"

"Jolanda Jones, there is room for both of you, for Smoke and his mother and both of you, yes! But you've got to tell me what's the matter. What happened to you?"

Jolanda Jones began to cry, her eyes wide open, still beseeching me for something, something, understanding and—something. The tears tripped over her lids and streamed down her face.

But I had absolutely nothing for her, nothing to say. The world she lived in was outrageously complicated, dangerous.

"Reverend," she whispered, "he's goin' to know I got the VD. He's goin' to know I didn't get it from him. He's goin' to know that I been messin' round with other men. He's goin' to kill me. Oh, Jesus, he's goin' to kill me. And—" She paused. She closed her mouth upon his final misery and lowered her eyes and grew terribly still. "An' he's goin' to be right."

There. That was it. That was all of it.

And I had no answer. Silence filled my little study, and blame came down on me. What solutions did I know that she didn't? None. Or what theologies of Western Christianity could speak a comfort to Jolanda Jones in this particular calamity?

What could I say? Saying anything just now would be the same as saying nothing, no matter how right or true or good or godly the words I chose. Jolanda Jones was crying. Words were useless. And I, while I sat across from her, was almost crying too. My skin burned with sorrow for her. No, I was no authority. No, I did not feel like a Reverend. Just sorry. Sorry.

I stood up. I closed the space between us. I took her hand. She gave it to me and stood as well. And then I hugged her, and her bones were small, and there wasn't a scrap of sass, not a piece of street inside this woman. She pressed her face into my chest, and she wept. I stroked her shoulder. We were children together.

Jolanda. I am so sorry. *John 4:31–38*

September 15

My Own Church

Three weeks later I heard a terrific banging on my office door—a kicking, it turned out to be. Nothing feminine about this summons. Something horsy, aggressive, imperious. I expected an angry neighbor or—I didn't know what. Not a woman. Certainly not the regal Jolanda Jones, in the slant of whose eyes met all that's best of dark and bright—

But there she was, and she was beaming a refulgent joy. It fairly took my breath away.

"I did it, Reverend!" she declared. "I did *do* it!"

In one arm she held Smoke, wild-eyed and feral as ever, himself exploding with her happiness. He laughed with his tongue between his teeth, spraying me.

In the other arm she cradled a portable television set.

"No VD, no phone calls to nobody—an' I left him!" she cried. "Hey, I left that sucker flat when he wasn't home to see. Took Smoke. An' I took my own TV!"

Ah, this was news. I myself began to grin.

"So, what I want to know is," Jolanda grew serious suddenly, almost devout: "Could my own church use a TV set?"

John 4:39–42

September 16

The Poet's Reason

Harlequin, Finding His Voice

I'll give my poetry the kind
Of strictures Jonson gave his mind
And give my mind the freedom he
Would give his poetry.

Then, if the thought is dead for all
The centuries of dying it
Had undergone before I called
It out of my young wit,

A dizzy erudition in
The way I say the thing may win

It life again and something new
For telling it to you.

Our busy-ness is to invert
The funnel masters used, to blurt
A little thought as if we had
A trumpet and were mad.

Proverbs 22:17–19

September 17

The Language Makes Public

First, there was the love for Jesus, the thing itself, alive and real.

And then, with the name of Jesus, came awareness of what was.

And finally language came to frame it. And to confirm it. One marries another by a spoken vow. The vow identifies the relationship; the speaking of the vow is one's willing, conscious, and public submission to that relationship: now one's *own* identity—so one declares—exists only within *its* identity. In this process language is remarkable; it bears into the public air what had been knit in secret, in the womb of the spirits. *Psalm 89:1–4*

September 18

Something Invisible

Children grow up in a relationship with the whole world external to themselves. But when that world is disturbed (as the planet Uranus is disturbed in its logical course by something invisible) the disturbance is comprehensible only if there is a Being, equal at least to the whole world, affecting it. Except for that Being, they dwell in an arbitrary chaos, in perfect meaninglessness, and must suffer the killing conclusion that they are themselves nothing, nothing, less permanent and less identifiable than gross dust. But children by nature do not and cannot live in such non-ness of being.   *Psalm 111:1–4*

September 19

A Fortress of Forms

A practical and obdurately ethical woman was our mother.

She had fought many a brave fight on her children's behalf, and now the bravest of all was for our souls, that we be found righteous in the assizes. That is to say: she kept an eye on us.

She made a fortress of the forms of our religion. She guarded the doors of that fortress like Peter with a short sword and a key. And though this may seem small to the world at large, to us it was the fate of the children of martyrs—that Mother on a Sunday, when other worshipers were too ignorant to know the proper times for rising, rose, rose grandly, and commanded her children to rise up with her. So we alone would stand in the midst of a whole congregation, gazing staunchly forward, making our stance a lesson to them all, heaping coals of fire, as it were, upon their heads—but suffering the scorch in our own poor foreheads.

Ah, Mother was Amos in Bethel. Mother was Paul in Jerusalem. Mother was Christ in the courts of the Temple. Fearless. And practical. Obdurately ethical. Ours.

We would be found righteous.

Or perhaps we would be found like her for sheer independence and outrageous spunk.   *Ecclesiastes 3:1, 2*

September 20

Wandering

And I did go wandering—but not in the obvious, geographic way my father took. In fact, I had already departed from my family several years before I left them for Milwaukee. Nobody knew my leave-taking, least of all myself: the spirit of this nomad was invisible. But quietly—as my family struck camp again and again—secretly, unknowingly, I had decamped the faith.

I lived still within the forms of my father's religion. My mother's fortress still surrounded me. And so far as I knew, there were no reasons why I should not also march the walls of the stronghold of Christendom. It was without a conscious deception that I planned to become a pastor.

Ecclesiastes 3:1–3

September 21

Memory and the Sea

This memory starts as we are driving a narrow highway through tall, continuous forests of pine. I have made a bridge of my body, my toes on the back seat of the car, my arms and chin on the ridge of the front seat, my face between my parents' faces. They are gazing forward through the windshield. My father drives. My mother is talking—though memory preserves neither the timbre of her voice nor the words; rather, I see the tip of her nose dipping down as her mouth keeps forming soundless sentences. Forever and ever that tiny trick of her nose consoles me when I watch it, proof of my mother's presence.

Then my father says, "There!" I hear the cordwood tone of that command. "Look to the left," he says. "You'll see the ocean."

Almost casually I glance left. The forest is thinning as we speed through it, and a distant water flashes between the trees. Suddenly the pine is altogether snatched away, and I am startled by the sight. There, indeed, lies the monstrous sea, a nearly impossible reach of water, massive, still, impersonal, and infinite. *Ecclesiastes 3:1–4*

September 22

You're His "Image"

Oh, Grandpa was a wonderful man to "image." Superintendent of the cemetery in St. Louis, he was: master of the green lawns walled around with brick to six feet high; watchman, warder of the scattered stones, the gracious trees, the winding roads, the memorial shrines in which the memories were enclosed; king of the sleeping kingdom was he, to whom I was the green and golden prince—I the huntsman and herdsman as well, and grandly happy. Grandpa shot red squirrels when I visited him in the summers: single shots, most accurate pops in the silence of the cemetery. He skinned them and I watched him hang the pelts in the basement of his house, which was also on the cemetery grounds. And this is how strong the man was: during Prohibition (so my mother told me) he was called to the little illegal saloons that certain Germans maintained in the neighborhood around the cemetery. When Louie had a drunk he couldn't handle, big Bill Storck strode into the oily darkness (ah!) and lifted the drunkard bodily, like a basket of cabbages, one hand at the poor man's collar, one hand at his belt. Then he strode outside again and across the street to the cemetery wall, where, with little effort, he slung the drunkard up and over six feet of brick. And my mother said that Grandpa said: "Let a *Säufer* wake on a grave, and see if he changes his ways."

My mother grew pink with pleasure remembering such stories. And she said I was the "image" of this man, whom she obviously loved, whom I loved and honored with all my heart. It was good to be a little image of Grandpa Storck.

Ecclesiastes 3:1–5

September 23

Flying

In the children's book Potter, *the boy is befriended by an oriole, who leads him in a flying discovery.*

"Wings, Potter!" cried the Oriole. "Open your wings!"

He did. And what happened then was a wonder of the mighty God and a gift to Potter forever.

When just above the bushes his wings went out, they caught the air like sheaves of wheat beneath his shoulders, and suddenly he was sailing level to the ground at an easy speed.

Potter began to laugh. He tightened a muscle above his butt; his tail fanned forward, and he soared up. Mighty flaps of his wings—clumsy flaps, since the wing tips slapped above and below his body—powerful flaps, and he arose. He lunged higher and higher. Up the side of the house; up so high he cleared the elm; up and up and loose and free until the city lights turned below him, the river a ribbon of darkness, the woods like fur on the back of a bear.

Potter gulped the glory of God, the goodness of creation, and all of heaven stretched around him. He laughed like a loon, a little crazy to have let go of the earth, to float at the tops of the clouds.

Ha, ha! Swoop to the left, Dove-Potter, why not? He did. And swoop to the right, you light-hearted bird. He did. Then dive, child, dive like a hawk straight down from the clouds, your feathers thrumming at such high speeds, your eyes made narrow by streaking the winds. He did. He did: like an arrow piercing down to the earth and whistling the wind, he did!   *Isaiah 40:31*

September 24

Persistence

Douglas Lander drove the mule that pulled the plow that broke the earth to dig the hole on which was built Grace Lutheran Church. They dug that hole twice. The flood of 1937—when folks boated above such streets as Governor and Garvin—filled it in the first time. But Douglas was ever an even-tempered man and would do the same thing six times over uncomplainingly if five times first it failed.

"You can't command a mule," he chuckled even to the end of his days, "until you got its attention. An' you know how you get a mule's attention?" It was a tired joke; but Douglas was so sweet in its delivery, so pacific a man himself, so neat and small a ginger stick, that people grinned on the streets when he told it. He was a pouch of repeatable phrases. Besides, it was understood that he meant more than mules: the younger generation, the government, some recalcitrance in human nature, cocky young preachers—whatever the topic of his present conversation. He could trim a joke to any circumstance. "Hit it with a two-by-four."   *Ecclesiastes 3:1–7*

September 25

Not a Ghetto

Both Miz Lillian and Douglas—and she was as short as he was, though neater, thriftier, quiet, maternal—were fixtures of the inner city neighborhood, as standard as pepper shakers on a table. They *made* the mean streets neighborly. They gave the crumbling streets a history. Douglas could point to a rubble three blocks west of Grace, where the city had demolished some substandard house, and remember: "I lived there. Right over there. And I recall when Line Street *was* a line, black to the west of it, white to the east, and you better not cross 'less you got business takes you across. Now we black on both sides." He grinned. He lifted his sweet eyebrows. "One o' them things," he sang high tenor. "One o' them things."

Miz Lil spoke less of the past than did Douglas. Not because she did not remember, rather because she spoke less than Douglas in all things. She hadn't a compulsion to talk. She watched and kept her own counsel, and her words were weightier, therefore.

These were the flesh of the inner city, Douglas and Miz Lil, the living ligatures. For their sakes, do not call it a ghetto. Do not presume it a mindless, spiritless, dangerous squalor—a wilderness of brick and broken glass, brutality, hopelessness, the dead-end center, no! They made it community because they remained in confidence and honor.

The *Lamed Vavnik:* the Righteous Ones. They gave it civility, familiarity, and purpose—they caused it to be a good ground on which to raise fat children—because they remembered the names.   *Ecclesiastes 3:1–8*

September 26

The Widow's Stone

And then she broke the silence. Miz Lil began to talk. The pastor listened without interruption and slowly began to realize, even before she was done, the holy benevolence of her words. In the darkness he allowed himself to cry.

In fact, Miz Lil was speaking of grief. Carefully, touching the subject with infinite reverence, she said that her grief was a stone in the womb. Not *like* a stone, no. It was there—a lump as mortal as an infant between the wings of her old hips, but heavier: a painful, physical presence. "And you pray it would go away," she said. "It doesn't go. You plead to Jesus you can't bear the suffering. You bear it anyway."

She rocked and rocked in the darkness. There was the sound of a whispering fabric: she was rubbing her stomach.

"Finally you understand," said Miz Lil, "that this is the way it's going to be forever till you die. The stone is never going to pass. You're going to mourn forever. But you say, *This isn't wrong.* Finally you say, *This is right and good.*"

The sorrow that started as the enemy, it ends a friend. This is what Miz Lil explained as the night developed. Sorrow had become a familiar thing for her now, and the perpetual pain in her stomach a needful thing. It was there when she woke at midnight, there in the morning. She took it to church with her, and she brought it home. This particular baby would never be born nor ever leave, but would companion her forever. This was the loneliness that kept a widow from being altogether lonely—because it was, inside of her, a memorial of her husband. It was pain and wanted rubbing. It was sorrow and caused her to sigh. But it was also the love of Douglas— and stroking it was the same as stroking the husband whom you love.

"Douglas is not far from me," said Miz Lil, "nor me from Douglas—" In midsentence, she fell silent. There was only the sound of the whispering fabric. And the pastor in the darkness realized his tears.   *Ecclesiastes 3:9–11*

September 27

High-Rise Poverty

In the four selections through September 30, Wangerin does a guest-preaching stint at a prosperous big-city church.

But if you step outside the church and look left, you will also see a nearly unspeakable stacking of poverty: Cabrini Green, high-rise housing, warehousing, the desperate housing of the poor. Down the faces of these grim buildings is a dark, interior cleft, as though Vulcan had slashed each one from the hairline to the jawline with his hammer. But the architect did that. The architect caused this indentation as though some part of every floor in the building should be revealed to the world. "Is it nothing to you, all ye that pass by? Behold and see—" My heart recoiled when I saw that visible shaft. I felt ashamed, partly because I felt as well a fascination and watched for inhabitants to appear in the crack as a boy might watch for ants in an ant farm. I felt embarrassed for the multitudinous poor and for this society which solves them like a problem in structural engineering. Or maybe all my feelings and reflections came from shock at the scale of poverty. I knew the name Cabrini Green. But who knew it was so big, so big? And from this vantage, so globally silent? I was looking at the moon come down and grounded on the earth. I was, I guess, awakening.   *Matthew 8:16, 17*

September 28

The Baglady Interrupts the Preacher

An old woman; a woman crook-backed, hunched at her shoulders so that her face thrust forward; a woman behatted, but the hat just sat on her hair, because the hair shot out around her head in a white and spiky nimbus, stiff hair, angry hair, hair capable of stabbing. This woman's face was full of the mumble of words. Her mouth was working words as though they were gum. Her eyes were darting left and right, pew to pew as she approached. What was she doing? With a draining horror I understood: the woman was looking for a seat!

The woman came straight down to the front. She tucked her body sideways into the third pew on my right-hand side, never casting so much as a glance at me. She thumped to sitting and then proceeded to open the bag on her lap, to root therein all mindless of the place, the time, the worship, the people—and to place her worldly possessions on the seat beside her. She had a glittering eye, precisely like a weasel's.

Well. I raised an angry face to the congregation and only then discovered that they were as much the butt of this joke as I was. The poor usher, when he caught my eye, literally threw up his hands in apology. Some of the members sent me stricken looks, aggrieved that such a thing should happen in their church. Others raised eyebrows of incredulity. They didn't believe it either. They thought it must be a setup and that I myself had found a tricky way to make [my street-person sermon] real to them.

Ah, Jesus—nobody's joke, then? A baglady indeed?

Matthew 8:18–22

September 29

The Baglady Confounds the Congregation

But at that moment in the LaSalle Street Church I said nothing at all. I was silenced, and my story stopped.

The baglady had found what she was feeling for. She snatched it up between us—almost like some talisman against an evil—and she hissed a second sentence with startling clarity, and my neck began to tingle. But what she held was a half-pint carton of milk. And what she was doing was giving it to me.

I heard an expulsion of air, a sigh from the congregation. I interpreted their sigh. The drama around me diminished me, and I was moved, and the microphone sagged away from my mouth.

Behold: the impoverished is nourishing the preacher. Behold: the servant is being served.

I remembered the microphone and lifted it again. My voice continued in an amplified squeak: *"You can't pray because we have a time to pray," I said, and the little man collapsed before me*—

But this woman with spikes of white hair and tiny weasel eyes was willful, insistent. She shook the carton of milk. She wanted me to take the milk. I did. I took the milk in my left hand, then she nodded once, fiercely, as though satisfied with my obedience, and dismissed me by folding her arms across her bosom.

Matthew 8:23–27

September 30

God's Laughter

Angels, yes indeed! But when angels descend from Cabrini Green and not from condominiums, they don't bathe first; they don't approve themselves with pieties first; they do not fit the figments of Christian imagination: they prophesy precisely as they are and expect us to honor them whole, prophecies and blasphemies together.

I wanted so badly to laugh, because God was roaring a wonderful thunder, surely. The baglady had been a joke, yes—and the joke was God's.

When I had first approached her pew, all crippled with fear, this is what the crook-backed woman hissed at me: "It's damn if I will," she said. "It's damn if I want to, Preacher. You'll never get me to stop my swearing!"

What would the La Salle Street Christians make of that? My ears uncorked to hear her. But I drove my story onward nonetheless.

And when she handed me the carton of milk, when all of the people exhaled their sentimental sigh, she sharpened her weasel-gaze and hissed: "This—is—poison. Hee-hee! Hee-hee!"

The messenger of God was cracked. And so was I, to her shrewd eye. Oh, we were a subversive pair in this rational middle mix, Americans at worship. They had no idea what sedition they'd taken to their bosoms—

And God was pounding his thighs and weeping with the laughter surely.   *Matthew 8:28–34*

October

October 1

Jesus Describes His Work

Jesus said, "For the work that I do, I will have no house, no bedroom, and no bed. Foxes sleep in holes. In nests the birds do sleep. But I won't even have a pillow for my head."

Jesus said, "For my work, I won't need money, no possessions for me. And I shall have enemies, people who won't understand how much I love.

"But," said Jesus, "I shall have friends as well, and I will teach them. I will teach them to love one another even as I love them." *Luke 9:57,58; 10:1–5*

October 2

The Habit of Goodness

What we look for, you know, is a habit of goodness.

Not sporadic, isolated acts of goodness, however great. These leave no lasting effect on society. They occur at the whim of the individual, and whim is a light-weight, ephemeral thing. Unreliable. Whim seldom outlasts the feeling that engendered it—and many an act of goodness dies, when whim dies, on the vine.

The habit of goodness. Not goodness performed because someone is watching, someone authorized to criticize or reward: a boss, a parent, a spouse. God.

That sort of goodness is not good. Its first consideration is always the self. The self seeks praise. The self avoids guilt, pain, punishment. There can be no true joy in a "goodness" meant to protect oneself and to curry favor, since its deepest motives must be fear (of the stick) and a selfish desire (for the carrot). When desire is thwarted, it turns to bitterness or anger. When fear expands, it panics or breaks into rage.

What we hope and pray for, both in community and within ourselves, is a *habit of goodness*. This goodness is motiveless, in that it needn't be argued or explained. It is a way of life. It's the person's personality—utterly spontaneous in deed but characteristic in spirit.

There is no heroism in this goodness because there's no awareness of exceptional action. Goodness is natural. What other thing should one do besides this good thing? Why, there is no other thing.

You see? This goodness springs from a quality of being.

1 Thessalonians 4:9–12

October 3

Why We're Here

With the creation of light and dark, the day and the night, God caused *time* to be. (And in "time" events could now occur; history began.)

With the creation of a firmament to shape the world, to protect the cosmos from the wild waters of chaos above it, God caused *space* to be. (And in "space" things could now exist.)

By his mighty commands to things below the firmament, that the seas should keep their boundaries and the earth its various terrains, that every living thing should be fruitful and multiply according to the design of the Deity, God caused *place* to be, a viable environment, a living nature in which another sort of being might live and sustain its life.

Into a place precisely right for life, God put humankind.

Job 38:12–21

October 4

Emily Dichter, Author and Saint

This and the five episodes that follow tell of Wangerin's encounter with an elderly parishioner and what she taught him about writing, repression, and blessing.

I received by mail an invitation on pasteboard, signed with a flourish, to "lunch in her home with Mrs. Emily Dichter. Would you be so kind, sir?"

Sir? To whom could I be anything like *Sir?*

Nothing I could think of recommended me to Mrs. Emily Dichter.

Nevertheless, such an invitation felt like a summons.

Yes, I would be so kind. I accepted.

The woman did not live in the grandeur her card implied. But she lived in a valiant decorum.

Her daughter met me at the door of a four-room bungalow, took my "wraps," and led me through a little "parlor" stuffed with books, into a little kitchen where Emily Dichter sat in state behind a little table. We shook hands (I bowing at the waist). Her daughter had to guide the old hand toward mine: Mrs. Dichter was nearly blind. But she pierced me! I swear, she pierced me with her milky, ancient eye. I sat. She never took her eyes from me.

This close, I could see how thin was her cloud of white hair. And age had simply broken her spine like a reed. She crouched of necessity.

She said, "Are you content, sir, in every particular?"

I assured her that I was.

"Then," she said, "before the repast, let me make my introductions." We might have been a royal party, but there were no more than three of us here; no more than three of us could fit in here. Emily Dichter was nearly ninety years old then. Until her last days she spoke that way: with a Jamesian rhetoric so florid it could shame a king.

"My daughter," she announced, "is my amanuensis. She has sight and reads for me. She has dexterity and writes my words on paper. You, sir, you are an author," she said, astonishing me, but never removing her eyes from my soul. She called me an author! She named my dream as though it were true. But she didn't even pause: "And myself I shall introduce in due time. Let us eat." *1 Timothy 1:1–7*

October 5
To Dance in the Dark

Later, at the end of the meal, Emily Dichter announced:

"As I have published a small book, I am an author like you. I wish you to know this regarding me. It is good for those of a common interest to recognize each other."

An author! This took my breath away. I did not know authors in those days, though I dearly desired to know them. Why had no one told me this about Emily Dichter before? Did she know what a dazzling gift to me her second reason was? The company of a published author! She must have known. She must have seen that I was grinning.

But her third reason, while it perplexed me with a mystery, outshone the second as the sun outshines the moon.

"Third," she said, still fixing me with her blind eye, still steadying herself on the knob of her stick, "I offer myself to you as a mentor, sir, if you wish it and will accept. Take time to decide. But an elder author can perhaps inure the younger to difficulties before they arise. I may perhaps walk you the rounds like a Virgil, sir." She smiled at her conceit. And then she leaned across the table and whispered with intensity, "But do accept. Never!" she whispered. "You should never, never be sentenced to dance in the dark!" She leaned back. "No one should. Not ever."   *1 Timothy 1:12–17*

October 6

Loving Beyond Vengeance

Of course I accepted her proposal. The woman had acknowledged me an author. What would I not accept from such generosity and insight?

What she knew of writing, I was able quickly to equal. But what Emily Dichter knew of charity and sanctity and sheer endurance, I shall never equal. Great church, we ought to canonize such women for their outrageously loving spirits, for their suffering (Mrs. Dichter suffered!), and for this: that they could translate their pain not into vengeance but into blessing.

I give you my Matron Saint, whose mentoring was my epiphany.

Even from childhood Emily Dichter was compelled to write. This was no choice for her. This was what she was. And while she was young, in the last decade of the previous century, people generally tolerated her curious hobby. They expected adulthood and marriage to dispel her of fantasies, to school her in duties and in her prescribed role.

Emily was no fool. She knew precisely what was expected of her. This didn't mean, though, that she would cease what she could not cease. Rather, she concealed it. And she continued to write in privacy. After adulthood, no one read what she was writing. (I marvel at this woman.)   *1 Timothy 1:18, 19*

October 7

Writing in the Dark

And then she married. And then she had children to raise. And her husband was Teacher Dichter, principal of the school; therefore, she had a reputation to maintain. His reputation, her own interests being fiercely circumscribed by the community, and by the church.

She did not not write. She could not *not* write. But she wrote when the children were sleeping, in the afternoons when her husband was working. She wrote behind drawn drapes where no one would see her. She wrote in a perfect solitude—though writing by its nature yearns a reader.

But this was the case in those days: that writing was fine for students and essays and sermons and postcards; but *creative* writing was a frivolity. And for women—conscientious women, Christian and Lutheran women, pious women, the wives of church officials—creative writing was considered vainglorious, a vanity to be censured, a dereliction in wives and mothers, a sin, and a sign of that womanish malady: hysteria.

I am not overstating the case. For though the church could be as civil as a Sunday suit, it knew exactly what it wanted of its people, and it knew how, piously, to shame the deviate.

1 Timothy 5:11–16

October 8

The Author Dances in the Dark

Yet Emily Dichter wrote, and that's a boldness of spirit I can scarcely comprehend. She wrote. She must have been like Spanish moss, surviving on air. She survived, though her identity was buried inside of her. She wrote, and what's more, she began helplessly, devoutly to write a book. An actual volume. Months and nights, and no one knew: this woman was birthing in longhand a biography of Katherine Luther. The wife of a teacher was honoring the wife of the fifteenth-century reformer. In utter solitude Emily Dichter produced a book.

And when the thing was done, she determined that this, at least, should have its reader. She wrapped the manuscript and laid it in a box and mailed it to the only publisher she knew, a Lutheran press. Then she put on her housewife's face and with burning nerves awaited reply from the publishing house—a terrible and thrilling time. In a very real sense, she might come to *be* by her book. I know such existential passions now. I am a writer like Emily.

The publisher answered.

Emily Dichter waited until she was alone. And then she took the letter into her dining room, slit the envelope, unfolded the single sheet of paper, and devoured three lines of print. "Congratulations. . . ."

"I was so delighted. Sir, I was so ecstatic," Emily Dichter said to me, "that I put my hands atop my head not to explode. I laughed aloud. I twirled me round the dining room like any child. My skirts ballooned, my arms went up, my hair flew backward, I cried for joy to God in heaven—and I danced. I danced. Oh, how I danced that day."

But before she danced her joy, Emily Dichter went to the window and shut the drapes.

The community must not see such vanity. The community would despise the sin in her. Therefore, Emily Dichter, writer, splendor, God's bright eye—she danced in the dark. Alone.

This was the only book she ever published. Yet for the rest of her life she was an author!   *2 Timothy 1:1–5*

October 9

Honor Her!

Ninety years old, she said to me, "I offer myself as your mentor, sir." And she said, "You should never be sentenced to dance in the dark." Ninety! Emily Dichter, what you suffered, what you knew, and what you did with your knowledge! Woman!

She saw me. She pierced me to the core. Blind at ninety, that woman lived in a light of perception and mercy. She chose to preserve me from the sin that had buried her, to preserve me from the greater blindness of our heritage, the blunt insensitivity of our community, the prejudice and the oppression of our church. Is not this a wonder? She survived for fifty years on a single book. Identity bravely intact. In kindness, not in bitterness. Instead of vengeance or rage or despair, Emily Dichter chose to love and to bless. Yes, and I am blessed.

This is no less than epiphany. This is a miracle. This is a saint. Honor her!

Surely, great church, in the brightness of such saints we can see and confess our sins against women in the past, our demeaning of any who did not fit our easier categories, our dead-weight pressure upon lightsome spirits. Surely, in this sunlight, we shall not darken others hereafter. Surely we will recognize the personhood of each and each. In God's name, surely! *2 Timothy 2:1–7*

October 10

Meaning

Walter acknowledges the readers of his column in The Lutheran *magazine.*

An author may suffer fits of uncertainty.

In Albert Camus' novel *The Plague,* an old man sits in his bed and counts peas from one pan to another, cheerfully, as though the practice accomplished something. This is the way he divides his life: "Every 15 pans it's feeding-time." This is the way he occupies himself until he shall die: "What could be simpler?"

The narrator is impressed by the old man's honesty and self-awareness. Life holds no meaning whatsoever for this old man; therefore, he has created a ritual activity of nothingness: Its meaning is to while away a meaningless time.

An author can (perhaps any professional can) be suddenly struck with the fear that he is doing nothing more than counting peas from one pan to another, counting words from his brains to the paper—and that he *does not know* how valueless the practice is. The old man's ritual was absurd. But ignorance is worse. It is a hollow vanity. This is the fear of the author: Is the lonely work a vanity, and I a fool? Do I defraud myself?

But then this is the redeeming blessing of the church, the body of Christ: to receive the work of that author after all (the work of any professional in my vocation!) and in the reception to declare it valuable; to give that author place in the body whole; to call him "brother"; to call her "sister"; to companion him, to surround her with an active love.

Dear people, do you know the merciful kindness you give me every time you read this column? You turn dried peas to worthy words. We engage in dialogue. And in consequence, you grant me purpose and being—all this in the name and under the providence of the Christ who makes us one.

The holy catholic church, the vast community of Christians, preserves each of its members from meaninglessness by honoring the work of its members one by one, whatever that work may be, by acknowledging the benefit of their labors.

1 Corinthians 12:22–26

October 11

Nature's Beauty Doesn't Care

The day that followed was blue and beautiful—and mute. Clouds of impossible whiteness, sheer-edged against the sky, both high and eyeless, sailed heaven. They saw nothing. They were. They said nothing, knew nothing, cared nothing. They floated, and they were.

And the trees revealed a wild variety of emotion: umber, the burnt-brown, brooded; the Lady oak took red at the edges, a deep flame-red, while yet she kept green at her heart, and so she seemed a gentlewoman of a long experience; some of the maples burst yellow, effulgent, crying attention, demanding attention; some of the maples slurred a bright primary red, an almost unnatural red, upon themselves, like harlots laughing; some of the maples shed their leaves in the first draft and stood naked. Aspens were modest, giggling trees; but where they were, they were so many. They could afford to be modest. Pine and fir thrust green among the colors, unchanging, unwilling to change, criticizing by their contrast every other change. And the elm and the walnut, the willow, the gum, and the locust: the woods, the woods, the busy woods, the heartless forest and the trees, that whole congregation simply went about its natural business.   *Psalm 104:31–35*

October 12

Youth Ministry

This center was considered my ministry by those who employed me, who owned the basement hall in which we gathered; and at first I considered it a ministry too. I began with a certain idealism, prepared to make a holy mark upon the indigent, rapscallion youth, ready to model a better life in the nights when the youth came down to play. But fairly quickly idealism shattered against the faces of your people—and none of you left me time or gave me the chance for ministry, at least as I'd envisioned it. My work became a sort of policing action.

Well, on the very first night of my "ministry," six kids asked for a van-ride home, and I felt gratified to be of service. But five got out at the house they'd led me to, and the sixth, when we were driving away, began to shriek with laughter. "Cathouse!" he screamed, beating himself about the head. "I can't believe you was so easy. You took 'em to a cathouse!" I learned suspicion.   *Proverbs 9:7–12*

October 13

I Know You, Jimbo Gaddy!

Even before the door swung shut I heard a yelp, and then a single, unbroken wail of fear. And I knew. And immediately I was running.

I burst through the door. I was bounding up the steps when I saw your brother fighting Simon on the ground. Where were you? Jimbo, suddenly I knew exactly where you were, exactly what you were doing. Still on the steps I whirled around and looked up. In that same instant you had jumped from the ledge above me. You were flying down with a knife in your hand.

Your weight knocked me backward to the sidewalk. You landed flat on my chest. But I had the advantage of foreknowledge and threw you off. So we rose and circled each other, you with a ridiculous serrated kitchen knife and an ice-blue eye. Then this is what I did: I drew an enormous breath, and I pointed my finger at you, and I bellowed, "I KNOW YOU, JIMBO GADDY! I KNOW YOU! GIVE ME THE KNIFE!"

Astonishingly, you did. And on that night, I was very confident that I did know you.

You neither answered nor revealed the least emotion. You gave me the knife, and you gazed at me.   *Revelation 2:8–11*

October 14

I Didn't Know You After All

So then I didn't see you for a while. Weeks, I think.

But I remember that you returned to the center one more time. Your hair was slicked, but your eyes were dilated and black, and I guessed that you were high on something. You slouched. You might have been smiling, but I said in my soul that you weren't. Jimbo, I didn't believe the smile.

Suddenly you turned and hit me on the shoulder, a sharp, short knuckle-punch, which left a bruise. "Hey, man. Because!" you said right distinctly, and you nodded and you leered. I didn't think "smile." I thought "a thin-lipped leer."

"Because," you said again. "Because . . . we can rap, man, you and me. I like you because we rap!"

Rap. I promise you, Jimbo, that's the first time I had ever heard the word *rap.* I did not know what it meant.

Therefore, I said, "Yeah, we rap," and I hunched my shoulders and left you then, because I figured it for some sort of derision. And besides, you were leering. We never, never did rap after that. I never saw you again.

Rap. Now I know what it means. And now I know that I didn't know you at all. Once, in our relationship, you offered to talk with me. But I had grown hard and cunning and self-confident. I missed it. I didn't even recognize it. No, Jimbo Gaddy, ice-blue eyes, I didn't know you after all.

Revelation 3:19–22

October 15

Mary's Wisdom

There was a period, five or six years ago, when your older brothers received more letters than usual from aunts and uncles who addressed them in formal terms: "Master" Joseph and "Master" Matthew Wangerin. Talitha was perplexed by a title she had never heard before.

"If boys are masters," your younger sister said, "then what are girls?"

You solved it straightway, as easy as swimming.

"Masterpieces!" you declared.

And mom laughed at the aptness, since you are a piece of work; and I laughed for three or four seasons; and you—you laughed for the pure pink pleasure of it all, the center of attention, a round cheesecake of a child, dumpling cheeks, not a cloud in your blue sky. *Proverbs 10:1*

October 16

Gossip

If one must build himself up by tearing another down; if one's goodness must be proven by contrast to another's badness; if one feels religious by blaming the irreligion of others; if one's righteousness is planted in the unrighteousness of sinners, that one is unrighteous at the root.

Gossipmongers depend on evil rather than on God! Therefore, their foundation is rotten. The sin of another is more than mere pastime for them; it has become their salvation, that which by contrast declares them acceptable and good.

No one ever climbed to heaven on the wrongs of others. But gossipmongers try. *Proverbs 11:10–13*

October 17

Who Is Greatest?

Now Jesus began to travel the road to Jerusalem, and always the crowds surrounded him.

Here came fathers with children and mothers with wishes: "Maybe Jesus will touch my daughter, will kiss my son, and maybe he will bless them."

"No! No chance of that," said strong Peter, waving these parents away. "Can't you see how busy Jesus is?"

But Jesus covered Peter's mouth to make him quiet. "Peter, Peter," he said. "The greatest people in the kingdom of heaven are *children.* Let them come to me. Don't ever keep them away!"

Then Jesus hugged the children, kissed them sweetly, loved them deeply, and blessed them. They were his.

Matthew 19:13–15

October 18

Children's Laughter

Let the children laugh and be glad.

O my dear, they haven't long before the world assaults them. Allow them a genuine laughter now. Laugh *with them,* till tears run down your faces—till a memory of pure delight and precious relationship is established within them, indestructible, personal and forever.

Soon enough they'll meet faces enraged unreasonably. Soon enough they'll be accused of things they did not do. Soon enough they will suffer the guilt of powerful people who can't accept their own guilt, who dump it, therefore, on the weak. In that day the children must be strengthened by self-confidence so they can resist the criticism of fools. But self-confidence begins in the experience of childhood.

So give your children (grandchildren, nieces and nephews and neighbors) golden days, their own pure days, in which they are so clearly and dearly beloved that they believe in love and in their own particular worth. Give them laughter.

Observe each child with individual attention to learn what triggers the guileless laughter in each. A story? A game? Traditions? Excursions? Elaborate fantasies? Simple winks? What? Do that thing. Laughter—so easy in childhood—must echo its encouragement a long, long time. A lifetime.

John 17:16–21

October 19

How Can I Get Faith?

Among my letters comes one of a single sentence, written with a purple felt-tipped pen:

Dear Walt, How can I get faith? Karen.

And how shall I answer the question I can't ignore? What shall I say: pray for it?

I don't think so. So brisk a reply would cheapen the cry in the question and seem to dismiss the questioner. Prayer is a practice of faith. Without faith, prayer can feel as foolish as a plastic toy—or else as frenzied and futile as weeping into a telephone long since dead. Poor Karen, attempting prayer, might only suffer a vaster difference between herself and all the Christians who pray so easily.

So what shall I say? Love God with all your heart? Love your neighbor as yourself?

No, no, at least not yet. As good as these laws are for the faithful—those enabled by the Spirit to pursue them in peace—each is a yoke on the neck of the solitary woman who, if she cannot accomplish them, feels the more accused, the worse for weakness. We might as well say to the legless woman, "Run."

What, then, can I say? Read your Bible? Go to church?

Well, that's half an answer. But half a fallacy's in the form of it.

Dear Walt, How can I get faith?

Dear friend, this is how I answer you. With a parable.

When I was a kid in the second grade, I roared it all over the neighborhood, how strong were the arms of my father. I knew my dad, had watched him chopping wood and declared his strength superior to Jimmy's dad's for sure. But I didn't believe it. Not with my life.

In our backyard stood a cherry tree. Ten feet up a stout branch forked northward. Upon that fork I would lay me down—my "private place" where I went to be alone, to dream, to read, to bathe myself in the higher air of self-importance.

Now it happened on a summer's day that a thunderstorm caught me in my kingdom unaware. Suddenly the east wind assailed my tree, and tore the book from my hands, and made a small boy throw his arms around the forking branches for dear life, his head slung down between them.

"Dad! Dad!" I shrieked, and the rain swept up and whipped me. A low cloud cracked and blackened the earth. "Dad!"

My father appeared at the back door. For just an instant I giggled in the wind, relieved. "Hurry!" I cried. But my father didn't climb the tree as I'd expected, made no effort at all, in fact, to carry me down. He stood directly below me and raised his two arms and called above the thunder, "Jump." *Jump?* If I broke his sticklike arms I would hit the ground and then what? Then I'd die. Forget your jumping! I gripped the branches with my arms tighter than ever.

But the east wind makes no concessions to the sensibilities of little boys. It ripped that tree and bent it. Savagely it shook it. Then suddenly my own poor branch exhaled and split beneath me. "Daddeeee!"

I did not jump that day. In bloody panic, I let go. All help-lessly, I fell. I thought, *Here comes the bump,* and I simply gave up. But my father caught me.

Then—*then,* dear Karen, my father's arms were strong in-deed. And to say so was a creed in me. And to hug him, and to let him carry me, why, that was love and faith and life to-gether. We strode that storm bare-faced into the kitchen. Me, I was weak and strong at once, who had only been weak be-fore. Dad, he was as strong as he had always been. So, what had happened? I had fallen to land on the truth, and truth was a living being.

So, what had happened? Faith.   *Romans 8:14–17*

October 20

The Poet Recognizes the Danger
of Self-Accusation

Regarding Confessional Poets: The Fusion

The trouble with atomic bombs
Is lethal egocentricity:
When one remarks upon himself
There goes the near vicinity.

Romans 7:9–11

October 21

Warm in the Memory of Experience

No, we are warm yet in yesterday's retreat, yesterday's wor-ship service, when certain prayers and certain ceremonies melted us to tears and we said in our souls, *The Spirit of Jesus is here.* We are full yet with the rosy gratitude that a prayer

was answered, a sickness healed, a hopeless marriage renewed, a burden lifted, an impossible problem resolved, or a
human hugged us so tightly, so unexpectedly that we said in
our souls, *This is a miracle: this is none other than the presence
of the Lord!*

This is the handiwork of Jesus and privately we bowed our
heads, and privately we wept. Warm: we are for some time
warm in the memory of the experience . . . of the promise . . .
of the Spirit . . . of the dear Lord Jesus.

The experience happens, truly does happen, a thousand
ways; may even happen more than once. But always one
thing follows: Time.   *Romans 16:25–27*

October 22

When Warmth Cools

The days pass. Yesterday flows backward, like the river, into
last month, last year. And time itself instructs us.

When the experience (which we thought would continue,
thinking that *it* was the new plane of our relationship) does
not return, then slowly the warmth cools. Last month becomes a season lost. Then what we do still have feels very
cold within us. And what do we have? The memory—whose
reality is in the past. And the memory is of a promise—
whose reality is in the future. But we are in the present where
nothing is because what we do not have is the experience itself or immediate evidence of a persistent Jesus. *With our
eyes* we cannot see. Again, what do we have? Mementoes.
Promissory notes. Documents which one day long ago or
one day yet to come might prove valuable and true, but
which today are paper. Scriptures. Doctrines. Books of com-

mon prayer, literate, lovely, but lacking, we sadly confess in
the silence of our souls, fire.   *Hebrews 12:18–24*

October 23

Forgiving

Most of our errors about *how* to forgive arise from fear or
from faithlessness. We are personally afraid to confront the
sinner openly with his sin. If the sin hurt once, don't we risk a
second hurt by exposing that sin? Or we doubt ourselves (or
the God within us), doubt we can handle it right, doubt the
righteousness of our emotions, doubt that forgiveness can do
any good after all.

So we avoid true acts of forgiveness by the simple expedi-
ency of changing its definition. We call things "forgiveness"
which aren't; we do those lesser things and feel that we have
done enough. But we haven't.   *Matthew 9:1–8*

October 24

Healing with Sympathy

One of the reasons we (men and women alike) neglect and
even deny the task of healing is that we feel finally helpless
before it. We're not almighty; troubles and diseases will arise
greater than our resources to solve them. Nursing the little
sicknesses for a little while is well and good; but we know
that some problems simply cannot be solved, some maladies
cannot be cured (or we, at least, will be baffled by them and
impotent), some emotional distresses, some grievings, some
of the fears of our spouses would simply overwhelm us if we
tried to struggle with them. So we turn away from the hurt

and ignore the need. "Don't tell me about it. What can I do?" We set a hard face against the hurting spouse—or else we rush that spouse to every other professional in the community, whimpering about our powerlessness, matching her sickness with our own. And if there is no help anywhere (in the end comes death) we are filled with impotent rage or with despair.

All this comes because our concept of healing itself is wrong, and, therefore, we are blinded to one significant thing that we can do, however little skill we think we have.

We can sympathize.

[We can] experience with someone her own experiences; feel with someone his own feelings; suffer with someone the sufferings he or she knows in that same moment. It is, in the deepest sense, to abolish internal loneliness by entering into the experience of the one whom you love.   *Hebrews 2:14–18*

October 25

Mercy's Human Face

Mercy has a human face. A human face can gaze at me, directly and personally. Then when I return the look, and when I discover a tear in Mercy's eye, and when suddenly I realize that that is *my* tear, *my* pain, suffered by Mercy itself and warmed by Mercy's love—then Mercy changes me. Sympathy disarms me. The willingness to take my pain (my worldly sorrow, my punishment, my sickness, my death) first to share it, but then to take it from me altogether, that is a killing sort of love: it destroys me. I can't comprehend its motive. My iniquitous nature is well able to understand the law: give to get. It feeds on the law. But mercy confounds me. Why would one, who doesn't have to hurt, hurt? Iniquity can't make sense of it; yet there it is, a tear in a human face! Argument fails me. My mouth is shut. My nature starves within me. It simply withers for want of substance in this new relationship. And mercy accomplishes what the law cannot: I am, in spite of myself, humbled. I die. And I am changed.

This is no longer the realm of theology. This is experience, spiritual and personal at once. It happens, and we change. This is consequence of an actual covenant: that mercy has a human face.   *Romans 3:21–26*

October 26

Mercy's Effects

Young Matthew's stealing comic books has resulted at last in a spanking, in his father's tears and repentance for his anger, and his promise of faithful love to his son.

The law can do many things, of course. It can frighten a child till his eyes go wide. It can restrain him and blame him and shame him, surely. But it cannot change him. So it was with Israel. So it is with all the people of God. So it was with Matthew. Mercy alone transfigures the human heart—mercy, which takes a human face.

For this is the final truth of my story:

Years after that spanking, Matthew and his mother were driving home from the shopping center. They were discussing things that had happened in the past. The topic of comic books came up. They talked of how he used to steal them, and of how long the practice continued.

Matthew said, "But you know, Mom, I haven't stolen comic books for a long, long time."

His mother said, "I know." She drew the word out for gratitude: "I knooooow."

Matthew mused a moment, then said, "Do you know why I stopped the stealing?"

"Sure," said his mother. "Because Dad spanked you."

"No, Mom," said Matthew, my son, the child of my heart. He shook his head at his mother's mistake. "No," he said, "but because Dad *cried.*"

Hereafter, let every accuser of my son reckon with the mercy of God, and fall into a heap, and fail. For love accomplished what the law could not, and tears are more powerful than Sinai. Even the Prince of Accusers shall bring no charge against my son that the Final Judge shall not dismiss. Satan, you are defeated! My God has loved my Matthew.

Do you know why I stopped the stealing?

Sure. Because Dad spanked you.

No, Mom. No. But because Dad cried.   Luke 15:20–24

October 27

Seeing Sin

The sins we see easiest in others we learned first in ourselves; we know their behavior and their signs from the inside. Though they deny the personal fault, gossips spot gossips a mile away, as wolves know wolves by a familial scent. Is he neglectful? Impatient? Judgmental? Self-indulgent? Jealous? Scornful? Abusive? So, sometime and somewhere, were you—

Recall: that if you did not commit the sin against your spouse, yet you did, once, against your parents, your adolescent classmates, your friends, your colleagues at work, the teller in the bank, another race, another class of people, the poor. Or you did in your heart what you didn't have the temerity to do openly with your hands.

But recall these sins *not* to torment yourself, rather to rejoice in the forgiveness God has given you—you personally—since God was always at the other end of your sin, and did not return judgment for iniquity, but mercy.

Matthew 6:9–12

October 28

Where Does Forgiveness Start?

Christ came to you when he forgave you. But Christ becomes visible in you, so others might see him there, when you *do* as Jesus *did*.

The world says (and your worldly flesh agrees) that it is your legitimate right, your dignity, and your duty to bring suit against the one who injured you, to press her until she has redressed the wrong, to accuse her, to punish her until her hurt at least is equal to yours. This is just. This re-establishes the order her sin destroyed. This places the burden of reconciliation totally and righteously upon the one who started the mess—

—and this is not forgiveness. As scandalous as it seems to the world (as painful as it is to you), forgiveness places the burden of reconciliation upon the one who suffered the mess.

Matthew 6:14,15

October 29

Jesus Teaches Forgiveness

It was Peter who came to Jesus with another question.

"Lord," he said, "how often should I forgive my brother? If he keeps sinning against me, should I forgive him seven times?"

Jesus said, "I do not say seven times, but seventy times seven. Peter, my rock, this is the way that it is in the kingdom of heaven—" Then Jesus told this parable.

"Once upon a time," he said, "a king decreed that everyone who owed him money should pay it at once. But one of his servants owed him ten thousand talents, an enormous sum, an impossible debt.

"'Pay me!' said the king.

"'O sir!' said the servant, 'I cannot pay you.'

"The king frowned. 'Very well,' he said, 'then I shall have to sell you and your wife and your children into slavery!'

"When the servant heard that, he began to cry. He sank to his knees and folded his hands and wailed, 'Wait! Wait! I will work for it, sir! Have patience with me, and I will work and pay every penny I owe.'

"'Let me see,' said the king, and he fell to figuring. He added, and he multiplied, and he discovered that it would take this servant one hundred and fifty thousand years to pay back the debt if he worked for it.

"That made the king feel very sorry for his servant. 'No,' he said, 'do not try to work that long. Instead, I forgive you the whole debt.' He struck a line through his account books and said, 'You owe me nothing any more. Go in peace.'

"That servant bowed very often, being very happy, and left the palace.

"But as soon as he was outside, he saw another servant who owed *him* a hundred denarii. He grabbed the poor man by the throat and said, 'Pay me!'

"'O sir!' said the fellow servant, 'I cannot pay you.'

"'Ha!' he said. 'And I suppose you expect me to wait while you work for it?'

"'Have patience, sir, and I will pay you,' said the fellow servant.

"'Patience?' he said. 'I have figured it out. You would have to work a hundred days in order to pay me back. No, I cannot have that much patience!' And he had his fellow servant thrown into prison.

"When the king heard what his servant had done, he stood up and roared, 'Get him!'

"So then the servant was standing once again in front of the king.

"'You wicked servant!' said the king. 'I forgave you your debt because you asked me. Why could you not have mercy on your fellow servant, even as I had mercy on you? *Take this man away!*'

"The king gave the servant to the jailers. The jailers put him in prison. And there he sat until the whole ten thousand talents should be paid.

"Even so," said Jesus, "will my Heavenly Father do to you if you do not forgive your brother from your heart."

Matthew 18:21–35

October 30

After You Have Forgiven

Be realistic: change doesn't happen in a day with a single act of forgiveness. Be realistic, not depressed by that thought the day after you forgive. And then be wise. You have right now the opportunity to give a concrete *shape* to your relationship, to establish between you certain promises and certain habits which will characterize your interaction hereafter, which will give a foundation to your mutual trust, and which can forestall this sin's recurrence.

The event of forgiveness is not yet complete until you agree upon a covenant—almost a renewed contract—defining your future behavior together. Surely, you have at this point a deeper knowledge of one another; you know the destructive tendencies which previously were hidden; you know something of their causes and you have felt their consequences—and this is, now, a knowledge common to *both* of you. (A mutual recognition of one another's deeper personalities is a blessing of enacted forgiveness!) You are wiser. *Psalm 32:1–7*

October 31

Not Afraid

There was a moon on Halloween, which could be seen from my kitchen window even before the dark. A rising moon. Paul and I streaked our faces in charcoal to give ourselves fantastical grace and grimaces. But he said he was a pirate, and though we looked alike I said I was Sir Lancelot, wearing my father's shirt reversed as armor. It came down to my knees. I carried a double-barreled shotgun for protection. We each had pillowcases to gather candy in.

In an exciting darkness, then, we criss-crossed Overhill house to house, ringing doorbells, knocking on doors, and crying, "Trick or treat." The adults, with their living room lights aglow behind them, would bend down and drop wrapped candies into our pillowcases, smiling. The night was cold and windless and busy with the black forms of children, clutches of rushing children. No one was afraid.

Calmly I cracked the barrel of my shotgun, closed it, and discharged two loud bangs to prove it lethal. After that Jimmy Newman didn't argue anymore, and I really believed that the gun had been my grandpa's, because I couldn't think of any reason why it couldn't be true. I wasn't afraid. *Psalm 33:13–22*

November

November 1

The Artist of Faith

An artist of faith—a *real artist!*—may therefore cry: Listen, we have a myth that consoles and secures, one worthy of a lasting belief, one we can surely live by. It is "myth" insofar as it is the timeless, defining story by which we make sense of a senseless existence. But it is *truth* insofar as it happened. It is vaster than I am (says the artist). I did not create it; it created me. I may name it with my words; but it is the word which named me first: Jesus Christ the Righteous! But the artist of faith had better cry that in language as fine as that of the secular artist who sings the abyss.   *Colossians 1:15–20*

November 2

Hollow Beauty

An author's technical mastery may excite our admiration, as though this artist accomplished supernal things by making supernal prose. But words will finally, also, mean something. They will have influence beyond the prose itself, affecting not only the taste but also the spirit—the deepest presumptions and so the behavior—of the readers. Effective art is a subtle, pervasive persuader: it teaches people *how* to "see" by giving them a particular perspective, sight and insight, in an intense, controlled experience. Willy-nilly, art shapes the reader's view of truth. A hollow beauty, a beautiful void, can be subversive by persuading the reader of nothingness.

Ecclesiastes 1:2–11

November 3

How to Treat Women

Of our four children, which is the strongest, the most aggressive, audacious, daring and tough? The youngest. A daughter. A woman-child who stuns the rest by plain courage. I beg the world into which she will sally tomorrow: Honor her!

Because (I warn the world) if you do not, you will on the following morning be pulling quills from your hide. It is to your advantage, I promise you, to ignore the gender and seek the skill.   *Proverbs 8:1–11*

November 4

Hell is . . .

"I maintain," writes Fyodor Dostoyevsky in *The Brothers Karamazov,* "that hell is the suffering of being unable to love." And then he offers as incisive an explanation of hell as I've found anywhere.

Hell is finally to know what love is, to see the utter holy rightness of love, even to see love burning in the face of God as the godliest thing of all—but forever to be incapable of love. And there are no delusions anymore: I am not what I desire most to be; therefore, I loathe the thing I am. And I deserve the loathing! That is hell. I think I'd rather have fire than that; for the nearer the loving God comes to me, the more horrible is the difference between us, the more tormenting my *self* to me. I am my pain. Even in the midst of heaven, then, I'd be in hell, for genuine love would burn me by the contrast. Lonely, loveless, solitary, despising myself eternally—that is hell. *Hell is the suffering of being unable to love.*

1 John 2:24–3:2

November 5

Love Is . . .

Love is the willing ability to sacrifice oneself for the sake of another. It is the sacrifice that is observable! It is the sacrifice that validates the truth of a true religion, for sacrifice remains a riddle to the world except it be explained by faith. At the core of Christianity is not an angry threat but the cross of Christ, his love made manifest in sacrifice.   *Romans 5:6–11*

November 6

The Church and Democratic Ethics

Democratic and Christian ethics are different in kind, not merely in degree. Moreover, the three commandments of the democratic ethic are nice, not malignant. They're composed of good intentions, and the church has lately and passionately appealed to them. But if these are the commandments we commit to, then we are not a church. Here is form without substance, and goodness without God.

1. Thou shalt be tolerant.
2. Thou shalt be kind.
3. Thou shalt be compassionate.

Then what is lacking? What's the danger of making this our highest moral response? What could be better than to be

"Christlike"? Why, Christ himself! Jesus is infinitely better than the best imitation.

Look: Jesus need play no role in the democratic commandments. Their center is the unjudging, generous and sympathetic human heart. In fact, the name of Jesus becomes an embarrassment within the democratic ethic. And there is nothing eternal or heavenly about this "goodness," however Christlike it appears. Salvation isn't even an issue. What lasting good can human compassion accomplish? Its goodness dies when we do.

But this is the difference we must maintain between ourselves and the world: that all we do is done in and by and for the love of Jesus. We are not merely *like* Christ. In us abides the very spirit of Jesus. When we do well, it is not because we are good by nature but because we obey the Christ who redeemed our fallen natures, because this Christ empowers us, and because through us the living God would seek and serve and save the lost, the oppressed, the hungry and haunted. We do not so much love them, as we love Jesus and *he* loves them. Or again: We love them because we see in them the image of our Lord.

It's not enough to strive for justice as though the striving itself were goodness. This must be a direct consequence of the cross of Christ (the one true and victorious act against any oppression, for that it defeated sin). It's the cross translated into faithful action, glorifying the Redeemer. We start with Jesus. We end with Jesus. The "good" of our "goodness" is the God whom our every action confesses.

Failing that essential source, we fail to be a church. Finding it, we are. *Romans 6:1–7*

November 7
The Search for God

Poet, Venator

A fox is always a thing running-gone.
Too bad. I'd like her still to think upon.
But we're the ones who cut her from the brush
And said that that's to rest but she's to rush,
Or be rushed, or be running—as you will.
We couldn't think on something standing still.
Not us. If God himself begins to run
(Why not? Grant God an interstellar fun)
We'll after him, intent upon the kill.
Anything. We'll chase anything up-hill.

Acts 17:22–31

November 8
I Can't Hear You

My first sermons seemed to me possessed of a certain nascent power. I preached, I thought, with vigor. And I was particularly gratified to note that Sunday after Sunday bold Joselyn Fields would bow her head behind the organ, nodding, rubbing her chin, meditating. This was a lady of stark determinations, an ebony will, and a forthright honesty. What she did not like, she did not pretend to like. What she liked received her nod and her attention. And if I had captured the organist with my preaching, why, then there was no one I had not captured.

Yet, curiously, she never mentioned my sermons to me when the service was done.

There came the Sunday when I chose to direct my preaching altogether to her. I mean, I looked at her where she nodded behind the organ. I sidled toward her, away from the pulpit. I smiled. I peeped overtop her organ—and behold! The woman was reading music—nodding, meditating, selecting the offertory.

Preachers can feel very lonely for want of an ear.

"Mrs. Fields," I said at the end, "what did you think of the sermon?"

She sized me with a narrow eye and decided to state an opinion. "I know preachers," she said, "who make loud noises to the Lord. Please do the same. I can't hear you."

Proverbs 10:19–22

November 9

Is God on Schedule?

We, the professional faithful, the preachers so earnest for our responsibilities, have measured the arena of God's activity by our own; and the people, glad to be led in definitions, have allowed us to noose the mighty God and to remand him to a tiny space. To a tiny space, a discrete time, and a handful of particular, prescribed exercises. Because *we* meet the people formally from the chancel and the pulpit, there it is that God most evidently meets the people. Because we must necessarily schedule our time, sometimes serving, sometimes not, it is assumed that God operates also on some sort of schedule.

Proverbs 16:1–9

November 10

Meanings or Events?

Because we make much of pious or liturgical procedure, implying some form, good form, some formula, some proper votive attitude as needful for the manifestation of God, so the people assume that there are rules and requirements governing God's good will and his appearing, and that certain people possess the rights of propitiation, while others do not—but that God is circumscribed by them nonetheless. Moreover, because our own most usual apprehension of the Deity is by a noetic labor—studying, reading, analyzing, classifying, theologizing, propounding and providing *doctrine,* teachings— because our preaching is largely teaching, explaining and instructing, so the people may assume that God is a matter of the mind (or the heart, in more emotional deliveries), but not of the whole human in all its parts. We say, of a text, "This is what it means." And we imply that God comes present in the understanding of meanings, *even though these meanings be pointing to events!* Our manner communicates more than the matter we would deliver, because it is subliminal and qualifies every word we say.   *Amos 5:8–15*

November 11
God Made Smaller

Despite what we may think, and despite the freedoms we experience in so many areas of our culture, we remain, where religion is concerned, a people of the priest. By those singled out for the office we meet and perceive our God: the meeting is a conscious desire; the perception is an unconscious shaping; the consequence, except the priest be careful, is the contraction of God.

Contraction has through the ages been an effect of the priesthood, and often a desired effect. The three strictures to place, time, and the special rites of propitiation have always bound God to temples, festivals and ceremony. Evil priests found power in controlling the All-Powerful. And frightened people were happier not bumping into an arbitrary god unawares. But even when fraud and fear were *not* the motives, people believed that the Limitless had found limits and *therefore* was approachable. The priesthood was an order within greater society: God was less than the whole; he was contracted.   *Amos 5:21–25*

November 12

God Made Abstract

The shape of preaching most shapes our God. And what is the shape of so much preaching today? Why, it is the shape of the classroom: teaching. And teaching is always (in our consideration) one step removed from experience and from the "real." It is an activity of the mind. It prepares for what will be; or it interprets what has been; it is separated from both. The God who is met in doctrines, who is apprehended in the catechesis, who is true so long as our statements *about* him are truly stated, who is communicated in propositions, premise-premise-conclusion, who leaps not from the streets, nor even from scriptural texts, but from the *interpretation* of the scriptural texts—that God is an abstract, has been abstracted from the rest of the Christian's experience.

2 Timothy 2:8–18

November 13

Manifest Power

What does the psalmist mean when he sings, "He utters his voice, the earth melts"? Or Amos: "The Lord roars from Zion, and utters his voice from Jerusalem; the pastures of the shepherds mourn, and the top of Carmel withers"? That the word of God is more than mere instruction: it has manifest power before the eyes of the people and hard against their hearts. It created. It continues to shape creation in a most palpable way. *Amos 9:11–15*

November 14

Incarnation Is Not a Concept

Or what, for heaven's sake, is the incarnation, if it doesn't announce God's personal immersion in the events—the bloody events, the insignificant and humbly common events, the physical and social and painful and peaceful and daily and epochal events of the lives of the people? In their experience! And isn't the coming of the Holy Spirit the setting free of that immersion, so that it be not restricted to any sole place, time, or people, but breathes through *all* experience and temples in *every* faithful breast?

Of course. Of course. It is not hard to argue the immanence of God. Why, it is one of our doctrines.

One of our doctrines. There's the sticking point. So long as it remains a doctrine alone, a truth to be taught, immanence itself continues an abstraction—and is not immanent. God abides not only in the church, but in the books in the church, and in the minds that explain the books, and in the intellect.

Micah 5:2–4

November 15

The Worst Curse

And one day my brother laughed at me. No discernible reason. He just laughed. But it sent me into a white fury, and I

chased him. I thought he was laughing for his superior goodness—and he was right, and that made it worse. I thought he
was laughing also for his secret knowledge of me—and I was
angry. His very righteousness enraged me. So I punched him.
I made a sharp knuckle of my middle finger and punched
him on the bony part of his shoulder. He fell like a stone,
straight down, clutching at his upper arm. And then he
cursed me with the worst curse I'd ever heard; and the power
of the curse was in its truth. He said, "Nobody likes you!" He
said, "Don't you care that nobody likes you?" He disarmed
me and broke me with that single curse. I saw the great hurt
I'd given him, and the great evil that I had become, and I
hated myself.   *Proverbs 12:15–18*

November 16

The Anti-Home

*The following ten selections form a long connected piece, the story
of Horstman. The reader is encouraged to use this story as a med-
itation on the sin of betrayal, arising from fear and guilt. Wangerin
urges us to see ourselves in his own confession of a long-past evil.*

I went to the infirmary twice that year.

The second time was for the closing of a three-inch, self-
inflicted laceration of the right forearm. There was no doubt,
that second time, why I was there. No doubt, no hesitation,
little talk, much action. Blood and worry make a certain
breed of people lean, and the nurse belied her size with a
quick precision and a dash that surprised me.

But regarding the first time I went to the infirmary: the
cause was less clear then.

I was sick, that's sure. But whether in mind or heart or body
first, I didn't know.

I needed a respite. I needed, truly, some sort of hibernation from the horrors of a boarding school I did not love and which did not love me—and something broke down in me, and I didn't argue, and I didn't try to be brave. I simply accepted the week away from everything, from classes, the dorm, the refectory, the gym, the chapel, the harrier faces of the other boys, and I slept.

[Returning to school from my home in Chicago,] I feared deeply, deeply the alienation I would feel the moment my parents drove away: the open contempt of my classmates, the loneliness which was my only refuge from contempt, and the black mood, the melancholia, the heart's paralysis—homesickness.   *Psalm 86:1–10*

November 17

Innocent

Early in the year one of my roommates sat batting a tennis ball against the wall with his racquet, an innocent pastime, I would have assumed. But the proctor appeared and on the spot laid down a law with such force I was astonished. *"Strafarbeit,* Reinking!" he cried.

It chilled me with wonder: how powerful these proctors were, how stern their measures, and how terribly careful I must be regarding the rules! I sat at my desk, staring, afraid.

"No sports in the dorm, you got that, Reinking?" demanded the proctor, a fellow with a horsy nose which he thrust forward in his anger. "And you, Reinking—you got two hours *Strafarbeit* tomorrow after classes. See me then." *Strafarbeit:* punishment work. The proctor departed.

Reinking's face was red, though his posture swaggered. "What are you lookin' at?" he snapped at me.

"Nothing," I said, dropping my eyes.

"No, nothin'," he mimicked. "You never mess up, do you? You sit at your desk like Matilda. You girl!" My roommates could make that word sound vulgar, a contemptuous length of burp: *Girl!* Reinking said, "You're not so perfect. You'll screw up. You'll get caught with your panties down, swinging racquets the same as me—see if you don't."

"I won't," I said.

"Oh, kiss off, Wangerin." Reinking dismissed me with a gesture. "Kiss off!" he said.

But my righteousness was the one thing I clung to for salvation. I said "I won't" with serious conviction. Not only did I fear the consequences of "screwing up," the disgrace and the punishment, but I also preserved my self-respect and my identity that way—in my own mind at least. I was good, please. I was good. I was innocent and good. It explained with some honor the suffering I endured in this place: Wangerin in the world, yes, he was different. No, Reinking, I would not screw up. I would maintain my righteousness, even to the heavens.

Psalm 86:11–18

November 18

Words Annihilate

But keep a passive face. The best you can do is file it for the future, when your turn will come and you've earned the right of creative cruelty—

But I thought I would never exercise that right, if ever I got so far. I would remember my hurt and my humiliation; the chain of pain would stop with me, in me. Thus the difference between me and these: I would maintain my righteousness to the heavens. I would never bruise the spirit of another human. But these! Even these, the younger students at Concordia, my classmates: were pitiless. I saw them on an autumn afternoon annihilate a man.

Albert Burns was a mild professor of Old Testament who had never learned the expedience of a passive face. But this is the treacherous, frightening fact which I learned that day: that contempt can make a man indeed contemptible. The action calls forth its own validation. Yes, in the end he was a sadly contemptible figure.

"Burns beats his wife."

While Albert Burns was writing on the chalkboard, his back to the class, George Fairchild lowered his mouth into his hands and began a low and rhythmic murmur, barely audible: "Burns beats his wife," he murmured.

The classroom jumped to the percussive rhythm. Boys were drumming their desks to the chant. It was astonishing to me how directly they looked into Burns's eyes, unflinching, unabashed, in perfect harmony with one another. Many were grinning. George Fairchild had the gift of high, etched eyebrows, skull-close hair, a totally emotionless face. Nothing in that boy. Nothing. Neither remorse nor delight. He was not smiling. He looked indifferent, rather—and I feared him.

Burns walked toward the back of the classroom. I watched him come. He sat on the piano bench behind me, laid his left arm on the keyboard, bowed his head, and wept. The tears soaked into the thick hair of his forearm.

Burns beats his wife!

He was annihilated, brought to nothing. And all by the words of my classmates.   *Psalm 102:1–8*

November 19

Horstman

Returning to boarding school after a vacation, Wangerin collapses into the infirmary for a three-day sleep.

There was a boy beside my bed, sitting on a chair and staring at me.

"You're awake," he said, clasping his hands. "Good! Do you know how long you've been out? Oh, a long time, a long time. You'd be surprised at how long you've been sleeping!" Even so quickly did the boy's face shake off guilt. Now it was full of tics and wiggles, animation: it was difficult to read which mood was there, since one followed so quickly upon the other, a frown, dismay, a knowing grin. The boy had a larval face, squirming, bedroom-pale with stark black brows. "I guess you're sick, hey? *Honk! Honk!* Not dodging classes, faking it. No one could fake sleep that long—unless you're a marathon faker. *Honk!* Like the man of a thousand faces. Did you see that movie with Lon Chaney? You talk in your sleep, you know that? Listen, you want some tea?"

Tea? What? Who drinks tea?

I must have frowned.

"No, that's okay. I can make it," said the boy, his face a quilt of apologies, solicitation, pride. "I've got my own electric pot and teabags and cups. You want some tea? It's no trouble, really. You want some? I'll make you some."

He hopped up from the chair and bustled to the bedstand next to mine. He lifted a little pot on high, hanging with a rat's tail cord. He winked. "Water," he explained, and bustled from the ward.

That boy had said something that stuck in my brain, bothering me. What did he say? A menacing thing. It made me feel vulnerable. It made me want to talk with him some more, to question him—

Oh! He said I talked in my sleep! No, I didn't like that, because what was I revealing to someone I didn't know? And it caused a distressful sense of intimacy with this boy, to think that he had heard my dreams, that he had crept into my sleep. I didn't want to be close to anyone at school. I didn't like that.

Psalm 102:9–17

November 20

Horstman Gets Close

"You want me to plump your pillow?" he said behind me, and then, to my amazement, he reached right over my head with his left arm—so close that I could smell hair tonic—and began to squeeze my pillow between his hands.

This caused a storm of feelings inside me. "Don't!" I cried, shrinking from him. "Don't do that!" Spitting around the thermometer.

"What?" said Horstman, his voice suddenly so tiny that I looked at him. His face, too, was tiny. He was pinched right down to a miserable blister. He had snatched his hands behind his back.

I must have shouted at him. In spite of myself, I felt sorry to be cruel to Horstman.

Daniel *Horstman!* Yes! I remembered him!

Several weeks into the fall term there had been a banquet in the refectory, a gathering of students, all strangers in dark suits. There was beef and potatoes and corn, labored, rhetorical speeches—all of it heavy, oppressive to me. I, too, wore a suit and a choking tie. Someone had played the piano during the meal. He played a long, dramatic piece which descended from sweetness to declarative force, then rose to a lush and nearly impossible sweetness again. I had paid attention to that music. I let it make a space for me in the refectory, and I marveled that one so young could play with such dexterity, that he could play all by himself in the corner of the room while no one, apparently, listened, while everyone was talking and eating. That musician had been Daniel Horstman.

"You want a cup of my tea, Wally?" He looked at me, such naked appeal breaking his face that I turned my eyes aside, to the wall, to the singing teapot.

"That'll be fine," I said.

"Orange Pekoe?" he said so tentatively—as though Orange Pekoe might be another mistake—that I couldn't tell him I had no idea what Orange Pekoe meant.

I said, "What was the music you played at the banquet in September? What kind of music was that?"

The boy burst with a radiant light. "See? See? I told you most of the guys know me."

He handed me a cup on its saucer. "Rachmaninoff," he said politely.

"What?"

"Rachmaninoff's Rhapsody on a Theme by Paganini. That's what I played at the banquet." *Psalm 102:18–28*

November 21

Watch It, Wangerin

Reinking came to see me in the infirmary. I was shocked. I hadn't even imagined my roommates noticed my absence. That one of them should actually visit me was a charity so unexpected that it flustered me. I blushed and couldn't speak well.

"What," I stuttered. "What are you doing here?"

"Brought you assignments," said Reinking, sizing up the room, the ward. "Somebody had to. Professors are saying, 'Where's Wangerin?' We're saying, 'Who knows? He don't tell us where he goes.'"

In that instant I loved Bob Reinking—or felt something approaching love, though this athlete, this tennis player with his bowlegs and rolling shoulders would snort and drop to locker-room language if he had the least idea what I felt.

"How can you sleep," hissed Reinking, "with that fairy next to you? I'd watch it, Wangerin. I'd keep a careful eye on those greasy hands if I were you," he said, shifting weight from foot to foot.

My stomach constricted at Reinking's opinion. My face strove for slackness, the passive, noncommittal expression, cool unconcern. "Oh yeah?"

"Oh yeah," said Reinking on the balls of his feet. "Why do you think he stays up here all the time?"

"I don't know." Oh no! Guilt by association. But I really am sick, Reinking.

"I don't know either. All I know is, his roommates don't want him flitting round *their* room in the night. I think," leered Reinking, "they make life difficult for him. Ha, ha! I've seen him sit with that stone face on his bed two hours at a time. Ha, ha! Poor Danny Horstman. We don't do you like that, do we, Wangerin?"

By the time Bob Reinking departed, my feelings of gratitude had turned to water and fear. *Psalm 107:1–9*

November 22

Appeal

Then Horstman returned to the room and sat on the side of his bed, staring at me—the same, I thought, as he must have stared while I was sleeping. It unnerved me. I pretended to be reading. But my ears were hot.

"Aren't you going to talk to me?" said Horstman coldly, staring at me.

"Well," I said. "I'm reading now, you see—"

"Wally! *Wally! Wally!*" he shrieked.

This jolted me. This was a purely anguished wail. Horstman had actually clasped his hands before his breast in a begging gesture, and his face was swarming with tics of appeal. He stunned me, so blatant was the pleading.

"Wally, talk to me!" he cried. "I'm on an all-campus blackout. I am! I know I am! And what was Reinking doing here? He told you to black me out too. Talk to me!"

Daniel Horstman was suffering—so undisguised a suffering that it frightened me. The reality might have been exaggerated, but not the feeling. This was no hypocrisy. This was uncontrol.

"I don't," I whispered, "I don't know what blackout means."

"Silence!" he cried, jumping up and beginning to pace the middle of the room. "Nobody will talk to me. But I had to do what I had to do. Wally, you're sensitive, you're good. You can see that?"

"Dan, I don't know what you did."

· "You don't?" he roared almost angrily, lifting his lip with suspicion. "Then you're the only one."

"I promise you, I don't. I don't know what you're talking about."

He stared at me a while, then dropped his face into his hands. Long fingers. Trembling fingers, and white. He took a deep breath, then threw himself to pacing again and poured forth his miserable story.   *Psalm 107:10–16*

November 23

I Am Not Like You

Horstman tells how he has turned in another student for gross sexual misconduct, in which he had refused to participate. After the student's dismissal, Horstman is ostracized.

Poor, pitiful Daniel Horstman. Behold: I was larger than someone else on campus. Someone was according me a sort of stature.

For the rest of that day, Horstman and I talked. Horstman did most of the talking. He distressed me more than he knew by describing his roommates' abuse of him, distressed me because I feared the same for myself—had, in fact, suffered some of the same and hated the reminder. He chattered passionately about his interests, his music, his home where he lived alone with his mother (for whom I felt compassion, wondering whether she knew the reputation her son had on campus—then that made me think of my own mother, and that too distressed me) because his father had died. His hands flew when he talked. He seemed miles past misery, exhilarated, breathless, bursting with goodwill toward me. I kept a wary physical distance. But I did not discourage the talk. Poor, pitiful Daniel Horstman.

I said, "I don't want to go back"—and instantly regretted saying anything.

Horstman pulled a long and knowing face, as though to say, *I understand,* and, *We two suffer the Philistines together.*

No! We do not suffer together. No, we are different, you and I. I am not like you.

In that same moment Nurse Tillie Pfund pumped into the ward, followed by a student.

"Well," she said. "Here's three of you together, and all from the same class. I approve, what? It helps to keep each other company."

When she left, the student undressed, gazing at the both of us—at Horstman and me—from underneath high, etched eyebrows, from a totally emotionless face. He took a bed opposite and slid between the sheets in shorts. No pajamas. He gazed at us with a sort of effrontery. George Fairchild.

"We were just saying," said Horstman, ticcing geniality all over his face, "how Wally is nervous about going back to his dorm room—"

Oh! My face blazed. From that instant onward I despised Daniel Horstman. I was appalled by his flat stupidity, his outrageous presumption, his destruction of all I had labored for—and I hated him. I would not say another word to him.

And I didn't. I turned my back to him.   *Psalm 107:17–22*

November 24

Please, Wally, Talk to Me!

I heard the whistling breath at my left ear. I felt body warmth. Someone was staring at me in my sleep. Someone had his face bare inches from mine.

I opened my eyes. A wintry moonlight cast shadows over everything in the ward; the moonlight on snow is a luminance. I could see Horstman beside me, kneeling at the bedside, staring. His eyes were mica.

"Wally," he whispered. "You awake?"

I looked at him, then turned away.

"Wally, please," he hissed. "Don't black me out. Please. Talk to me."

I said nothing. His breath was sour. His heat was like disease.

"Wally, whatever I did, I'm sorry. What did I do? I'll play the rhapsody for you. Is it Fairchild? We don't have to talk in front of Fairchild. And we can go off campus when we're out of here."

I said nothing. Daniel Horstman seemed incapable of not being intimate. This was horrendous language to use, perilous in a boys' school—like making dates. I set my face like flint.

"Wally," Horstman hissed directly in my ear. "For Jesus' sake! Please, please, please, please, Wally, talk to me!"

He put his hand on my shoulder then, and I rose up in revulsion, the blankets sliding off me. In deep shadow across the room I saw the face of Fairchild, sitting up in bed and watching us, his cold eyes sunk in two black holes—and a horror shot through me.

"Kiss off, Horstman!" I cried out loud. I pushed him. He stumbled backward and fell to the floor. I shouted with a shaking passion: "Just kiss off! You hear me?"   *Psalm 107:23–32*

November 25

Wangerin, the Outcast's Nemesis

Released from the infirmary, Wangerin covers his rule-breaking ball-throwing by deliberately cutting his arm on a broken window.

By the time we found Tillie Pfund, the T-shirt was soaked, bright as a red bandanna. And I was humiliated to be returning so soon—the second time that year, the same day I had left the place.

"I thought I discharged you," said Tillie Pfund. Then she saw the bleeding and she said no more. She became lean with efficiency and speed.

"Oh!" she murmured when she had unwrapped the T-shirt.

I had done that too—that cut. She said, "Oh," and I was mortified by shame.

But it is required that I record the entire truth—and this story is not true until it's done. One more emotion seized me in that day.

While Tillie Pfund was cleaning the wound, bent close (since I was too embarrassed to tell her she'd find no slivers of glass in there), George Fairchild came and leaned against the doorjamb of the examination room. He watched for a dead five minutes, his lifted eyebrows, his drooping lids, his cold, emotionless face. I spent that five minutes feeling as though I sat on a toilet under scrutiny. I blinked furiously.

But then Fairchild folded his arms across his chest and spoke.

"I guess you know you did it to him, Wangerin," he said.

I didn't understand.

"You did it right and tight," he said. "Danny boy took his teapot. Know what that means?"

I didn't.

"He left," said Fairchild, as impassive as the sky.

"Without permission," Tillie Pfund said to my arm. "Lads are growing too big for their breeches these days."

"I'd say he took off," said Fairchild. "I'd say Horstman's sneaking home this minute. What do you think, Wangerin? You should know," he said. "You are the nemesis of Daniel Horstman, erstwhile student of Concordia."

All at once I felt a rush of a new blood in my face.

Whether or not George Fairchild had the gift of reading human nature, this is the emotion such high talk caused in me: pride. A swelling pride that seemed more healing than medicines. I sat the straighter under Tillie's ministrations. I closed my right hand into a fist, expanding the forearm muscle so that my wound split wide like a red mouth smiling.

For this was the first time Fairchild had ever chosen to speak to me directly. And oh!—with how exalted a language had he acknowledged me! *Psalm 107:33–43*

November 26

The Power of Story

Once, for some little sin, my mother commanded me to sit on a straight-backed wooden chair till she should return and release me. I was left alone in a sunlit room, in a strange house. But there was a picture book beside me. I read it to while the time away. A dangerous diversion!

In the book a boy (no older than I) was eating a Thanksgiving dinner most thanklessly. Nasty, gluttonous kid, he stuffed himself with stuffing, yams and candied apples, crammed himself with gravies and sauces and turkey, no thought for the other guests. Oh, people warned him against such greed, but this was a selfish and sinful kid (whose mother should have sat him on a straight-backed chair!), and he ignored them. He gobbled and swallowed and wolfed and gorged himself—and he swelled. I saw it. His eyeballs protruded. His ears stuck out. His belt snapped. People took fright, but not the boy. When he had grown as round as a globe, he forced down pumpkin pies, and having stretched past natural limits, he burst, exploding Thanksgiving all over the room.

Which room? My own sun-flooded room! When I was done with the story, I was sweating, panting and rubbing my belly; for I had experienced both greed and its consequences, the popping of my personal, precious, immoderate gut.

This is the power of story. My critical reason knows that a picture book is just a picture book (and a movie's a movie, and TV is just TV); my reason remembers the exploding boy as a fiction. But my imagination absorbed the experience; my character keeps it as a genuine event of my childhood; and my irrational flesh is still afraid of overeating because my dumb stomach has still a real horror of bursting.

But "we won't be influenced by what we read," says the mass of America. "We're too intelligent." And I respond: not if we haven't trained that fine intelligence. The freedom to watch, taste, read *anything* lays on each of us the grave responsibility to be critics with conscious standards: What is the good, why is it good, how does this good track back to God? *Proverbs 8:32–36*

November 27

Humility and Reverence

It's cold. The ground is frozen now. A light snow has dusted it, which shall be some moisture if the weather relents and lets it melt before it simply evaporates. It's winter, now, after a terrible season of heat and drought. Scientists surmise that we ourselves may be responsible for the enmity of the weather, that we have unbalanced its delicate, interdependent elements, the ordered exchange of energies. They suggest that headlong technology creates a waste, which the environment cannot process.

I am no scientist. I attend to the spirit of the people rather more than to their engineering skills, mechanical expertise. I weigh and evaluate the spirit rather better than I can empirical phenomena.

Nevertheless, to the scientist, sadly I say, "Yes. It is possible." Possible, and given the power, it is likely. The spirit of this race is fully capable of the sin that does not love its own environment, but makes of itself a god to be satisfied, and makes of the earth a sacrifice the gods devour. The spirit of this race is well able to justify the slaughter—first because it doesn't confess that the earth is alive, so there was no slaughter in the first place; second because it has made a morality of its economics, has made of its money a *summum bonum,* and is more concerned for the healthy flow of cash than the healthy, regenerative flow of rivers and streams.

The race, did I say? No, not all of the race. Those presently in power, perhaps; but not everyone lacks humility and reverence. Therein is hope. *Ecclesiastes 3:9–22*

November 28

The Frozen Heart

Elisabeth, mourning her mother, is kidnapped by the Water-Troll, who wants to comfort her, but is wounded in his attempt.

Ahhh. Soon in her soul the child is saying, *Ahhh. Of course.* She's remembering the stories they tell by firelight: *This is the Water-Troll!*

While she watches the suffering beast, Elisabeth's soul is flooded with understanding: this one answers the water of tears. Yes. This one listens to the talk of all waters. He rises like mist in the night. Yes, yes! He can leak through a double-locked door, he can leak into a troubled heart, he can melt a frozen heart in pity. Of course the water drips around them. This well is the source of all of the water of Dorf—and this one is the Water-Troll.

Little Elisabeth leans over the Troll and begins to cry. She is crying because of his pain—the first such tears she's wept since her mother's death turned all her tears to bitterness.

One by one the tears splash on the Water-Troll. They startle him, and his green eyes open.

"What, child?" he growls. He raises a claw. "Art thou still crying? But I wanted to dry thy tears. Ohhh, pretty Beth," he sighs. "I did not want thee sad. I wanted to tell thee, this life is lovelier than bad. I wanted to say, 'One someone loves thee, Beth, and does not lie.'" The great Troll closes his eyes and groans. "But what hath ugliness done for thee? Why, nothing but frighten thee, and what is the good of that? Begone, my Queenling," he groans. "Go home. Forgive a Troll and forget him. Go."

But the little Queenling neither leaves nor moves. Instead, she smiles. Through the rain of her tears she smiles as though the sun were shining. And that which happens next in the well they never tell by firelight:

> *"Oh, Troll," she says; and on his chest*
> *She lays her head as if to rest.*
> *Indeed, he is the ugliest,*
> *But he needs comforting.*
> *So Beth begins to sing.*
> *For him she sings, "Alack-a-day,"*
> *For him a pretty roundelay*
> *To take the pain away:*
> *"Alas, and lack the day—"*

Psalm 138:1–8

November 29

The End Time

After this I looked, and behold! a great multitude which no man could number, people from every nation, tribe and tongue standing before the throne and the Lamb, crying aloud: "Salvation belongs to our God, who sits upon the throne, and to the Lamb!"

An elder said to me, "Who are these, clothed in white robes, and whence have they come?"

I said, "Sir, you know."

And he said to me, "These are the people who have come out of the great tribulation. They have washed their robes and made them white in the blood of the Lamb. Therefore they are before the throne of God, serving him day and night within his Temple. And he who sits upon the throne will cover them with his presence. They shall nevermore hunger, nor thirst any more; the sun shall not strike them nor any scorching heat. For the Lamb will be their shepherd, to guide them to springs of living water; and God, even God himself, will wipe away every tear from their eyes."   *Revelation 7:9–17*

November 30

Wally's Plan for Judgment Day

On the other hand, when I was a child of ten or eleven years old, I was terrified by admonitions of the Judgment Day.

Generally it was late autumn or early winter when the pastor bethought himself to warn the world of flames and the falling stars, black suns and bloody moons, quakes, and the ruptures of tombs. Sin, it seemed, caused certain people to despair in the face of such disaster, and sin it was that caused the jaws of Hell to gape for them. *Jaws of Hell!* I saw those jaws, though the beast to which they were attached was too imposing even for my imagination; it filled the rest of creation, so far as I was concerned. And seeing that I harbored in me something very like despair in the face of such disasters, then I was a sinner—no doubt. Those jaws, with fangs like the columns in our church and drool like the rush of a flood, were open for me. The throat was backed by a purple curtain, a Byzantine reredos of marvelous complication, and a stone altar for a tongue. The throat of the Jaws of Hell looked exactly like the chancel of our church. I was destined to enter there. But by God, I was not, if I could help it, *going* to enter there. I had a plan.

Before the Son of Man transfigured this chancel into the yawning mouth of Hell, two jaws gaping for me particularly, *I would see him coming!*

Therefore, I always sat by a clear patch in our stained-glass windows, and I peered perpetually to the east. The instant I saw the corner of one cloud touch ground, whether shaped like a wheel or shaped like a throne or shaped like the prow of a boat, *bang!* I was going under the pew!

Then, while mighty footsteps of the Son of Man gave lurch to the earth and shook the foundations of our own church, *whizz!* I would slip straight backward under six pews, break for the basement door, and shut myself in the boiler room.

Obviously, the Son of Man shall concern himself with weightier, more majesterial matters than boiler rooms and boys—at least at the beginning of his manifest reign. He had kings to deal with, presidents, and schoolteachers. Now, I didn't fool myself into thinking that he would never get around to me. As great as my terror was for Hell, even so great must my sinship be. Such sinners the Lord would have listed somewhere.

But consider: millions, billions, trillions! Get it? By the time I peeped out from my dank hiding place, why, I'd be lost in the crowd. I wasn't coming out till I felt the rumble of nations outside, till I heard the myriad cacophony of seven foreign languages at least. I'd stretch the wait with sacred patience. But when I did come out, how much land do you suppose a trillion people covers? Shoulder to shoulder, I think they'd carpet the state of Texas, and not a blade of grass show through. Now, where do you think the Son of Man is going to stand to see all those folks? Well, high up, is my guess. Very high up. I expect he'd be sitting somewhere near the sun. *Distant,* wouldn't you say? Olympian. Unapproachable. Exalted "on high."

No, he wasn't going to notice a boy of lightning reflexes and slippery strategies. No, he wouldn't miss one sinner. No: if I couldn't see his face in the uttermost remoteness of his glory, neither would he see mine. No, I was not going to be swallowed by the Jaws of Hell, whose tongue was a stone in the shape of a casket. *Ezekiel 43:1–9*

December

December 1

Waiting for a Friend to Arrive

I had a dream. It was a simple dream, more feeling than detail, but it seemed to last a long while.

Simply, a friend of mine was coming to see me, and I was excited by the prospect. I didn't know who the friend was. That didn't seem odd. I suppose I didn't occupy myself with the question *Who*. Just with the anticipation, and with the certainty that he would come.

As the time for his arrival drew near and nearer, my excitement increased. I felt more and more like a child, beaming with my pleasure, distracted from all other pursuits, thinking of this one thing only. I found that laughter fell from me as easy as rain. I wanted to stand on the porch and bellow to the neighborhood, *My friend is coming!* Joy became a sort of swelling in my chest, and all my flesh began to tingle.

A wild kind of music attended my waiting. And the closer he came, the more exquisite grew this music—high violins rising higher by the sweetest, tightest, most piercing dissonance, reaching for, weeping for, the final resolve of his appearing.

And when the music had ascended to nearly impossible chords of wailing little notes; and when the familiar scent was a bounty around me; and when excitement had squeezed the breath from my lungs, I started to cry.

And he came.

Then I put my hands to my cheeks and cried and laughed at once.

He was looking directly at me, with mortal affection—and I grew so strong within his gaze. And I knew at once who he was. I was a perfect flame of the knowledge of his name. It was Jesus. He had come exactly as he said he would.

I cherish this dream and think of it often. I was a man full grown when I dreamt it. *Isaiah 9:1, 2*

December 2

In the Beginning

This is Wangerin's paraphrase, for children, of John 1:1–18.

In the beginning was the Word,
and the Word was with God,
and the Word was God.
He was with God at the beginning of things.

All things were made through him,
not one thing made which he did not make!
Life itself was in him,
and this life was the light of men,
and this light still shines in the darkness,
for the darkness has not overcome it!

He was in the world,
the world that was made through him,
yet the world refused to know him.
He came to his own,
yet his people refused to receive him.

But to those who received him,
to those who believed in his name,
he gave power to make them the children of God!
So these children were born not of blood;
not of the will of the flesh were they born,
nor yet of a human will
but of God!

And the Word became flesh
and he dwelt among us,

blazing with grace and truth!
And we saw his glory,
the Son in his glory,
the singular Son of the Father,
whose fullness has given us
grace upon grace upon grace!

For Torah was a gift through Moses,
but true grace came through Jesus Christ.
For no one has ever seen God:
The only Son,
who leans on the breast of the Father,
he has made him known. . . .

John 1:1–18

December 3

Incarnation

The incarnation certainly does not mean that God dwelt in the world as a hookworm in a hog—that is, in, but apart from; in, but different from; in, but not *of* created existence nor of the sin that had disfigured it. No, that were a lesser miracle, being the lesser sacrifice, and somewhat parasitical. Other gods, the false gods, came only to be fed and to be praised. This God, at the incarnation, came to feed and to serve. This God, born of a woman, accepted for himself all the conditions of this existence. He was not just in the flesh; he *was* flesh. No foreign matter, he, but matter itself. No *seeming* human, as the Docetists taught; but human, *doulos* to all that jerks us left and right, and obedient even unto the starkest and most signal change, the Change Progenitor, the one that causes terror in every other change we suffer, to which all other changes tend: death.

The world is forever a flowing thing. Until the end of it, when the trumpet shall shock it still, all our lives and our experience are borne upon this flux. It is the unspeakable love of God that he comes to meet us *in the very terms* of this world.   *Matthew 1:22, 23*

December 4
A Victory for All

Most of the sweet, victorious tales in this world are fairy tales. In them the child is allowed to imagine evil overcome.

But there is one tale which is no one's imagination, which is true and therefore very powerful: the story of Jesus. Here we do not say to the child, "Imagine." We say, "Believe!" We do not pretend that a little girl had a fairy godmother to help her. Rather, we announce in fact that a real child has a real God to help and to love her.

You, my child, there is a victory for you!

The story of Jesus. It is a beautiful tale, a terrible tale, and then again a tale more beautiful than any other. For, that God should come to love is beautiful. That he should fight the devil, suffer the hatred of a sinful world, and die—these things are too true (as children know) and terrible. But wait! That he should rise to life again, triumphant over evil, and that he should wish to share the triumph with his children is the most beautiful news of all.

There is a victory for all of us.   *Isaiah 9:5, 6*

December 5

Giving Birth

There are two kinds of suffering which attend the physical bearing of children into this world. The first is that a woman must make space in her body for a baby; and doing that, she sacrifices a host of personal goods: her shape, hormonal equilibrium, energy, her freedom to sleep in any position, beauty (so she sometimes feels) and, with these, her self-esteem.

Did I call such sacrifice a suffering? Well, it is, I suppose.

Then, the second suffering of bearing children is the opposite of the first. Having made space for the baby, she must now empty the space. It does not matter how much she has invested in carrying the child. At the end of nine months she's asked to give it up, to separate herself from it, to deliver it whole and squalling into existence. "Go out of me," her muscles say, her womb, her leaning forward, her very self says to the infant: "Go out of me, in order to *be*."

And this is suffering. (The work is so hard.) Yet this also contains the sharp spasm of joy. (Here is life!) And I am astonished that two such things can be together.

Romans 8:22–25

December 6

The Little Adam

So the baby is born. Straightway he's a little Adam relating to nature, breathing in the air the plants breathed out. Nature feeds him and keeps him whom God commissions one day to "dress and till and keep" her in return. Little Adam, little farmer, little scientist, surgeon, something.

The baby is born, a tiny Eve now brought into relationship with another human being, receiving the hugs of her mother, bone of her bone, flesh of her flesh. Immediately there is the benefit of community, parental first, social thereafter. Adam and Eve each need the other as deeply as people and plants do, helpers "fit" for one another, folks who find themselves in the faces of the other. This *is* life: relationship.

The baby, I say, with a shock is born—and by the sudden distress of relationships does, to some degree, experience his being, feel his life and his self.

My son flew out of his mother. Or so it seemed to me. He flew out and up and over her, then dropped to her bosom; and all this terrified him, and it filled me with a fear on his behalf.

The baby slipped into the doctor's hands, blue, smeared, glistening, its fat face mashed shut. Immediately the nurses raised it up in a sweeping circle over its mother, aspirating the nose and mouth so swiftly, so skillfully, holding the child face upward, aloft—

"A boy!"   *Genesis 4:1–3*

December 7

Falling into Birth

And there, right there, just as they lowered him to Thanne's bosom, I saw the fright, and deep in my father's bowels I understood.

His fat eyes popped open. He sucked air. He threw out his tiny arms as if to catch himself. *He was falling!*—he who had never fallen before. I gasped. All the relationships were changing so radically that it must have seemed for a moment that there were none, that he, at the moment of birth, was dying!

For until this instant his life was experienced in such close relationship to another that he had only to move to feel it, feel the walls of the womb that embraced him. And all sound must have been muffled by those walls, except the ordering, comforting beat of the heart-drum above. And the temperature had been temperate, and light was softened, and motion was rather like rocking.

All at once his body is assaulted. He discovers his nostrils by the jabbing in them. He feels chill wind on his skin. The light crashes his eyes. The sounds are hard and foreign—*and he's falling!*   *Psalm 31:1, 2*

December 8

Freedom?

The sinful world celebrates self above all other things (since self is the final judge of goodness, the recipient of every "good" thing). Likewise, it puts the love of the self above all other loves. It reverses the necessary order of creation and holiness by saying: "*First* I must love my self before I can love anyone else." It acts like God, living and loving in a solitude. Other kinds of loving become the choices of the self, only so long as the self considers itself served by them; for no other loving, no other relationship is seen as necessary for life. The only code this self obeys is that which proceeds from and preserves its self, that which fulfills and enlarges the self. A perfect independence, a complete self-sufficiency—*I need no one but me*—is considered the highest sort of freedom.

And there is the wretched deception: one so "free" is merely one alone. Beginning and ending with the self isn't life at all, but isolation. Which is death.   *Psalm 22:9–11*

December 9

Gifts

We call the giving of gifts and the volunteering of yourself to your spouse a task, the sixth task of marriage, something that must be done. And we're right to do so.

But it's a paradoxical task. From the receiver's point of view, from your spouse's point of view, the value of a gift is exactly this, that it *didn't* have to come. You didn't *have* to give it. Nothing forced you; you did it of your own free will. It was not expected. In fact, a gift is always more than could have been expected. This gratuitous element of the act is its very nature and its virtue for the marriage. Nothing more genuinely gives *you* to your spouse than the gift no law commanded, but which your free will chose to give.

Ruth 4:13–17

December 10

True Gift-Giving

And then there are two memories, side by side:

I am standing at the kitchen door, holding the publisher's letter that promises to print my book. You've just stopped me to ask an earnest question. Your face is upturned, your eyes dead on mine. "Wally," you say, touching the letter, meaning the book, "this isn't going to come between us, is it?" I am surprised by the intensity of the question and deny that anything should come between us. "Well," you say, not fully convinced, not wholly persuaded by this occupation of mine, "you're an author now." Did you have second thoughts about my desire to write?

Well, but the second memory is of the interior of our house when I happen to be home, once, and you are not. You've rearranged the furniture, and I stand gazing at the change you've made. I'm shaking my head. I'm shaking my head over you, astonished by your kindness. This house has two bedrooms; one is the children's, one is ours, and these are the only two rooms with doors and privacy. But here, in what used to be the sitting room, is all our bedroom furniture— and what used to be our bedroom has become a study, in which I am invited to write. Thanne! You've given up your bedroom. How can I answer that kind of love? I can't. I can only bow my head and stand in its light. And write.

Ephesians 4:21–33

December 11

How to Tell the Christmas Story, I

Tell this story in a generous voice. Hush your voices, men, when you enter its passages; and women, almost whisper. When you speak of loving, seem to love. Describing sorrow, be sad. Let fear come through a harried voice, and gladness come with laughter, and triumph sound like exultation.

Half of the life of the story is the story's teller. Your voice and face and body give it form. It is you whom the children hear and see. They will not distinguish. It is you who will love or not, and so the story will or will not love.

Touch the child, sir, when you tell it. Ma'am, tell it to children. If you do not tell it at all, it isn't. It doesn't exist for them. Then tell it. Do not neglect it, but tell it.   *Luke 1:1–4*

December 12

A New Thing

Once upon a time the world was dark, and the land where the people lived was deep in darkness. It was as dark as the night in the daytime. It had been dark for so long that the people had forgotten what the light was like. This is what they did: they lit small candles for themselves and pretended it was day. But the world was a gloomy place, and the people who walked in darkness were lonelier than they knew, and the lonely people were sadder than they could say.

But God was in love with the world.

God looked down from heaven and saw that the earth was stuck, like a clock, at midnight. "No," he said. "This isn't good. It's time to make time tick again. Time, time," said the mighty God, "to turn the earth from night to morning."

And God was in love with the people especially.

He saw their little candlelight, and he pitied their pretending. "They think they see," he said, "but all they see is shadow, and people are frightened by shadows. Poor people!" he said. "They wonder why they are afraid." God watched the people move about like fireflies in the night, and he shook his head. "Poor people, pretending to be happy," he said. "Well, I want them to be happy. It's time," declared the Lord our God. "It's time to do a new thing!   *Malachi 3:1–5*

December 13

How to Tell the Christmas Story, II

Parents, if you haven't already told your children the story, who has? What sort of Gabriel brought it to them? Don't you know that the teller shapes the tale?

Grandparents, are you satisfied to let mumbling Rumor garble this marvelous story for your grandchildren? Should they piece it together themselves, from Christmas carols and that dead set, that mercenary invasion, that box of empty sentiment and silliness, the television? "The true meaning of Christmas"—indeed!

Fathers, make a holy time in which nothing distracts you and nothing delights your children except this story. Mothers, prepare a holy space in a corner of your home. Time and space will prove the story important. Grandma, Grandpa, present a holy attitude. You reach to an ancient bedrock for this story. Both the age in your face and the love in your eye will convince the child of that, and of its truth.

Then tell the story whole, beginning to end, all of a piece, and seamless.

Say, "Child, I want to tell you a story beautiful and true. It actually happened; it happened for you."

Say, "Once upon a time, the angel Gabriel was sent from God—"   *Mark 1:1–3*

December 14

Gabriel Comes

So there was an angel flying through the night. So swiftly he flew that nobody noticed. Across the continents the angel went, to a particular province named Galilee, to a city named Nazareth, and then in that city to one particular house, to one particular woman sleeping in that house. Her name was Mary. She was young and blameless and lovely in her bed, as innocent as the lily. Her lashes were long and black. She was a virgin, but she dreamed of a man named Joseph, because they were betrothed and would marry in four months' time. She was smiling in her sleep.

The angel Gabriel appeared at Mary's bedside and began to grow bright.

Light beamed in her bedroom. So Mary frowned a little. She turned in her sleep and she sighed.

Brighter and brighter grew the angel, until he blazed like the sun.

"Hail," he said.

But the angel's voice was like thunder.

Poor Mary awoke with a terrible start. Her eyes flew open, and she saw the brilliant light beside her, and she heard the glorious greeting in her ears, and she caught her breath, did Mary, because she was afraid— *Luke 1:26–28*

December 15

How to Tell the Christmas Story, III

Do you see? Do you see? The reason why the story must be told by a human mouth to human ears with human faith and affection is that a story is always more than information that some poor kid must labor to understand. A story is a world, my dears, both radiant and real—a world into which the child is invited, and she enters.

And it is the telling of the tale that causes this world to be.

The telling encourages the child to believe its being.

The telling calls her into it so that she more than knows: she actually experiences.

In the instant that the child imagines the light that Mary sees, and cares for Mary, and fears with her—in that same instant your child has departed this veiled existence and entered the world where God is unveiled, bright and present and active and loving. And which of these worlds is real? Why, both. But the latter gives meaning to the former. The latter is revelation.

The child must be enchanted.

And the story must continue to be told.

Continue, then, in a husky human voice—   *John 1:1–5*

December 16

Listening to the Angel

When the angel said "Hail" in the middle of the night, like bright explosions in her bedroom, poor Mary jumped and covered her mouth and could not talk, because she was afraid.

God in heaven whispered, "Hurry, Gabriel. Comfort the woman."

So the angel said, "Hush, Mary." The angel softened his glorious voice and murmured like rain in the night, "Mary, hush. The dear God loves you, don't you know? God favors you, and the Lord is with you."

God favors me? Mary was trembling. Her mind was racing in the unnatural light. This greeting of the angel troubled her. *What does it mean? What is he saying?* she thought. *Why would an angel come to me?*

"Mary, do not be afraid," said the angel, still more gently—and the light grew warmer than bright, and it touched her, just on the forehead, with a single beam of kindness. So Mary grew calmer; her mind grew quiet; and she began to listen.

Luke 1:29–30

December 17

A Song for the Telling

"Behold," said the angel, "you will conceive in your womb and bring forth a son, and you shall call his name Jesus."

A baby? thought Mary. *A baby?*

"Quickly, Gabriel," said God in heaven. "Tell her quickly what this means."

And quickly the angel did a comely thing: he stopped speaking, and he started to sing. So marvelous was the meaning of this baby, that it wanted a song for the telling.

"Mary," sang the angel:

> *Mary, the child of thy labor shall be great;*
> *The Son of the Most High shall he be called;*
> *And God shall give him the throne of his father David;*
> *Over the house of Jacob shall he reign*
> *Forever and ever: his kingdom shall have no end.*

A baby? thought Mary in spite of the music. How dear was the promise. How deeply she longed for it. But there was a problem she couldn't ignore. Desire was troubled by that problem, and Mary astonished herself. She actually spoke to the angel.

"How can this be?" she blurted—and the angel stopped singing, and God in heaven began to smile.

Well, maybe the angel didn't understand the nature of human bodies. Some things had to happen first for other things to happen second. "How can this be?" said Mary meekly on her bed. "I'm not married, you see. I don't have a husband yet."

That was the problem. Not the greatness of the baby, not his kingship, nor that the kingdom would last forever—but that the baby needed, first, a father.

There came a strange sound in Mary's bedroom then, like the creaking of the walls, or the cracking of the universe. It was an angel chuckling. For the thing that he was telling Mary was a miracle, after all. *Luke 1:31–34*

December 18

Laughter for Joy

"With God," the angel assured her, "nothing will be impossible."

So Mary, kneeling on her bed; Mary, bowing as lovely as the lily, whispered, "Behold—" Deep, deep inside her stomach she felt the giggles coming. "Behold," she said, "I am the handmaid of the Lord. Be it unto me according to your word—"

Which word was: Mary is going to have a baby! Yes!

So the angel was done, and he dimmed. The bright light faded from her bedroom. Gabriel vanished altogether. But Mary didn't mind the darkness now.

A baby!

Oh, she jumped from her bed, and the giggles tickled her throat. Oh, she clapped her hands and twirled about, and her dark hair flew like a glory around her head. Oh, the virgin was laughing now, for the virgin was going to have a baby!

So now there was a blameless, beautiful woman running through the world, the dark world, as fast as she could go to her friend, her cousin Elizabeth.

And just as the angel had sung his celestial song for her, she sang a song for Elizabeth.

"My soul," sang Mary, "O cousin, my soul doth magnify the Lord. My spirit rejoiceth in God my Savior. He is keeping his promises to us. Elizabeth! I'm going to have a baby!"

So then—in the middle of the gloomy world there were two women laughing. They laughed till they couldn't laugh any more, and then they began to weep for gladness.

And God looked down from heaven and saw them. And the Lord God smiled.   *Luke 1:35–38*

December 19

How to Tell the Christmas Story, IV

This, good parents, is the reason why you are telling your child the story, why you are weaving its marvelous world around her: because of love.

It isn't enough just to say it. That piece of knowledge fits like a stone in the pocket, but not in the heart. It is necessary that she should be loved, that she dwell within the light of that love, that love lift her up and take her to its breast, that she breathe love and laugh love and sleep in its sweet dominion—and so experience its security, its peace, and so believe in love.

This is not a matter of the intellect, that she should think about it.

This is a matter of the heart. It isn't explained. It happens.

This is not a lesson to be learned. This is an event. And Jesus, whose story this is, encounters your child when she enters his story.

But you, good parents and goodly grandparents—this is also the reason why you must tell the tale unto your children.

For between you and the child already is trust, and sympathy, and a common memory, and mercy and discipline together, and triumphs, and failures, and anger, and forgiveness. These are the threads of an active love. But when it is you who tell the story in your own voice unto your own child, these also become the delicate threads that define and shape the story, in her mind first, and then in her heart. They weave Jesus. Better yet, Jesus rides the weave; so human experience is elevated to heavenly experience. God becomes the truer, holier, brighter parent.

You tell the story to your child, then, in order to deliver your child to God, that God should adopt her and keep her forever and forever safe.

Because you love her, you see.

But the baby isn't born yet. Talk on, dear parents. Sing on, sweet Gabriels, till the whole of the song is sung. *Acts 1:1–11*

December 20

Joseph Hears the Angel

In those days the dark world had some dark rules by which a man could put a woman away—and then it would be as if they had never been married at all. If a woman had a baby by someone besides her husband, then her husband could put the woman away. That was the rule.

One night Joseph lay in bed and thought about this rule.

He said the words out loud. He said, "I will put her away," and he almost started to cry.

Then God in heaven turned to his angel.

"Gabriel," said God.

And the angel said, "What, Lord?"

"Go down," said God. "Go down right now. Tell Joseph the truth. The man is blinded by the darkness. He thinks that Mary has committed a sin. Go! Go!"

So a light grew bright in Joseph's sleep, and the brightness was a dream, but the light was the angel Gabriel, so close to the man that he shined inside his mind.

"Joseph, son of David," said the angel.

Joseph slept on; but Joseph heard and saw, and he remembered. And the more he heard, the happier he became, until there was a man in Nazareth who was smiling in his sleep.

"Joseph, do not be afraid to take Mary for your wife," said the angel. "The baby conceived in her is of the Holy Spirit. Mary didn't sin. Mary doesn't lie. Mary is going to have a baby boy, and you shall call him Jesus, and this is what his name means: that he will save his people from their sins."

Listen, listen! Sin is the darkness of the world! This baby shall be its light, for he shall shine in the dark and take its sin away. *Emmanuel* is the infant that shall be born, which means: *God with us.*

Joseph, God is keeping his promises. Joseph, something wonderful is happening—   *Matthew 1:18–25*

How To Tell the Christmas Story, V

In the hearing of this marvelous, seminal, progenitive story, the child comes to know her Lord and his love. But in that relationship she also comes to know herself. Who is born in the story? Why, Jesus. But who is born in the telling of the story? Why, your child is—reborn. For here she receives and is persuaded of a name: Beloved of God. And herein the children of God are shaped and since it is God both shaping and empowering them, what then? Then theirs is the image of God again. The image broken in sin is renewed in the faces of the children.

Ah, parents, how could you not sit down and tell your children such a story? However could you justify neglecting it? For this is the Gospel itself—which, if they do not hear it, how can they believe? And telling it is nothing less than proclamation.

So tell it, tell it, with calm simplicity and a cosmic serenity. With faith. And thou dost name thy children in the telling, as thou thyself wast named.

Tell it with a generous voice, especially this passage to come, as familiar to thee as the rising of the sun.

And hush thy voice, O man, when that thou enterest this passage.

And woman, almost whisper.

For this is the fullness of time, the fullness of heavenly love for us: the birth.   *1 John 1:1–4*

Telling the Story

Now it came to pass in those dark days, that there went out a command from Caesar that all of the people should be counted.

"A census," he decreed. "Citizens, go to the cities of your ancestors, to be counted according to families there."

So people began to travel.

So Joseph, too, obeyed the command. He and Mary traveled south together, to the province named Judea, to a particular city of David called Bethlehem, but in that city to no particular house at all, for they had no house in Bethlehem. Joseph was a descendant of David; that's why he came to Bethlehem. But there were hundreds and hundreds of others descended from David; the city was crowded with people, and that's why there were no houses nor rooms at all where Joseph could lay his Mary down to rest for a while and stay.

Even the inn was full.

But the night was dark and cold. The night was deep and lonely.

And Mary was huge with her child and tired.

She wasn't grinning any more, was Mary. She was groaning. "Joseph," she whispered, "it's time. Oh, Joseph," she said, "the baby is coming. It's time."

"Mary, can you wait a little longer?"

"No," she said.

"Mary, there's no place for us."

"It's time," she said.

So Joseph went running through the streets of the city. People were sleeping. Nobody noticed. Nobody answered his knocking.

So this is all he could find: a stable where travelers tethered their beasts when they slept. A little shelter against the night.

"Mary," he said when he led her there, "do you mind?"

"No," she said.

"Can you lie on the straw?"

"It's time," she said and knelt down.

So there it was that she brought forth her firstborn son; and she wrapped him in swaddling clothes and laid him in a manger, because there was no room for them in the inn.

Luke 2:1–7

December 23

How To Tell the Christmas Story, VI

In the beginning, before there was a world at all, God spoke. And this is the first thing ever the Lord God said. God said: "Let there be light." And there was light.

Light is the first thing God created. And this, and all things, he made with his creating Word; for he said it, and it was.

In him was life, and the life was the light of every people.

The light shines in the darkness, and the darkness has not overcome it.

Nevertheless, there came an aeon, once upon a time in human history, when the world was dark, and the land where the people lived was deep in darkness, and the light of God was hidden. It was dark as the night in the daytime. It had been dark so long that the people had forgotten what the light was like.

But God was in love with the people.

Therefore, God spoke again, the second time. But the Lord God said what he had said in the beginning, before there was a world at all. He said, "Let there be light!"

And so the Word came down into the world that the Word himself had made.

For the Word became flesh and dwelt among us, full of grace and truth; we have beheld his glory, glory as of the only Son from the Father.

This, dear parents, grandparents, is all that we have said: that every time you tell the story, the first light shines again. Your words give opportunity to the Word, that the children might behold him. For to all who receive him, who believe in his name, he gives power to become children of God.

This is what we've said. No more than this.

And so you shall, in faith, continue your own saying, even to the end.   *Hebrews 1:1–4*

December 24
Shepherds Hear the Angel

And there were shepherds in that same dark country, abiding in the fields, keeping watch over their flocks by night.

And God turned to his angel. And God said, "Gabriel."

And the angel answered, "Yes, Lord?"

And the Lord God said, "Go down. All of the people must know what I am doing. Tired and lonely and scattered and scared, all of the people must hear it. Go, good Gabriel. Go down again. Go tell a few to tell the others, till every child has heard it. Go!"

And so it was that an angel of the Lord appeared to the weary shepherds. Their dark was shattered, for the glory of the Lord shone round about them, and they were sore afraid.

The angel said to them, "Don't be afraid."

But the light was like a hard and holy wind, and the shepherds shielded their faces with their arms.

"Hush," said the angel, "hush," like the west wind. "Shepherds, I bring you good news of great joy, and not only for you but for all of the people. Listen."

So shepherds were squinting and blinking, and shepherds began to listen, but none of them had the courage to talk or to answer a thing.

"For unto you is born this day in the city of David," said the angel, "a Savior, who is Christ the Lord. And this will be a sign for you: you will find the babe wrapped in swaddling clothes and lying in a manger."

Suddenly the sky itself split open, and like the fall of a thousand stars, the light poured down. There came with the angel a multitude of the heavenly host, praising God and saying:

> *Glory to God in the highest,*
> *And on earth, peace—*
> *Peace to the people with whom he is pleased!*

But hush, you shepherds. Hush in your wonder. For the choral singing soon was ended. The hosts ascended, and the sky was closed again. And then there came a breeze and a marvelous quiet and the simple dark of the night. It was just that, no terror in that then. It was only the night, no deeper gloom than evening. For not all of the light had gone back into heaven. The Light of the World himself stayed down on earth and near you now.

And you can talk now. Try your voices. Try to speak. Ah, God has given you generous voices, shepherds. Speak.

So then, this is what the shepherds said to one another:

"Let us," they said, "go over to Bethlehem and see this thing that has happened, which the Lord has made known to us."

Luke 2:8–14

December 25

What Did Mary Ponder?

So the shepherds got up and ran as fast as they could to the city of Bethlehem, to a particular stable in that city, and in that stable they gazed on one particular baby, lying in a manger.

Then, in that moment, everything was fixed in a lambent, memorial light.

For there was the infant, just waking, just lifting his arms to the air and making sucking motions with his mouth. The holy child was hungry. And there was his mother, lying on straw as lovely as the lily and listening to the noises of her child. "Joseph?" she murmured. And there was Joseph, as sturdy as a barn, just bending toward his Mary. "What?" he whispered.

And the shepherds' eyes were shining for what they saw.

Exactly as though it were morning and not the night, the shepherds went out into the city and began immediately to tell everyone what the angel had said about this child. They left a trail of startled people behind them, as on they went, both glorifying and praising God.

But Mary did not so much as rise that night. She received the baby from Joseph's hands, then placed him down at her breast while she lay on her side on straw. With one arm she cradled the infant against her body. On the other arm, bent at the elbow, she rested her head; and she gazed at her small son sucking. Mary lowered her long, black lashes and watched him and loved him and murmured, "Jesus, Jesus," for the baby's name was Jesus.

"Joseph?" she said without glancing up.

And Joseph said, "What?"

But Mary fell silent and said no more. She was keeping all these things—all that had happened between the darkness and the light—and pondering them in her heart.

Luke 2:15–20

December 26
Wherefore White

Wangerin explains why the color for Christmastide in liturgical churches is white.

For that the lily *candidum,* Madonna's lily, when it opens to the daily Gabriel of the sun, is white; and it is good, as God did, still to start with Mary: *Ave gratia plena.*

For that the Holy Spirit, coming low to overshadow her, if it had visibility at all, was whiter than the piling cloud: it was a vapor of the Deity, it was a wind, the breath of God.

For that the snow, which sometimes cloaks this season, covering the parti-colored tantrums of humanity in one hue only, cool and smooth, is white.

For that the glory that shone around the shepherds was unquenchable, a white flame from the throne of God—

For that all the stars did next throw down their spears, take up a canticle, and sing above the midnight of the shepherds; and these, the multitude of the heavenly host, were white.

For that their song was *Et in terra, pax!* Peace! was the pleading of the stars; peace! concluded their doxology: Peace to the people with whom he is pleased. And the figure of peace is a dove. And the dove is white—

For that if wars should cease on one day, the next day's dawning would be white as fleece—

For that the holy deed remembered in this season admits of no division, none other instrument than God's pure love alone, no human help, though humans have the benefit: the only-begotten Son was a gift from the Father of Lights, with whom there is no variation nor shadow due to changing, white—

For that the eyes of all are whiter than the skins of any.

For that the teeth of children when they laugh are ivory, and their laughter is a pearl—

—Therefore at the Christmastide we drape our holy furniture and stole the necks of those who preach in white.

Luke 1:46–55

December 27

Reprise

Christmas and his Incarnation
Dimple time, make time a vortex,
Suck time backward through itself, and
We return through its forward going:

We, by mercy, pass its latter sadness first; we
Meet its middle as our own, most penitential;
We arrive then at its first, the simplex,
Our last home and holing.

This is the marvel of our celebration
And the grace of God:
To take us back

Through headlong time,
To make us small
And tuck us home
Again.

O baby, rest your nappy head;
Your eyes be rollin', you half dead;
Your mama loves you, wide and deep—
O baby, baby, steal to sleep:
Your story's done
  Begun   *Revelation 12:1–6*

December 28

Two Pictures

This and the following two selections fit together to show an impor-
tant contrast.

The scene is simple, the furniture rude, the people sweaty
and few.

A plain photograph of the birth of Jesus would be altogether unremarkable—except that it showed a woman bearing her baby in a public place. That might cause a remark or
two. Some could find the photo offensive (riffraff, you
know, as shameless with bodily functions as the homeless in
New York; or if they can't be blamed for their poverty, a
blight on human dignity). But no one would call this photo
holy.

That which the camera could record of the Nativity of Jesus
does not inspire awe: It's either too common or too impoverished. To modern scrutiny there is nothing much meaningful
here.

If, for us, reality is material only—if we gaze at the birth with a modern eye that recognizes nothing spiritual, sees nothing divine, demands the hard facts only, data, documentation—then we're left with a photograph of small significance: a derelict husband, an immodest mother, an outdoor shelter for pack-animals, a baby left in a feed-trough. Simple, rude, dusty and bare.

But if we gaze at Christmas thus, then our own lives must be bereft of meaning: nothing spiritual, nothing divine, no awe, never a gasp of adoration. We are, as it were, a shell of existence, hollow at the core. Today, a fruitless rind; tomorrow, quintessential dust.   *Revelation 18:1, 2, 9–20*

December 29

Seeing the Glory

Our seeing reveals our soul—whether we conceive of one or not! So how do we see Christmas?

If we do not recognize in the person of this infant an act of Almighty God—the beginning of forgiveness for a rebellious world; if we do not see in Jesus the Word made baby flesh, nor honor him as the only premise for any Christmas celebration, then we see with that modern eye merely. Stale, flat, unprofitable.

If the "true meaning of Christmas" is for us some vague sentiment of charity and little else, we see with that modern eye merely. Human goodness is a poor alternative to *Immanuel,* the active, personal presence of God among us. Human goodness is unstable. God is not.

If the "spirit of the season" is for us a harried getting and spending, an exchanging of gifts, we see with that modern eye merely. Instead of the love of God to redeem us from dying (and so to give birth in us to an everliving love) we have that halting human love which might redeem a day from loneliness, but which itself must die.

If we reduce the glory of the incarnation to craven phrases like "Season's Greetings" (for fear of offending some customer, some boss, someone who finds not Christ in Christmas), then we offend God by seeing with the modern eye merely. Likewise, "peace" and "joy" and "happiness" are shapeless wishes, irresolute and unsubstantial, so long as they avoid the Prince of Peace and the joy of his salvation. For the world can make an illusion of joy, but illusions, when they shatter against experience, leave people worse than before—and this world has never, never compacted a lasting peace.   *Revelation 19:1–10*

December 30
The Center

No. I will not see the scene with that empirical, modern eye. My picture won't be undimensioned, as flat as a photograph, no. But I will paint mine like a child, wide-eyed, primitive and faithful. And I will call it true—for it sees what is but isn't seen.

My painting is immense. Stand back to look at it. It is composed of seven concentric circles, each one lesser than the last, and all surrounding Jesus.

The widest circle is the whole world, dark and cold and winter-fast. All creation yearned for this birth. Inside that is a round of angels, countless as the stars, bright with a white light, gazing inward, full of news. Heaven attended his advent here.

The third circle is constructed of beams and boards, a stable signifying poverty, none of the wealth of the world. This king was low-born, to lift the low on high. The stable is filled with a warm and orange light.

Within the stable is a ring of animals, sheep and cattle gazing, like the angels, inward—for nature made a harmony with this Nativity. And I hear in the growl of the beasts a choral praise and piety, the music of earth and all spheres.

The circle in the circle of the animals is a gathering of shepherds, whom I paint with the faces of children, smiling and shining and breathless and reverent. For these are the people of every age who heard the news and believed, who believed and rushed to see, who saw and beheld: it was the Savior in very flesh. Two of the shepherds are giggling, and one weeps.

Circle six is a man and a woman, one standing, one reclined in weariness. The man is Joseph, the stepfather who lent house and heart and lineage to Jesus. The woman is Mary, his mother, regal and transcendently beautiful, for heaven crossed all the circles to choose her; and she, when heaven came, said, "Let it be." The sixth circle is the historical, that it happened. And this is the beginning of meaning in history.

The smallest circle of seven, meaner than the others, is a manger made of wood. Wood: for Jesus was material indeed, bone and flesh and blood. But wood: for wood one day would kill him. And this is the truth which can't be seen, but which my painting depicts in an outrageous wood: His life, rounded by a cradle and a cross, saves ours thereby. We are in the picture.

And then, in the perfect center of my circles and of all of the spheres of the world, in the center of time and eternity, in the center of thought and love and human gesture—like the

heart that radiates life to the extremities, the whole of creation—Jesus! The Babe! The Infant King! Immanuel!

Revelation 20:1–6

December 31

Waiting for the Last Advent

In that day, the Lord shall make the whole world new.

When I grew to be an adult, I dreamed that I met Jesus. A
lovely dream, but it was just a dream.

The advent itself is ahead of me still, and that shall be no
dream. It is a promise now; it will be the single most overwhelming event in the universe when it occurs. I confess that
I tremble at the thought of the coming of One who shall dis-
populate the graves and assemble the peoples and transfigure
the whole of creation. But it is the grandeur, the uttermost
awe of the thing that causes me to tremble. I am not afraid.
And I will not hide. I wait in a purple contemplation, peering
through a clear patch in the stained-glass window. I watch,
and I wait.   *Revelation 21:1–8*

Books by Walter Wangerin, Jr.

Fiction

The Book of the Dun Cow. New York: Harper & Row, 1978.
The Book of Sorrows. New York: Harper & Row, 1985.

Poetry

A Miniature Cathedral and Other Poems. New York: Harper & Row, 1987.

With Paul Manz, *Una Sancta: A Mass in Thanksgiving for the Unity of the Body of Christ.* Chicago: Christ Seminary-Seminex, 1986.

Children's Books

The Bible for Children. New York: Checkerboard Press, 1981.
Branta and the Golden Stone. New York: Simon & Schuster, 1993.
Elisabeth and the Water-Troll. New York: HarperCollins, 1991.
In the Beginning There Was No Sky. Nashville: Thomas Nelson, 1986.
Miz Lil and the Chronicles of Grace. New York: Harper & Row, 1988.
My First Book About Jesus. New York: Checkerboard Press,1983.
Potter. Elgin: David C. Cook, 1985.
Thistle. New York: Harper & Row, 1983.

Short Stories

The Manger Is Empty. New York: Harper & Row, 1989.
Ragman and Other Cries of Faith. New York: Harper & Row, 1984.

Theology

As for Me and My House: Crafting a Marriage to Last. Nashville: Thomas Nelson, 1987.

Mourning into Dancing. Grand Rapids: Zondervan, 1992.

The Orphean Passages: The Drama of Faith. New York: Harper & Row, 1986.

Reliving the Passion. Grand Rapids: Zondervan, 1992.

Articles

"Hans Christian Andersen: Shaping the Child's Universe." In *Reality and the Vision,* edited by Philip Yancey. Dallas: Word Publishing, 1990.

The Lutheran (monthly periodical), numerous articles beginning in 1988.

Sources by Book

Sources by Day

14 S, 69, 70

15 S, 91, 92

16 S, 103-5

17 S, 136, 137

18 S, 145-46

19 S, 150

20 S, 161

21 S, 184

22 S, 189-90

23 S, 241

24 S, 318

25 S, 332-33

26 S, 338-39

27 L, Feb. 28, 1990

28 RP, 21, 22

29 DC, 92

March

1 MC, 130

2 OP, 14-15

3 RP, 25

4 RP, 31

5 RP, 31

6 RP, 40-41

7 RP, 43

8 RP, 46

9 RP, 49, 50

10 RP, 54, 55

11 RP, 59, 60

12 RP, 68-69

13 RP, 72

14 RP, 81-82

15 RP, 82

16 RP, 83

17 RP, 89

18 RP, 99-100

19 RP, 114

20 RP, 122

21 RP, 125, 126

22 RP, 133-34

23 RP, 149

24 RP, 156

25 OP, 12

26 L, Mar. 30, 1988

27 L, Mar. 30, 1988

28 L, Mar. 30, 1988

29 RF, 3

30 RF, 4-5

31 RF, 6

April

1 MD, 65

2 ME, 155

3 OP, 3-4

4 OP, 16

5 OP, 1

6 OP, 2

7 OP, 7

8 OP, 74

9 OP, 8

10 OP, 12, 13

11 OP, 10-11

12 OP, 6, 7

13 OP, 7

14 OP, 20, 21, 22

15 L, July 13, 1988

16 MC, 132

17 RV, 5

18 RV, 10

19 RV, 14

20 RF, x-xi

21 L, Sept. 28, 1988

22 RF, 76

23 MD, 41

24 MD, 79

25 MD, 47-48

26 MD, 48

27 MD, 17-18

28 MD, 89

29 L, Jan. 24, 1990

30 P, 45

May

 1 OP, 290

 2 L, Aug. 9, 1989

 3 L, Aug. 9, 1989

 4 RF, 101

 5 NS

 6 NS

 7 L, May 24, 1989

 8 L, May 24, 1989

 9 OP, 58-59

10 OP, 60-61

11 OP, 65

12 MD, 25

13 MD, 90

14 MD, 109

15 MD, 93, 95

16 MD, 140-41

17 MD, 162

18 MD, 190

19 MD, 189

20 MD, 196-97

21 MD, 212

22 MD, 222

23 ME, 113

24 OP, 282-83

25 MD, 273

26 MD, 274

27 MD, 275

28 OP, 233

29 OP, 265-66

30 MH, 18, 19

31 S, 204

June

 1 RF, 57

 2 OP, 113, 114

 3 MD, 111, 112

 4 MD, 115, 116

 5 OP, 157

 6 OP, 158

 7 OP, 163

 8 RF, 104

 9 RF, 105

10 MH, 31-32

11 MH, 71

12 MH, 216

13 MH, 142

14 MH, 145

15 MH, 219-20

16 MH, 202

17 RF, 117, 118

18 MH, 126

19 L, June 14, 1989

20 L, Mar. 1, 1989

21 L, Mar. 1, 1989

22 OP, 122

23 OP, 138

24 ML, 176, 177

25 RF, 66, 67

26 RF, 70

27 OP, 203-4

28 P, 29

29 L, Oct. 1, 1992

30 L, Aug. 10, 1988

July

1 L, Feb. 8, 1989

2 US

3 US

4 US

5 US

6 OP, 77

7 L, Feb. 8, 1989

8 L, Feb. 8, 1989

9 L, Apr. 20, 1988

10 L, May 23, 1990

11 RF, 93

12 RF, 94, 95

13 RF, 96, 97

14 RF, 124, 125

15 RF, 125, 126

16 RF, 126, 127

17 L, Jan. 4, 1989

18 RF, 137

19 RF, 138

20 RF, 139

21 RF, 29, 30

22 RF, 12, 13

23 RF, 13

24 RF, 14

25 RF, 15

26 L, Mar. 1, 1992

27 L, Mar. 1, 1992

28 L, Nov. 13, 1991

29 L, Feb. 20, 1991

30 L, May 3, 1989

31 L, Jan. 25, 1989

August

1 ME, 171

2 MD, 133

3 MD, 73

4 L, June 14, 1989

5 MH, 147

6 MH, 124

7 P, 28

8 L, Mar. 2, 1988

9 L, Mar. 2, 1988

10 S, 272
11 S, 273
12 S, 274
13 S, 275-76
14 S, 276
15 L, June 14, 1989
16 L, Oct. 18, 1989
17 OP, 109
18 OP, 105
19 OP, 76
20 OP, 67
21 OP, 270-71
22 OP, 121
23 MH, 147
24 MH, 117-18, 119
25 OP, 272
26 OP, 274
27 OP, 280-81
28 L, Apr. 1, 1992
29 L, Apr. 1, 1992
30 ME, 88-89
31 ME, 184

September

 1 ML, 92-93
 2 ML, 93
 3 RF, 100-101
 4 ML, 52
 5 ML, 51
 6 ML, 149
 7 ML, 90

 8 P, 31
 9 ML, 126-27
10 ML, 128-29
11 ML, 130, 131
12 ML, 133-34
13 ML, 134
14 ML, 140-43
15 ML, 144-45
16 MC, 125
17 OP, 45
18 OP, 45
19 ML, 116-17
20 ML, xiv
21 ML, xii
22 ML, 12
23 P, 24
24 ML, 26
25 ML, 27-28
26 ML, 32
27 ML, 108
28 ML, 112
29 ML, 113
30 ML, 114-15

October

 1 FB
 2 L, Oct. 17, 1990
 3 MD, 51
 4 ME, 97-98
 5 ME, 99
 6 ME, 99

7 ME, 100
8 ME, 100-101
9 ME, 101-2
10 L, Nov. 8, 1989
11 S, 29, 30
12 ME, 92
13 ME, 94
14 ME, 95
15 ME, 80
16 L, June 1, 1992
17 FB
18 L, Jan. 24, 1990
19 L, Nov. 2, 1988
20 MC, 127
21 OP, 154
22 OP, 154-55
23 MH, 93
24 MH, 223-24
25 ME, 119-20
26 ME, 132
27 MH, 99
28 MH, 99
29 BC, 303
30 MH, 111
31 ML, 71-72

November

1 L, July 11, 1990
2 L, July 11, 1990
3 L, Jan. 1, 1992
4 L, Sept. 26, 1990

5 L, Sept. 26, 1990
6 L, Nov. 29, 1989
7 MC, 129
8 RF, 58-59
9 RF, 72
10 RF, 72
11 RF, 72, 73
12 RF, 73
13 RF, 74
14 RF, 75
15 ME, 168
16 ML, 146-47
17 ML, 150
18 ML, 152-54
19 ML, 155-56
20 ML, 158-59
21 ML, 160-61
22 ML, 163-64
23 ML, 165-66
24 ML, 168-69
25 ML, 173-74
26 L, Apr. 12, 1989
27 ME, 85
28 EW, 35-38
29 BC, 414
30 ME, 160, 163

December

1 ME, 159-60
2 BC, 232-33
3 OP, 11-12

4 FB

5 RF, 99

6 MD, 33-34

7 MD, 34

8 MD, 58

9 MH, 240

10 MH, 249

11 ME, 27

12 ME, 28

13 ME, 29

14 ME, 30

15 ME, 30, 31

16 ME, 30

17 ME, 31

18 ME, 32-33

19 ME, 33, 34

20 ME, 35

21 ME, 37-38

22 ME, 38-39

23 ME, 39-40

24 ME, 40-44

25 ME, 42

26 ME, 67-68

27 ME, 56

28 L, Dec. 19, 1990

29 L, Dec. 19, 1990

30 L, Dec. 30, 1990

31 ME, 172

Index by Title